THE DRUG COMPANY NEXT DOOR

The Drug Company Next Door

Pollution, Jobs, and Community Health in Puerto Rico

Alexa S. Dietrich

NEW YORK UNIVERSITY PRESS
New York and London

NEW YORK UNIVERSITY PRESS
New York and London
www.nyupress.org

References to Internet websites (URLs) were accurate at the time of writing.
Neither the author nor New York University Press is responsible for URLs that
may have expired or changed since the manuscript was prepared.

LIBRARY OF CONGRESS CATALOGING-IN-PUBLICATION DATA
Dietrich, Alexa S.
The drug company next door : pollution, jobs, and community health in Puerto Rico / Alexa
S. Dietrich.
pages cm
Includes bibliographical references and index.
ISBN 978-0-8147-2499-6 (cl: alk. paper)
ISBN 978-0-8147-2473-6 (pb: alk. paper)
1. Pharmaceutical industry—Environmental aspects—Puerto Rico. 2. Pharmaceutical
industry—Risk assessment—Puerto Rico. 3. Pollution—Social aspects—Puerto Rico.
4. Pollution—Economic aspects—Puerto Rico. 5. Environmental policy—Citizen
participation—Puerto Rico. I. Title.
TD428.P54D54 2013
363.73'1—dc23
2012050536

New York University Press books are printed on acid-free paper,
and their binding materials are chosen for strength and durability.
We strive to use environmentally responsible suppliers and materials
to the greatest extent possible in publishing our books.

Manufactured in the United States of America
10 9 8 7 6 5 4 3 2 1

For Thelma Trotty-Selzer, my first formal teacher of anthropology, who taught me to always question what I thought I knew, and to never forget both the beauty and responsibility of being human.

And for Mary Lerner, my mother and my first informal teacher of anthropology, who every day models the importance of empathy in all endeavors.

CONTENTS

ACKNOWLEDGMENTS

This research would not have been possible without access, at a minimum, and trust, in many cases from people at all levels of the project. Virtually every person I met contributed to my thinking in some way, because virtually everyone had ideas about the role of the pharmaceutical industry in Puerto Rican life. Many of those people will go unnamed in these acknowledgments, sometimes out of respect for the confidentiality I promised them, but that does not diminish the level of gratitude I feel for their help and support. The research could not have been accomplished without them, though the conclusions I make in the book (as well as any errors) are my own.

Before living in Puerto Rico, I gained insight from industry insiders in my hometown, and benefited from being able to compare the experiences of people there with those in Nocorá. On my arrival I quite literally depended on the kindness of strangers for a safe landing in the field. My most heartfelt thanks to Deepak Lamba-Nieves, who let me sleep on his couch until I found a place to live, and who sang "Don't Stop Believin'" in a karaoke bar one night when I needed to hear it. Deepak was, and continues to be, a source of humor and insight about Puerto Rico and life in general. Thanks also to Beliza Torres-Narvaez, who broadened my cultural horizons, and was a great sounding board. Erlyn Ramirez gave me my first mallorca and then adopted me practically as her own daughter. She and "las lobas de San Jorge" (especially Hilvita Conde, Sonia Aponte, and Silvia Henríquez) fed and sheltered my body and soul in more ways than I can count. Sonia Aponte gave me early feedback on ideas about environmentalism, and Silvia Henríquez gave me the opportunity to experience NGO work in La Perla firsthand.

My work in the town I call Nocorá benefited from the generosity and friendship of many people, activists and non-activists. On the activist side I would especially like to thank Don Pedro and Don Luis, who always welcomed me into their homes, worked tirelessly to give me information, but were adamant that I should draw my own conclusions. Doña Monin said little about the work, but always gave me food and affection, and arranged a wonderful interview with the recordkeepers of "the stench." Other members of the local environmental group were also welcoming and supportive, and researchers from the University of Puerto Rico–Arecibo were very open to including me in their projects, such as measuring water quality. I learned a great deal about the potential for multidisciplinary environmental fieldwork from them, as well as the pitfalls of action research. Public Health educators from the University of Puerto Rico–Ciencias Médicas campus were also supportive and provided insight along the way.

A number of employees from various government agencies and companies took time to speak with me, or to invite me to events that proved helpful in my research. Thanks especially to members of the Department of Health in both San Juan and Arecibo, the local EPA offices, Environmental Quality Board, the Planning Board, the Aqueduct and Sewer Authority, and the Special Communities agency. Members of the Palenque neighborhood were also welcoming, and helped me understand the variety of ways a community could be organized. Members of the Catholic community organization in Arecibo did likewise. Employees at the local library allowed me to distribute my survey and helped me locate various documents. Employees of the Centro Cultural gave energetically of their time and knowledge, particularly lending to my sense of historical continuity and current cultural values. Finally, however critical I may be of their actions, I received a great deal of cooperation from both the alcalde's office and the municipal legislature. If anything, I believe their openness demonstrates that the majority of those working in those settings do feel they are working for the public good, and will be open to critical recommendations. As the conclusion of the epilogue demonstrates, I also believe that Nocorá shows a great capacity for renewal.

I feel justified in the hope I feel for Nocorá in great part because it is a community that, in my own experience, is full of good neighbors. My own neighbors, in particular Mari, Carlos, and Paola, made every day a good day, in the millions of tiny ways that living in the company of good people can. Finally, Brunilda Morales and her family were as helpful and supportive of me as if I were their own. The gratitude I owe them is more profound than I can say.

While I was in the field, and when I returned, many friends and family members in Atlanta and New York helped me keep my sanity with words of love and support. In particular, Mary and Dennis Lerner, and Ed, Zach, Liz, and Matt Dietrich, always believed that I would "get it done," even when they weren't exactly sure what I was doing. Erin Finley and Jess Levin both sent encouragement and music that kept me going. Peter Brown and Peggy Barlett visited me in the field, and in doing so helped affirm the value and relevance of the project.

Both Peter and Peggy, with very different but complementary styles, provided critical support and mentorship at a variety of points, and Kate Winskell gave without limits of her time, both as a person and as a professional. I am unquestionably a better anthropologist and person because of them. Dan Sellen gave early support as a committee member and letter writer, and David Nugent played an important role in the last stages of the dissertation. Lesley Sharp, too, has always been an unfailing supporter of mine in medical anthropology, long after her official role as a mentor had ended. An invitation to speak to a seminar class of hers at Columbia gave me an important opportunity to test out early conclusions.

Many people gave portions of the manuscript an extra read at various points and provided opportunities to test out ideas. Thanks to Marina Welker, Leah Horowitz, Peter Little, and Adriana Garriga Lopez (with Jessica Mulligan and Victor Torres Velez) for coordinating various panel presentations. Thanks also to Leah for her hard work that helped turn that particular set of papers into publications. Thanks to Merrill Singer for some early feedback and critical questions about an earlier article (Dietrich 2008). In the capacity of unofficial but "above and beyond duty" feedback, Erin Finley, Sarah Willen, Kate Winskell, and Mary Lerner deserve special mention. They always read with both insight and care, and the writing improved greatly. Michael Scholl also gave a crucial reading to an early chapter at a crucial time.

At Emory University I benefited greatly from a fellowship with the Center for Health, Culture, and Society, which gave me the opportunity to study epidemiology. The staff at the Center were wonderfully generous and supportive, making the School of Public Health like a second academic home. Joan Herold and Michele Marcus supervised my epidemiology Master's thesis, and taught me a great deal about the practice of public health. On the anthropology side, I received generous support for coursework, short-term research, and supplementary training. I would also like to express my gratitude for the biocultural environment of Emory's graduate program in anthropology. It was not without tension or conflict, but it was ultimately an extremely fertile environment in which the project germinated.

The main body of research was funded by the Wenner-Gren Foundation (Grant 7071) and The National Science Foundation (Grant 0314446). I also received grants from the Rockefeller Archive Center and the Centro de Estudios Puertorriqueños (Hunter College) for archival research on Puerto Rico's pre-industrial history. It should be noted, however, that any opinions, findings, and conclusions or recommendations expressed here are my own and do not necessarily reflect the views of those funders.

In the writing process I benefited from several programs coordinated by the NYU Faculty Research Network, and received funds from Wagner College to attend them, and to make short trips to Puerto Rico. The Maureen Robinson Fellowship for junior faculty (Wagner College) also bought me vital time to write. My colleagues at Wagner have been a great source of support and fellowship in balancing teaching and research, in particular Celeste Gagnon, Margarita Sánchez, and Donna Toscano. Philosopher extraordinaire Sarah Donovan deserves special mention, as she gave invaluable suggestions to make the Introduction more readable. Students in my Culture, Power, and Place seminar gave supportive feedback on chapter 1, and Ford Anderson notably gave feedback on early drafts of other material. Nick Richardson and Amy Eshleman could always be counted on for positive reinforcement and help with furniture.

Arlene Dávila offered several early suggestions to strengthen the book proposal, which contributed to its success. My editor at NYU Press, Jennifer Hammer, approached me about the project and then helped bring the book from proposal to manuscript. Thanks also to her assistant Constance Grady for answering my last-minute questions, and to Alexia Traganas in the Production Department for giving me some extra flexibility as I tried to finish the manuscript in the aftermath of Hurricane Sandy. I am especially grateful to the anonymous reviewers of the manuscript at several stages, who pointed out flaws and made extremely helpful suggestions for specific ways to improve the book. I am also grateful for the permission to publish here revised and updated versions of two chapters that were previously published: chapter 1 (from AltaMira Press) and chapter 4 (from the Wiley-Blackwell journal *Development & Change*).

All the hard work in the world cannot alone help you finish a project like this. Prior to the completion of this book I lost three people who constantly supported and challenged me, and served as unwavering reminders of what it means to care about the world: Environmentalist Sarah Peisch, my stepmother Sarah Dietrich, and my grandmother Lotte Rugh. I miss them enormously, but their lives will always serve as an example to me. My son Owen, with his relentless inquisitiveness and remarkable gift of articulation, is a constant source of inspiration. He is a true scientist in miniature. Finally, I owe an enormous debt of gratitude to Jennifer Ida, thanks to whom I discovered my love of Puerto Rico, and my love of anthropology, all over again.

KEY EVENTS TIMELINE FOR NOCORÁ'S
ENVIRONMENTAL HEALTH

1964   The *Central*, the sugar processing plant, and base of the local
            economy, closes.

1970   The Federal Clean Air Act (CAA) authorizes significant
            federal and state regulation and oversight of air emissions
            (expanding the role of the federal government from previous
            acts).

1971   The U.S. Environmental Protection Agency is established.

Early–   Construction of pharmaceutical complex begins in earnest
mid-1970s   in and around the Salvador la Cruz neighborhood (see map,
            figure 1.2).

1972   The Federal Clean Water Act (CWA) establishes the basis
            for the National Pollution Discharge Elimination System
            (NPDES), which regulates industrial wastewater.

1977   New primary-level (domestic/weak waste) treatment plant
            and ocean outfall pipe completed in Tipan, with plans for
            expansion.

1981   Secondary-level treatment phase inaugurated at the Nocorá
            treatment plant.

Early 1983 Tipan residents organize and file a complaint with EPA about
            local air and water quality. The plant is inspected and numer-
            ous problems are reported.

Late 1983   Tipan residents again contact EPA, alleging that the air and water quality are still severely affected. Office-based personnel respond, emphasizing the economic importance of the pharmaceutical industry for Puerto Rico, and downplaying the complaints.

1984   A more organized *Comité para Defender el Ambiente Nocoreño* (CDAN) begins trying to collect their own evidence of damage to the environment and to the plant's influent pipes.

1986   The Federal Emergency Planning and Community Right-to-Know Act is established, through which the Toxic Release Inventory (TRI) is created.

1990   EPA published first "Effluent Guidelines Plan" covering a variety of industries. Environmental groups file lawsuits alleging the plan does not meet CWA requirements.

1991   *Grupo Uniendo Iniciativa Ambiental* (GUIA) is established in the Bajas municipality, next door to Nocorá.

1992   Consent Decree requires EPA to establish a special rule especially for the waste effluent of the pharmaceutical industry.

1995   CDAN begins collecting daily reports of air quality from neighbors across Tipan.

Mid–late 1990s   CDAN associated with GUIA. They participate actively in a "committee on the odors" organized through the alcalde's office, and including representatives of the pharmaceuticals. The problems in Tipan come to the attention of environmental activists, including some lawyers, focusing on wastewater treatment complaints.

1997   CDAN members survey the households of CDAN, collecting data on household health problems and willingness to participate in a possible class action lawsuit.

2000   Through association with the wastewater activists, CDAN
            engage a lawyer, filing a public nuisance lawsuit against all
            the entities involved in the management of the wastewater
            treatment plant, including the consortium of pharmaceutical
            companies, on behalf of all of Tipan.

2008   The class of Tipan is declared, and the lawsuit is settled,
            emphasizing enhanced monitoring requirements.

ATSDR   United States Agency for Toxic Substances and Disease Registry
CAA   Clean Air Act of the United States
CDAN   *Comité para Defender el Ambiente Nocoreño* (grassroots environmental group located in the Tipan ward of Nocorá)
CDC   United States Centers for Disease Control and Prevention
CSR   Corporate Social Responsibility
CWA   Clean Water Act of the United States
DoH   Puerto Rico Department of Health (*Departamento de Salud, DS*)
EPA   United States Environmental Protection Agency
EQB   Puerto Rico Environmental Quality Board (*Junta de Calidad Ambiental, JCA*)
GRO   Grassroots organization
GUIA   *Grupo Uniendo Iniciativa Ambiental* (regional environmental NGO)
NGO   Nongovernmental organization
NPDES   National Pollutant Discharge Elimination System
PB   Planning Board of Puerto Rico (*Junta de Planificación, JP*)
PIP   *Partido Independentista Puertorriqueño* ("*pipiolos*"; Puerto Rican Independence Party)
PNP   *Partido Nuevo Progresista* ("*penepés*"; New Progressive Party, promotes statehood)
PPD   *Partido Popular Democratico* ("*populares*"; Popular Democratic Party, founding party of the political status quo, The Commonwealth or "Free Associated State")
PRASA   Puerto Rico Aqueduct and Sewer Authority (*Autoridad de Acueductos y Alcantarillados, AAA*)
TRI   Toxic Release Inventory

A NOTE ON PSEUDONYMS

Three may keep a Secret, if two of them are dead.
  —Benjamin Franklin, *Poor Richard's Almanac* (1735)

In anthropology it is traditional to utilize pseudonyms in ethnographic writing, in the most basic sense, to protect our subjects. The practice also has a tie to the notion that we, as anthropologists, enter a community at a given time, and leave it essentially as we found it—and that it lives on, unchanged, in the ethnographic present of our prose. The writing process in this sense, as well as the research process, has been rightly critiqued. However, I believe that it is incumbent upon every anthropologist, indeed every researcher, to revisit the question of pseudonyms for themselves: Who am I protecting (if anyone) by using pseudonyms? (Possible answers to this question include not only our subjects and informants, but the researcher herself, or the university or sponsor of research.) Is the changing of a name, or obscuring of circumstances, sufficient? And is it justified? Does the conformation to this tradition in any way compromise the research? Or perhaps even make a mockery of the effort to protect the subjects from very real consequences of our research, much more widely accessible now in the information age?

In the case of this study of the impact of the pharmaceutical industry in Puerto Rico, the question of pseudonyms has been one that I have struggled with almost constantly. It began when I realized (and confirmed with one of the authors of the previous studies) that I was working in a town that had been previously studied, not once, but twice. These studies, one carried out in the late 1940s and one in the 1950s, would provide crucial background material to understanding the emergence of a very particular industry (pharmaceuticals) in this small, otherwise unremarkable, town. Using the same name for the town would maintain continuity with previous studies, creating an unusually rich ethnographic record.

* * *

There is no way that anyone who knows Puerto Rico, or for that matter who knows the pharmaceutical industry, will not be able to make a strong guess as to where it is that I have done my fieldwork: the community I continue to call Nocorá could only be one of two or three municipios on the entire island. Its identity could therefore be considered an open or public secret (see Taussig 1999). In this case it is not the content of the secret itself that is important (for, as Bellman [1984] notes, the paradox of secrets is that they are meant to be revealed), but rather the purpose of the secret and its deployment. I initially retained the tradition of the pseudonym for every person and every business residing in the town of Nocorá for a few basic but very important reasons.

As mentioned earlier, I wished to retain the narrative continuity, and ethical integrity, of previous ethnographic studies of the same town. Most important, I wanted to make absolutely clear that while my purpose in this research process was to examine, and at times critique, the role of the pharmaceutical industry in the local community, this is not a work of investigative journalism. My goal is not to accuse any one company, nor celebrate the achievements of any other. That type of reporting would contribute precisely to a process I intend to criticize—the excessive and damaging role of competitive self-interest shared among the drug companies through which, at the end of the day, communities and consumers are both the losers. As far as both the identities of the companies themselves, and the individuals (some of whom are representative ethnographic composites), I would warn any readers, including companies themselves, against jumping to conclusions about who is who. Using individual pseudonyms for *private* individuals was also in compliance with the Institutional Review Board (IRB) approval I received for the project. There are a few cases, such as when referring to some of the larger environmental organizations whose actions form context, rather than direct data, for the study, in which I do not use pseudonyms. For these few instances a substantial part of the material used is drawn from publicly available sources.

It is also worth noting that in the time period of my main field research, a number of the parties described in this book were engaged in a lawsuit. Several members of one of the grassroots groups with which I worked had a gag order placed on them, preventing them from discussing the case in the press. Out of respect for this circumstance I have always been very cautious about revealing my sources within the group, and although the case is now resolved, I continue to use the same conventions for the sake of continuity. There have been, however, several events of great public significance and notice in the time since my fieldwork. In order to document these events, particularly in the epilogue, I have cited a variety of sources that name Nocorá by its actual name.

Understanding Political Ecologies of Risk in Puerto Rico

Puerto Rico is a combination of both [a permanent underclass and a privileged class] and many Puerto Ricans feel the awkwardness of generous but unequal treatment. All Americans should share that . . . it is a testament to the distance of Puerto Rico and the insensitivity of Americans that so few do.

 —Robert Pastor (1992, 220)

Stories of accommodation, collaboration and outright defeat are just as important [as heroic stories of resistance] because they give us ways to understand our position as caused rather than just existing.

 —Aurora Levins-Morales (1998, 31)

The High Cost of High Tech

The sun was disappearing and the crowd began to gather for the first night of the annual patron saint festival of Nocorá in Puerto Rico, as the air crackled with excitement and the potential for a thunderstorm. But while the locals clustered in groups around the wooden racing horse machines, bought *bacalaitos* (codfish fritters) and beer, and waited for the live music to start, I had finally arranged an introduction to "the biggest environmentalist in Nocorá." Don Lirio listened attentively as I described my interests, and then hastened to invite me to the next meeting of the *Comité para Defender el Ambiente Nocoreño* (Committee to Defend the Environment of Nocorá, CDAN), digging in his pockets for a piece of paper on which to draw a map to their headquarters. "We can tell you much about the pharmaceuticals," he assured me, meaning the local drug companies, "and also about the particular environmental problems of our barrio, about *la planta*. We have a more than 20-year struggle." He paused. "If you have a camera, you should bring it," he said. "We'll show you many things . . . and then you can make up your own mind what you think."

Figure I.1. Life in the buffer zone. Tucked behind the first row of trees, an outpost of the pharmaceutical complex looms over my recently constructed neighborhood. Photo by the author.

The production of pharmaceuticals is among the most profitable industries on the planet, even in the midst of the recent global economic crisis.[1] Drug companies produce chemical substances that can save, extend, or substantially improve the quality of human life. However, even as they present themselves publicly as environmental stewards, their factories have long been a significant source of air and water pollution—toxic to people and the environment. In Puerto Rico, the pharmaceutical industry is generally considered the backbone of the island's economy: in the small town of Nocorá, the main field site for this project, there are more than a dozen drug factories representing a small number of multinationals, the highest concentration per capita of such factories in the world. These corporate citizens have brought their human neighbors a degree of economic stability, paid for with longstanding acceptance of significant environmental contamination.

The problem of pollution in Nocorá has been widely recognized, and has taken many forms. The area closest to the factories, Salvador la Cruz, is a mix of industrial, commercial, and residential zoning, and the ground, air, and water have all been severely contaminated. The town's two Superfund sites of ground pollution, the highest concentration on the island, have finally been remediated. Nocoreño public schools have been ranked in the 11th percentile of the nation's worst schools for local air quality, and the top two sources of the implicated pollutants are drug factories.[2] Water contamination, too, has been significant, but it has become harder to quantify, or to tie to any one factory. Since the early 1980s, the factories have sent their liquid wastes, including a wide range of hazardous chemicals, to be processed at the regional wastewater treatment plant in the coastal neighborhood of Tipan. The treatment facility is typically referred to by local residents simply as *la planta*.

Ultimately both Tipan and Salvador la Cruz, and indeed all of Nocorá, have been strongly affected by the presence of the drug companies as corporate neighbors. The experience of those living in Tipan, however, is unique, because their place in the local social and cultural context is significantly different from any other group of residents. This distinct relationship has helped create a grassroots movement of protest aimed at protecting the environment, in spite of unquantifiable social pressure to quietly accept pollution as part of everyday life. The movement has had some success in holding the factories accountable for their actions, but as a result the neighborhood has paid a price. In exploring the dynamics among residents, local government officials, and corporate entities, it became clear just how embedded the pharmaceutical industry had become at every level of the community, from individually unhealthy bodies and families, to socially unhealthy politics and economic policy. This study— one of few uniting the concerns of critical medical anthropology with those of political ecology—demonstrates concretely how the well-being of human citizens can be sacrificed for the benefit of corporate entities. By understanding how these dynamics became established and accepted by a silent majority of Nocoreños, I argue that there is potential to forge new pathways in the seemingly inevitable association between corporations and communities. But that potential will go unrealized unless fundamental changes are made that re-create social contracts, and promote trust-based mutual accountability among residents, government, and corporations.

A Complex Problem: Pollution, Health, and Corporate Accountability

I returned with my friend Benicia to our folding chairs, and I noticed she was smiling. "It will be good for you to talk to Lirio and his group," she said. "He is very, very dedicated. You'll learn a lot."

She suddenly grabbed my arm and instead of sitting down, pulled me in another direction, waving at another man I did not know. "I want to say hello to Francisco, too, and I'll introduce you. We're colleagues, but he used to work in Environmental Health. If anyone knows about *la contaminación*, he does."

Francisco also nodded with vague interest in my project, and when I said, "I want to learn about the impact of the pharmaceuticals on the lives of Nocoreños," he slowly drew his fingers across his neck, saying nothing, and making a tight grimace. I glanced over to Benicia, and she unhelpfully widened her eyes, but made no attempt to interrupt our conversation. I leaned closer to Francisco. "Do you mean that these are questions I shouldn't be asking?" I asked in a low voice, hoping I didn't sound nervous.

He grinned and shook his head. "It's that I can tell you in one sentence how they impact our lives." He paused, and leaned toward me until our faces were quite close. "*El impacto es . . . nos matan.*" The impact is . . . they're killing us. He tone was calm, quite simply matter-of-fact. "Oh, not today, not tomorrow, but little by little . . . it will kill us all."

Francisco's assertion that the pollution coming from the pharmaceutical factories in Nocorá, Puerto Rico would eventually kill the town's 23,000 residents was not intended as a metaphor. However, it is notoriously difficult prove a causal connection between environmental risks and health problems using standard epidemiological research methods. To do so is not the task of this book, nor was it the goal of my 16 months of ethnographic field research undertaken in Puerto Rico between January 2004 and May 2005.[3] Francisco's words were, however, an appropriate starting place for asking some of the questions that would continually drive the research: What impact do people believe a demonstrably polluted environment has on their health? What evidence is there that reasonably supports these beliefs—qualitatively, if perhaps not quantitatively? These questions quickly beg two follow-up questions: How do these beliefs influence the way people view their corporate neighbors, which, in spite of their multinational corporate nature, now claim to be part of this small community? And conversely, how do those beliefs influence the actions of those same companies—actions that cannot help but structure, in turn, the society in which they are located? In a global environment of ever-increasing awareness of corporate influence, ethnographic answers to these questions have the potential to contribute to a number of important policy debates—about the environment, finance, governance, and health. There is no doubt that corporations have wrought powerful changes at every level of human society and ecology. But we are far from either understanding their full impact, or being capable of counteracting their more poisonous effects.

Although they are often criticized for their high profitability, pharmaceutical manufacturers benefit in public opinion from their association with health care. Although the pharmaceutical industry offers modern society undeniable benefits, one should never lose sight of the simple fact that they are leading members of a broader industry—the chemical industry. Chemical producers have had an unfortunate and well-documented history of turning a blind eye to the environmental and occupational consequences of their business,[4] a process sometimes known as "externalizing."[5] Because of the unique relationship of Puerto Rico to the United States, the island is also a place where the enforcement of U.S. federal environmental regulations and the public trust they ensure are often violated in the name of economic development. This may seem like a harsh indictment—but both ethnographic and documentary evidence support the claim. In a striking and recent example, the Caribbean-based nongovernmental organization (NGO) CORALations successfully sued the U.S. Environmental Protection Agency (EPA), with the U.S. District Court of Puerto Rico finding abundant evidence of "actions indicative of noncompliance on the part of both Puerto Rico and the EPA" with the Clean Water Act.[6] Local EPA officials adhere closely to the pro-development narrative that ecological issues must be harmonized with economic necessities. As the CORALations case suggests, the result is that even the local outpost of the institution charged with enforcing federal standards in Puerto Rico does so ambivalently.

As many other previous studies of Puerto Rico have demonstrated, there is much to learn by analyzing this special case. As a place that is arguably politically and economically midway between developed and developing, simultaneously colonial and postcolonial, what happens in Puerto Rico does not "stay in Puerto Rico." Rather, it has the potential to predict what might happen as other parts of the world become more heavily industrialized, but remain economically dependent on the larger markets of countries like the United States. The case of Nocorá in particular suggests that sacrificing the environment in the name of economic development and corporate prof-its ultimately produces unhealthy communities—individuals who become physically ill and lacking faith in their society. Unfortunately, as corpora-tions are becoming so much a part of the way we view the world, the case of Nocorá also illustrates why, paradoxically, we behave as if their survival were tightly linked with our own.

Creating a Culture of Pollution

The first time I ever noticed Nocorá was the second time I drove through it. Having spent a typical family Sunday afternoon at the rural mountain home of a friend's grandparents, we drove in the near-total darkness back down toward Route 4 to get on the AutoExpresso back to San Juan. As we emerged from the canopy of leaves covering the road, and approached the intersection of Salva-dor la Cruz, the night sky was suddenly lit up as if it were daylight. Through laughter at my astonished question of what this was, I was told that it was the pharmaceutical companies, which run 24 hours a day, seven days a week, making so many of the brand-name prescription drugs that we *gringos* take for granted.[7] My friend Lydia, a dedicated urbanite, scoffed as she told me the ten-second version of the history of Nocorá. "This town was nothing before the pharmaceuticals came; it was basically a little *barrio* of Bajas (the larger town to the east)." As a medical anthropology student with a strong interest in Puerto Rico, I needed little further impetus to begin the first steps of research that would eventually bring me to understand daily life in Nocorá first hand.

Medical anthropologists[8] as well as practitioners of critical medical anthropology[9] have analyzed the nature and impact of legal drug products, their roles in the market and in social life, and intellectual property issues (to name a few areas). However, there has thus far been little work bridging the critical medical anthropology of pharmaceutical products with the political ecology of health. At the center of this book is the examination of the com-munity health of Nocorá, addressing several key questions with respect to drug *production*. What damage is caused by (the creation of) these products? How is the damage caused, how is it assessed, and how can further dam-age be avoided through new public health and/or environmental policies?

In this book, by-products, rather than traditionally defined commodities, are the focus: that which is produced as a side effect of the making of those "useful" things that "can be turned to commercial or other advantage."[10] In the process of pharmaceutical production there are various toxic by-products, many of which are washed away in wastewater following the process of chemical synthesis, or in the flushing of solvents used to clean manufacturing equipment during routine maintenance. Important research has been directed at the environmental, health, and social impacts of what might be termed "harm industries" such as mining, tobacco, and arguably oil.[11] But communities playing host to polluters like the pharmaceutical industry face an even more complex sociopolitical landscape. In their increasingly image-conscious associations with health care providers and public health organizations, drug manufacturers easily position themselves not just as economic saviors, but literally as lifesavers.

The research project came together as I learned more through EPA documents, newspaper reports, and even local websites about what Nocoreños refer to in their general discourse as *la contaminación*. Federally recognized pollution problems[12] caused by members of an industry with the mission statement, "Disease is our enemy. Working to save lives is our job"[13] present an interesting conflict, to say the least. Critics of corporate capitalism view such apparently contradictory public relations statements as just part of the expected behavior of corporations. Indeed, as public relations (PR) guru Edward Bernays is said to have observed, the goal of PR is to engineer consent by the broader public. Therefore, I was also intrigued by the industry's shift toward the transformative rhetoric of "Corporate Social Responsibility" (CSR).[14] By embracing the language of "community," as is now common practice through CSR, corporations make themselves particularly good subjects for anthropological research. Anthropologists are now wary of the ways in which the term "community" can be used to make controversial ideas sound good and relevant to those outside the industry. But the term can still help us understand how people think about, and operate within, their local environment and social context.

It is useful to think about the key variables that influence culture, and therefore help to define particular communities, as belonging to economic, sociopolitical, and ideological segments of a society. In this sense economic variables mainly include material factors that influence how people make a living and fulfill their basic needs. The ecological environment, natural resources, technologies, and sources of labor are some examples. Sociopolitical factors include institutions through which people are organized, and through which certain groups ultimately have power over others. In most modern societies this can include governments, educational systems, and even corporations.[15] The ideological aspect of culture basically describes how people in that group think about things across all aspects of life and experience, and what types of models they use to understand the world. When anthropologists talk about communities, they are typically talking about groups of people who not only share these fundamental aspects of culture, but who have some intangible quality that holds them together as unique, identifiable groups. This quality has been given various names, and is usefully thought of as "social glue." Here I will often refer to this "glue" as *communitas* (the Latin term for community), the term made popular by anthropologist Victor Turner.[16] In research among communities, communitas is often most visible in the outcomes of group-shared practices, such as rituals, that produce a heightened sense of togetherness and belonging. The idea of community also acknowledges that "space and place continue to serve as important loci of struggle" providing "an important referent for the construction of memories and identities."[17] It is the complex combination of economic fundamentals, social organization, and how people think about things that influences how people behave. All of these aspects of culture and community also have enormous impact on the many dimensions of health.[18]

In the case of Nocorá, corporations are embedded in *every* aspect of this community dynamic, but their ultimate impact is highly contested by the rest of those claiming membership in the community. They have both polluted the environment and improved the economy. Their philanthropic actions cement their place in political rituals and their relationship with elites, while failing to address the needs of local residents and workers. They have a powerful influence on discourses of expert knowledge in public health and environmental science, through which policymakers and other elites often question or discredit resident concerns about pollution.[19] In this light one could argue that, on balance, the actions of corporations do more to disrupt the smooth functioning of healthy communities. Therefore, it was of particular interest to try to assess the various ways in which they participated in that community, and how they were ultimately viewed by local residents. As such, this project sought to address a question that is increasingly salient in our public debate: do corporations meet local social standards expected of responsible community members, as is becoming common parlance in their public relations?

Corporate personhood and citizenship[20] are important concepts for thinking about how corporate entities behave in society, and how we should expect that they treat others. It is therefore important to pay attention to the points at which the pharmaceutical companies claim membership in the Nocorá community, when they wish to be exempted from responsibilities, and when and how their acts of self-interest are justified. With these core anthropological concerns about community at the heart of this project, I argue that the health and well-being of local residents has never been assessed, discussed, or otherwise considered independently of the town's relationship with the drug industry since its establishment. As such the dominant narrative of "community health" emphasizes the relative economic impact of the drug industry, while downplaying environmental damage. In contrast, "community health" as viewed by those residents who owe the least to the pharmaceuticals is extremely concerned with long-term environmental impact.

This is by no means the first investigation into the impact of institutions into the everyday lives and bodies of Puerto Ricans.[21] But it particularly brings the corporation into focus, analyzing the impact of one of the most important institutions of globalization within Puerto Rican society in recent decades.[22] Many of us are used to thinking of globalization as a recent phenomenon, a mass movement of political, economic, and other cultural changes riding on a wave of technology and mass-market capitalism. But globalization has been shaping the lives of Puerto Ricans for more than 500 years, creating a society that has seen broad environmental changes, reducing old risks, and creating new ones. Therefore, the concept of risk is central to understanding the impact of the pharmaceutical industry on Puerto Rican society.

Theoretical Concerns
Environmental Risk in Anthropological Terms

The literature on risk is substantial, encompassing both "scientific" risk[23] and perceptions of risk in a global modern society fraught with potential dangers.[24] All risk is culturally constructed.[25] In order to understand how risk operates in human society, we need to consider the different contexts in which different types of knowledge about risk come into play and how they ultimately influence action. Many variables can influence how people define and interpret the riskiness of a particular behavior, or substance. But one of the most significant variables is whether or not the person making that judgment trusts the source of the information about that potential risk.[26]

An emerging public health consensus of ecologically informed multivariate risk[27] belies the traditional description of chronic pollution as merely a "nuisance." Nevertheless, the effects of chronic pollution can be difficult to quantify. It is particularly in the broader context of health evaluation that medical anthropology contributes to understanding risks not easily

measured. While statistics remain an important tool for addressing environmentally rooted public health problems, they cannot be the only tool. In the
words of one of my informants, an epidemiologist with many years of experience in community-based research,

> Health problems, some of them you can quantify, but not all. You can
> never quantify the impact of a health problem in all its dimensions. As a
> researcher you have to know that what you're dealing with [in a statistical
> analysis] is just a portion of a health problem. . . . Once you've identified a
> problem, okay, then you have to ask, "What is the perception of the prob-
> lem, how does it affect a person in her community?" You can't quantify
> these things. This is not included in that famous p-value.

Research by anthropologists can contribute to a better understanding of
community health risks in a number of ways. This book especially draws
on insights from the field of Critical Medical Anthropology (CMA), which
analyzes the ways in which culturally embedded social and economic structures contribute to health. Of particular interest are the processes through
which patterns of harmful behavior go unquestioned, and are presumed
to be somehow "natural."[28] More recently, anthropologists have begun to
explore the health problems that are embedded in environmental inequali-
ties.[29] For example, the deeply interactive nature of human economic activity
and global climate change[30] has created potential for powerful "syndemic"
processes to produce new epidemics of both infectious and chronic disease.[31] The notion of syndemics, or the mutually augmenting occurrences
of more than one health problem, has helped anthropologists and public
health workers understand, for example, how the re-emergence of tuberculosis was intimately tied to the rise of HIV/AIDS.[32] Changes in the environment can cause acute physiological health problems, but more insidiously,
may become syndemic to a series of long-ranging problems that cause more
subtle, but equally severe, damage to a community.

While environmental damage can have serious impact on ecosystems,
and thus on human society, human bodies remain a key site of experience
of pollution, and institutions like the state have profound impact on the control of both people and the environment. In this sense, bodies exist on many
levels and are at same time an individual body, a social body, and subject to a
body politic.[33] The individual body becomes a slate onto which the actions of
the state (or other power, such as a multinational corporation) may become
inscribed in many forms. In the case of my research in Puerto Rico, both the
bodies and the natural environment of Nocoreños bear a substantial burden

as a result of the pharmaceutical factories' activities. These activities are not restricted to manufacturing—the companies play a multifaceted role as polluters, economic providers, and social actors.

There has been, ironically, a tendency in public health to assign too great a role in the disease process to an ahistorical, naturalized local ecology. In contrast, insights from human geography[34] show that the places in which we live have increasingly become "spaces of vulnerability," making the concept of adaptations to the environment far from value-free.[35] The less control people have over their environments, the less it makes sense to view the selective processes of relying on certain behaviors, which may have additional negative consequences, as "natural."[36]

Does Corporate Social Responsibility Exist?

Ethnographic research on corporate-community relations has brought a number of key questions into relief, such as the production of what has been called "toxic uncertainty."[37] In their exploration of the environmental suffering in the Argentine shantytown of "Flammable," Javier Auyero and Débora Swistun illustrate the deep contradictions inherent in living in a poisoned and impoverished environment, in which local corporate patronage (in this case of an oil company) further distorts the fabric of social relations. Published after the conclusion of my fieldwork, *Flammable* demonstrates some themes in common with the experience of Tipanecos described in the following chapters, and is groundbreaking for its illustration of the grayer areas of living a contaminated life. Residents of Flammable received radically conflicting messages about health, safety, and corporate concern. For them, making the best decisions for their families' futures felt like a virtually impossible task. The ethnographic case of Nocorá builds on this work in a few distinct ways, providing an opportunity for scholars of environmental health and corporate dominance to draw useful comparisons of the different contexts, as well as work through ideas for future work in the field. Among the areas further explored here are the influence of the corporate social responsibility movement itself, the ritualized performance of local government actors and companies, and consideration of the significance of the industry itself (pharmaceuticals) being associated with a generalized public good. Additionally, in Nocorá the community of suffering itself is highly varied. Competing social movements that de-emphasize the environment and/or embrace the industry further complicate corporate-community relations.

When consumers begin to demand more accountability, corporations have been shown to change their behaviors. However, large institutions can also drive social change. If corporations take the lead in sustainability, it has been argued, the expansion of that shared cultural narrative will follow.[38] Because these narratives of community, health, economy, and environment are all very actively negotiated on the ground by companies, community leaders, and residents, the greatest impact will occur when representatives from each group of "stakeholders" all begin to advocate for change. This book identifies many barriers to such combined efforts, and therefore suggests how they might eventually be overcome.

Research Design and Methods
History

My project design included both qualitative and quantitative data collection (including participant observation, interviews, archival research, and surveys). Although most anthropologists now ground their ethnographic research in historical context, in this work a historical perspective was particularly important. Not only had previous ethnographic research been conducted, but the economic and ecological histories of Nocorá were key to understanding how the pharmaceuticals had come to have such a significant presence in the town. I gathered this material through interviews with residents and those who had worked in the industry, as well as through interviews and archival research with groups who had, at different times, taken an interest in the environmental problems of the region. The local *Centro Cultural* had a topical newspaper archive, and I also had access to a number of relevant files based on earlier work by the environmental advocacy group Misión Industrial. Additionally, Centro employees and the heads of several large environmental NGOs provided additional information through interviews. These sources, as well as the two previous studies,[39] provided incomparable cultural insight into patterns still visible today, and processes that have produced the current state of both society and environment.

Defining Stakeholders

In defining stakeholders for the purposes of the research design, I initially focused on three components of the local population: (1) the companies themselves; (2) local government representatives and administrators; and (3) local residents and their interest groups. At the time of the research, the dozen or so factories were owned by four multinational pharmaceutical corporations, all of which have their headquarters in the United States (in all cases there were multiple factories located in each industrial complex, and two companies controlled two distinct complexes each). I initially targeted my interviews with managers responsible for community relations, and through these contacts was sometimes able to interview those working directly on environmental issues. In addition to interviews, I was able to observe and sometimes participate in a number of local activities sponsored by the companies, such as educational fairs, plantings, and corporate team events such as health fund-raisers (e.g., Relay for Life).

In approaching government officials my methods were similar, and I relied on both interviews and participant observation in government-sponsored events, as well as public meetings. As with the pharmaceutical representatives, I paid particular attention to when government activities and residential or workers' activities overlapped. Among local government officials I worked with the *alcalde* (mayor), municipal legislators, and local Department of Health officials, as well as "regular" employees of those agencies. I also interviewed Commonwealth-level officials in the Planning Board, Department of Health, and both local and federal environmental protection agencies.

Although not initially part of my research design, I found when I arrived that I had underestimated the importance of regional and Commonwealth-level NGOs as representing potential stakeholder positions. In the time between writing my grants and my arrival, the Corporate Social Responsibility movement had arrived in force in Puerto Rico. I conducted interviews, and was able to do extensive participant observation, including taking part in a research advisory panel, with an organization I call *TransformaRSE*. The organizers of this NGO were working tirelessly with corporations, including most of the pharmaceuticals located on the island, to promote transformative corporate behavior. I also found that several regional NGOs were working to promote both community development and corporate social responsibility, and I was able to work with one in particular, which I call *La Vida Cristiana*. Additionally, I discovered that a regional environmental NGO, which I call *Grupo Uniendo Iniciativa Ambiental* (GUIA), had gained national recognition for its work, and I was able to spend some time at their activities, as well as getting to know their director. GUIA was a small operation with a disproportionately high level of influence in the environmental scene in Puerto Rico, and was considered by some to be a front for the pharmaceutical industry. As we will see, the reality was far more complicated, though the organization did indeed have close ties to the industry, EPA, the Commonwealth Planning Board, and the Commonwealth Environmental Quality Board (EQB).

Finally, I attempted to focus my attention on the non-institutional level of Nocoreño society in several ways. When I initially conceived of the project,

I had assumed that any grassroots activity would be in the neighborhoods adjacent to the factories. As will become apparent, in this I was dead wrong. Having learned through a serendipitous contact in the Department of Health that the local environmental movement was located in the coastal ward of Tipan, the group I call *Comité para Defender el Ambiente Nocoreño* (CDAN) became a central focus in understanding the environmental, and thus cultural, impact of the pharmaceutical industry. The intertwining stories of CDAN and Tipan as a whole are emblematic of a wide range of what we might call cultural "problems" inherent in the current state of the political economy of Puerto Rico. Furthermore, in discussions with pharmaceutical representatives it became apparent that there were several factors that caused the companies to try to distance Tipanecos as potential stakeholders, in spite of their seemingly obvious environmental connection.

It was also important to gather data in locations that did not necessarily represent the unique relationship of Tipan to the pharmaceuticals. Therefore, the sampling strategy for this aspect of the study was generally purposive, with the goal of gaining a broad sample of stakeholders within the Nocorá community. I did several door-to-door samples in the ward of Tipan, the location of the pharmaceutical industry–sponsored wastewater treatment facility. This approach, using the survey described below as an entry point, served to access residents who were not actively involved in grassroots activities, counterbalancing time spent with activist residents. I also sought out conversations with other stakeholders in locations, such as the library and cultural center, where people used services that were sponsored by the companies. This group included residents of some neighborhoods near the factories that had previously been exposed to as much air pollution (in Toxic Release Inventory (TRI)-reported poundage) as the wastewater treatment plant has received water pollutants. I particularly worked in the barrio of La Planchita, which borders one of the factories, and where there is a well-organized community group, but where there has never been significant grassroots environmental activism. Finally, in seeking to supplement my qualitative methods, I conducted an opinion survey[40] among the resident groups mentioned earlier, as well as among a majority of health care workers from the local health center (which is located in the heart of the pharmaceutical corridor), and a signficiant portion of the elementary school teachers and principals in the Nocorá school district. These were locations in which the companies claim to practice much of their citizenship activity/ philanthropy.

In addition to in-depth interviews and surveys (which also yielded many qualitative comments and observations), I conducted participant observation in a wide variety of community-based activities around Nocorá and in a few neighboring municipalities, as well as in the everyday social contexts that are the bread and butter of traditional anthropological field-work. In the quasi-industrial neighborhood in which I lived, several of my neighbors were employed by the companies, but were newcomers to Nocorá. Through them I gained a sense of how length of residence could contrib-ute to overall attitudes. This ethnographic investigation of the community of Nocorá gives ample cause for concern about trends in corporate-community power relations,[41] as well as developments in the growing field of "Corporate Social Responsibility" (CSR). The pharmaceuticals have shown themselves quite adept at mastering the emerging rhetoric of CSR, but both words and actions must be examined, and compared, in order to assess whether, and by what standards, a corporation acts in socially responsible ways.

While I am trained as an epidemiologist, I did not conduct a traditional epidemiological study[42] of either Nocorá or Tipan, although I did examine health data from a variety of other sources. Given limited resources and the complexity of measuring the long-term physiological impact of pollu-tion, attempting to measure the physical suffering of Nocoreños statistically would have distracted from the intent of the ethnographic study, and I was not convinced it would have been productive. Indeed, it would have played into the very cultural problem I was ultimately able to describe so clearly: the overemphasis on the quantification of the effects of pollution.

Organization and Chapter Summary

The following chapters present several different points at which the pharma-ceutical industry has entered Puerto Rican society, as evidenced by the case of Nocorá. In addition to the usual ethnographic stories and quotations that are used to illustrate various arguments in each chapter, between chapters I have also included short vignettes from my fieldwork as introductions to the analytic theme of each chapter. These narrative pauses, structured as separate micro-chapters, serve to give readers a small story to bring into their reading of each successive full-length chapter, enhancing their understanding of why each analytic point matters to lived experience.

Chapter 1 tells the contemptible story of Tipan and its long history of struggle with pharmaceutical-related air and water pollution. It describes the emergence of a grassroots movement to improve the functioning of the regional wastewater treatment plant, where the pharmaceuticals deposited untreated chemical wastewater from 1981 through the late 1990s. I argue that Tipan has a community health burden that may not be easily quantified through traditional epidemiological methods, but for which a variety of evidence exists. However, the pharmaceutical companies and the local government have marginalized the health and ecological concerns of Tipan in their efforts to support long-standing, environmentally insensitive methods of achieving economic progress. This theme is elaborated throughout the book. The purpose here is to draw the reader immediately in to the experience of living in a contaminated environment and to illustrate the frustration and suffering caused by a struggle against corporate giants and their local allies.

Chapter 2 elaborates on a number of key points in the history of Puerto Rico and Nocorá specifically, crucial for understanding how it is that the pollution problem developed in the first place. My experience in teaching this topic to students is that they often have trouble understanding *how* such a thing could be allowed to go so far, and how regulatory agencies, government, and the companies themselves could have avoided confronting the problem for so long. The economic development of the island has had significant impact on environmental and health-related ideologies and sociocultural relationships. These dynamics have created a situation in which Puerto Ricans are generally willing to trade short-term economic gains for the long-term negative potential of serious pollution.

Continuing with this theme into chapter 3, local politics play a large role in framing social relationships in Nocorá, and the relationships between the factories and residents are no exception. This chapter briefly introduces the reader to Puerto Rican electoral politics, tying them into broader observations about economic development and culture. I trace the instrumental role of the alcaldes of Nocorá in the founding of the pharmaceutical complex, and the power they wield in the community. I also explore the question of whether or not the drug companies can be, in anthropological terms, "members" of this small community, as they claim to be, and as local politicians would like them to be seen. Of particular importance is the centrality of their participation in local rituals and token good deeds, demonstrating how performance and perception drastically influenced Nocoreño beliefs about whether the companies are, on balance, beneficial or harmful.

Chapter 4 zeros in on the sometimes unexpected dynamics that exist *between* non-profit groups that are supposedly working toward the same goal (environmental protection). Through their cultural and political influence, the pharmaceutical companies in and around Nocorá have created a cultural perspective about the environment that serves them. However, the conflicting relationship between the Tipan activists and a larger NGO that is tied to the pharmaceuticals is not a simple one in which the larger NGO "sold out."

This chapter introduces legal and dispute resolution theories that can help the reader think in a more nuanced way about social conflict, an antidote to perceptions that such problems exist solely as either "black" or "white."

Continuing the discussion of power-laden relations between Nocoreños and the drug companies, chapter 5 examines the arrival of the Corporate Social Responsibility (CSR) movement in Puerto Rico in the early 2000s. A number of ethnographic examples from working with and observing Puerto Rico's only CSR NGO, as well as the CSR-related activities of the pharmaceuticals, demonstrate the social and economic complexities masked by simplistic, feel-good CSR phrases like "triple-bottom-line" (i.e., company, customers, and community all benefit from successful business). The chapter emphasizes the unique case of Puerto Rico, while at the same time encouraging the reader to consider the many possible consequences of the global CSR phenomenon for local communities, including the problem of "greenwashing."

The concluding chapter returns to the core issue of environmental impacts on health and brings forward the pervasive problem for activists, residents, and pharmaceutical employees alike: the knowledge required to prove that there is a relationship between the environment and poor health is in the hands of "experts," many of whom are in some way beholden to the industry. Those who are not beholden often have "captured" perspectives: their sincere beliefs, built upon the perceived economic necessity of the drug companies, lead them to discount evidence and experience presented by non-expert citizens. Workers who live in and around Nocorá are additionally vulnerable because their own skepticism about the companies can cause them to ignore restrictive safety measures, supporting the claims that if someone is not healthy it is "her own fault." In conclusion, I suggest strategies through which activists and educators can work to promote a more equitable redistribution and production of knowledge. This approach would benefit both residents and employees exposed to pollution and unhealthy pharmaceutical work environments. I also describe some philanthropic and programming opportunities for the drug companies to support these efforts, in the event that they are legitimately interested in changing the long-term patterns in their community relationships.

Following the main body of research, I have included an epilogue, drawing on my most recent post-field visits and contacts to briefly describe some important events in Nocorá in the years 2006–2012. These stories, in light of changing levels of global awareness of corporations, invite the reader to consider what lasting impact, in some cases if any, these social movements have had for environmental health in Puerto Rico, and for other communities with powerful corporate neighbors.

Figure 1.1. Measuring water quality in Tipan. Photo by the author.

Little by Little

A few weeks after finding a place to live, I was chatting with my landlord, a shy man named Samuel, about 15 years my senior. He asked me how I liked Puerto Rico and how I was fitting in. "I like it a lot," I told him, "though in some ways it's different than where I'm from."

"Well, it's very different from New York . . . even I know that," he said with a grin. Samuel was born and raised in Nocorá, and his family still lived on a farm in Tipan. His mother worked at the local library, and sold real estate, and Samuel managed the herd of cattle they had built up over the years.

"Ohh, yes, but I mean where I grew up," I said. "I'm from a small city surrounded by lots of farmland. And my father grew up on a dairy farm." Upon learning of this bovine connection Samuel suddenly lit up, and we chatted for a few minutes about the potential for using science to improve animal management. As it turned out, Samuel had pioneered the use of artificial insemination for cows in Puerto Rico.

"Of course," I said, turning from his pet subject to mine, "my town also has pharmaceuticals." He waved his hand. "Everywhere has something," he said. He paused, "But you're adjusting well?" he asked again, seeming concerned. "You like Nocorá?"

"Oh yes, absolutely," I reassured him. "Sometimes people talk a little too fast, but," I shrugged, "*poquito a poco*. . . ." This was another phrase I had picked up since arriving, the ending of a sentence with a shrug and the phrase "little by little." In spite of complaints, in spite of difficulties, I got the distinct impression that many of my neighbors felt that if one was patient, things would get done. The constantly-under-construction states of their houses were testament to that belief.

"That's right," he said with another grin. "Little by little we go, until the end of the world. And then, that's it!" Laughing to himself, he jumped in his car, yelled out the window to call him if I needed anything, and drove off.

I often thought about Samuel's comment and how it reflected life in Nocorá. His view seemed to echo a well-known Puerto Rican proverb, or *refrán*, that the best thing God did was to make one day follow another. For most Nocoreños, this indeed seemed to be how they made the best of their environment. For the residents of Tipan, however, living near the wastewater treatment plant added a more profound sense of urgency to their experience of pollution.

1

The Dose Makes the Poison

How Making Drugs Harms Environments and People

[N]ow we also hold ourselves accountable for how we produce
those medicines.

[F]ocusing on the economic, social, and environmental impacts of
our businesses and operations.

[W]e must operate our business in a manner that protects human
health, the environment, our employees and the communities in
which we operate.
    —Representative quotes from pharmaceutical companies'
    public relations literature

Although it is a subject that most people would rather not think about,
wastewater treatment is rapidly becoming a premiere global environmental
problem.[1] On a tropical island like Puerto Rico the problem is only magni-
fied, and this problem has been compounded by the increasing need to deal
with the industrial waste that also enters the water system. Treatment and
management of both domestic and industrial waste has improved in recent
decades. Nevertheless, a number of Puerto Rican communities must bear the
burden of the compromise made between the financial costs of waste management, and the human and environmental costs of failing to manage them
to a high standard.[2] The competing priorities of health and economic realities
often put these communities in the position of feeling that they must compromise their local environment for the sake of either saving public funds or
not alienating the companies that produce the waste.

    In Tipan, the coastal ward of the town of Nocorá (see map, figure 1.2), the
residential neighbors of the municipal water treatment plant have had few
incentives to abide pollution without complaint. From the earliest days of its

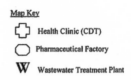

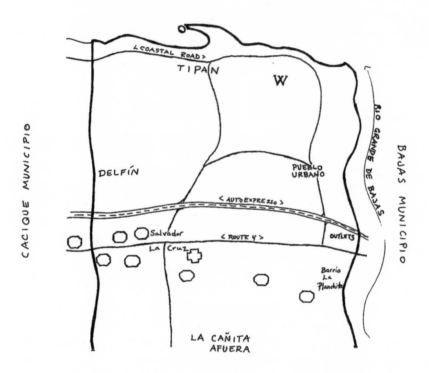

Figure 1.2. Map of the Municipality of Nocorá (not to scale). Drawn by the author.

operation, unbearable odors drifted out of the plant's open-air tanks, a problem that neighbors have always linked to the processing of pharmaceutical waste. "This is a treatment plant that is meant to treat human waste," Lirio Mendez explained to me as we approached the plant one Sunday afternoon. He and some other members of the organization, *el Comité para Defender el Ambiente Nocoreño* (CDAN), were giving me a tour of the environmental low points of Tipan. We pulled midway up the road to the plant, just beyond the trees that blocked the tanks from sight of the main road. He pointed to me and said, "Here, take your picture here."

As I was focusing my camera, I suddenly heard shouting. The guard at the station 100 yards farther on was yelling, and running toward us. I quickly took the picture and hopped back in the car, decidedly freaked out. Don Lirio reassured me with a wave of his hand, and indicated to keep driving up toward the guard. Meanwhile, this man in uniform continued shouting and gesturing angrily that I was not allowed to do that, taking down my license plate number, and generally looking like he was going to burst a blood vessel. Don Lirio and Reynaldo San Pareil both began speaking in calm, rational voices to him, explaining that as residents and members of the *"Comité de Olores"* they had a right to visit the plant, and that it was a public facility. Don Lirio finally lost patience when the guard swore at us, telling him that he was completely out of line, and lecturing him on being polite to women. Feeling that they had won their point, the aging activists returned to the car, and we drove back down the road toward the beach.

"I'm sorry, but I wanted you to see that," he said as we turned onto the main road. My suspicion that I had been set up was confirmed. "I knew something like that would happen, and I wanted you to see how they are, how secretive. Other people don't understand, they don't come here and they don't know." Don Lirio, like many CDAN members, often expressed the belief that if only people knew, if they really understood how the plant was managed, as he was trying to demonstrate to me, then they would realize the necessity of what he and the Committee were trying to accomplish; why they often said, *"Luchamos por todo Nocorá"* [we are fighting for all of Nocorá].

* * *

Tipan, coincidentally the subsite of both previous studies of Nocorá,[3] had its beginnings as an informal settlement of sugarcane workers near the beach. It became more official in the 1950s by the allotment of land parcels and government-subsidized building projects in which neighbors collectively provided the labor to build one another's houses. To the east of the original Tipan settlement (hereafter "Barrio Tipan") lies Tipanito, a more recent settlement of "urbanized" *parcelas*,[4] on the other side of an area of mangroves closer to the water. Barrio Tipan and Tipanito comprise, as of the 2000 Census, 359 housing units. Tipan (in general referring to the whole area) has been the site of the only grassroots environmental movement in Nocorá, in spite of the concerns in the population at-large about pharmaceutical pollution. This chapter explores the development of the wastewater pollution problem, and the emergence of the environmental movement of Tipan. This is a case of a neighborhood whose health has been compromised by the pharmaceutical industry both on the individual level and throughout the broader social structure. As such it is an excellent case study through which to interrogate and expand notions of what is meant by "community health," a concept that is widely spoken of, but not well-defined.

Health in the Cultural Context of Pharmaceutical Production

Conventional medical anthropology has traditionally made a distinction between "illness" and "disease" (i.e., between reported health problems and clinically diagnosed health problems). This distinction is useful because it illustrates the fact that a person's experience of ill health may not match a standard clinical description. However, it has contributed in a detrimental way to the idea that health problems recognized by authorized clinical (or in this case public health) sources are "culture-free [and] politically neutral."[5] This distinction is replicated time and again in epidemiological encounters with environmentally damaged communities, in which the standard tools of public health often fail to quantify the social, psychological, and indeed physical suffering of residents of polluted areas.[6] As such it is vital that we examine the role of the drug makers as much more complex and diffuse than they themselves would present. Those who live in Nocorá are exposed to harm because every aspect of their lives has been touched by the drug companies. For residents of Tipan, the economic benefits do not make tolerable the harm to their bodies and their social status.

In some cases failure to account for physical harm done is the consequence of the limits of methodological approaches for measuring environmental exposures, especially past exposures. In the most well-known example, cancer clusters, the U.S. Centers for Disease Control and Prevention state clearly that even after a cluster is confirmed, "[f]ollow-up investigations can be done, but can take years to complete and the results are generally inconclusive (e.g., usually, no cause is found)."[7] I will argue that in cases like that of Tipan in Nocorá, however, the power structure of the local community, and the influence of corporations within local government, may play a more direct role in whether or not a community's health complaints receive a fair evaluation from the public health establishment.

By examining the experiences of community-based activists in a cultural context largely framed by the pharmaceutical industry and local government, this chapter shows how the community health interests of Tipan have been pushed aside in favor of a broader narrative of economic progress both for the municipality of Nocorá and for its patron industry. In the category of "community health interests" I include negative physical health outcomes likely related to the pollution (based on community-gathered data, as well as data from my fieldwork). However, what is most obviously being damaged is their overall quality of life and shared sense of well-being as much as their physical persons in an epidemiologic sense. This damaged quality of life extends from the individual and family contexts, into the broader political environment, in which Tipanecos experienced marked discrimination. In spite of their isolation as strong critics of the industry, Tipanecos nevertheless shared many of the economic concerns of their Nocoreño compatriots should the pharmaceutical industry leave Puerto Rico. They asked only that the pollution be competently managed.

In considering the broad impact of the power wielded by the pharmaceutical corporations in Nocorá, in Puerto Rico as a whole, and indeed globally, I suggest that they have no need to ally themselves with government in ways that work against people. They could use their influence to materially improve the lives of their residential "neighbors," and yet often have chosen not to do so. Their pervasive unwillingness to think outside the traditional patron-client model of corporate-community relationships with regard to Tipan proves them not to be transformative corporate citizens[8] as their public relations materials would like to advertise (and as exemplified by the quotes on the chapter title page). Rather they are an industry skilled at public relations and crisis management. In anthropological terms, even as they contribute to the economic base of the local culture, they disrupt the environment, and greatly influence social and political relationships. This chapter presents the ethnographic story of Tipan, and the themes raised here will continue to be unfolded and examined in the chapters that follow.

Life-saving Drugs and the Problem of Toxic Waste

The economic situation of Nocorá had long been dire, and by the 1960s local leaders were still in search of a long-term solution to chronic unemployment. While petrochemical refining companies were drawn to the southern coast, the large quantities of high-quality groundwater located in northern coast aquifers served to lure drug manufacturers. The available water was in need of little treatment prior to industrial use, and the companies were permitted by the commonwealth to drill their own wells, and extract tens of millions of gallons, daily, cost-free.

Once established, the drug companies had to plan for the disposal of their copious liquid waste. Typical of accepted waste management practices at the time, one popular solution was for industries to inject liquid wastes into wells drilled especially for that purpose, or into water wells that had been sucked dry by the industry.[9] Doña Graciela, a retired teacher and non-activist resident of Tipan, recalled a school field trip to one of the factories during that era. "I'll never forget," she said. "They were just injecting it into the ground. It was just how it was then."

Injection of waste into underground caverns was one solution; discharging it into the nearby Bajas River was another, and disposing of it in sinkholes which are natural to the region[10] or depositing it in local landfills[11] were still others. When closer attention was drawn to the direct streaming of waste into nearby bodies of water, the companies had the waste loaded onto barges and dumped at a specified site offshore.[12] Local fishermen maintained that, because of the roughness of the ocean in that part of the coast (an area known for surfing), the barge often did not go out as far as it was supposed to, exacting a terrible price on the local aquatic life.[13] It became apparent in the mid-1970s that even under circumstances of "best" dumping practices another solution was necessary, in part because the accumulated contamination from the various practices described above had breached the very aquifer so necessary to the industries. Additionally, in 1974 the federal government had given the U.S. EPA the authority to regulate underground injection for the purpose of protecting drinking water resources.[14] This, in addition to other mandates of the Clean Water Act, proved significant with regard to the North Coast aquifer: by 1987, data from the U.S. Geological Survey indicated that in the Nocorá region, 29 percent of drinking water wells had been closed due to contamination.[15] The need for waste disposal was expected to rise significantly by the early 1980s as the municipal government, in conjunction with *Fomento Industrial* (Puerto Rico Indusrial Development Company, PRIDCO), were planning to build even more chemical factories in the same area.[16]

There was at this time a local wastewater treatment facility for the municipality, capable of handling only domestic wastewater and rain runoff. There is some evidence that new factories being built were nevertheless being given permission to hook up waste pipes to the original treatment plant.[17] Additionally, while the Puerto Rico Environmental Quality Board (EQB) did regulate the companies, in a newspaper interview the then head of the EQB admitted that compliance was measured by data supplied by the industries themselves, a process known as "passive" data collection. Echoing a concern I often heard during my fieldwork decades later, EQB officials lamented, "We do not have enough inspectors to do it ourselves."[18] In a compromise that recognized the inadequacies of a new primary treatment plant to process industrial waste, the industries of Bajas and Nocorá agreed to sponsor the additional construction required to make the plant a secondary treatment facility.[19] The new plant was financed chiefly by a cooperative group of the local pharmaceutical companies, which formed a separate nonprofit corporation (the Nocorá Consortium) to administer the funding for the building and continued maintenance of the treatment plant. At a capacity of 8.3 million gallons daily, by the time of my fieldwork approximately 70 percent of the treatment plant's influent came from the industries located farther inland, mainly the pharmaceuticals.

Early Signs of Trouble for the Nocorá Wastewater Treatment Plant

The planning for the new treatment plant did not go unnoticed by environmental activists, at the time often mobilized through networks that also supported political independence.[20] Unfortunately, as with many environmental mobilizations in Puerto Rico, many people interpreted the concern solely as "*cosa de independentistas*"—simply anti-American or anti-corporate agitations by those who wanted to break away from the United States. Don Lorenzo, a longtime socialist activist living in the town center, lamented: "They never listen, just because we're socialists. But this wasn't anti-capitalism. It wasn't about socialism." His sentiment was echoed in barrio Solita of the neighboring Cacique municipality, where a domestic treatment plant was located, and where residents much later became active in community planning and social justice movements. "Activists came through here when the water company was going to build our plant, with flyers, knocking on doors—and everyone said, 'Oh, they're just agitating.' But now we're sorry we didn't listen."

Ricardo Solano, a chemist who was one of the founding members of the activist group CDAN, remembered the establishment of the wastewater treatment plant a little differently than the official version. According to him, a secondary treatment protocol was not initially deemed sufficient. "The government promised us a tertiary-level treatment plant," he told me with quiet vehemence. "We had community presentations, we asked questions. They promised us a sophisticated plant, capable of treating whatever the industries sent down the pipeline. And they never delivered it." My informants representing the wastewater treatment industry maintained that *properly managed*, the plant should have worked. Said one U.S. engineer familiar with the project, "That facility has been poorly operated and poorly maintained. By the late 1980s, the plant was being operated better, but then pharmaceutical production increased immensely. By that time the plant couldn't take the load being produced."

The plant was planned in two stages, and the primary treatment facility became operational in August 1977, receiving permission from EPA to
accept domestic waste, industrial waste from the food processing factories,
and some "weak wastes" from one of the pharmaceutical factories. Following
treatment, the wastewater from the plant passed through a pipe to an ocean
outfall 815 meters (about half a mile) offshore.[21] The building of the outfall
pipe was the source of one of the earliest controversies involving the plant
and the residents of Tipan.

"It was supposed to be a mile and a half," Reynaldo San Pareil, the former
president of CDAN, told me. "The fishermen will tell you. They know that pipe
isn't what they said it would be. It's from them that we've learned about many of
the effects of the plant, things they see because they're up so early, things they
see because they're on the water." The fishermen of Nocorá were particularly
adamant about two things: (1) the building of the outfall pipe had not gone as
planned, so they were extremely skeptical as to where the treated wastes from
the plant were ending up; and (2) since the establishment of the pharmaceuticals,
even after the treatment plant was supposed to fix the pollution problems, the fish
and other local sea life had gone from a one-time overabundance to nearly zero.

Figure 1.3. During my fieldwork "fish kills" such as this one were still a common site in
the canals running through Tipan. Photo by the author.

I heard the same story many times about the building of the pipe, the basic version of which was as follows: In the preliminary plans (which convinced the community that they would suffer no harm as a consequence of the plant) the outfall pipe was designed to extend approximately 1.5 miles out to sea to ensure an adequate "mixing zone" for the treated waste.[22] The mixing zone for wastewater has the theoretical benefit of further diluting the waste with high concentrations of water (in this case the Atlantic Ocean) so as to reduce the waste-to-water ratio to near negligible levels. However, during the construction of the pipe, the ocean was so fierce that one construction boat was lost, and the completion of the original design distance was deemed impossible. The project was amended, presumably with the approval of the commonwealth's Environmental Quality Board (EQB),[23] and the final distance is now cited at a half mile from shore, at a depth of 27 yards.[24] For some this was simply evidence that the Puerto Rico Aqueduct and Sewer Authority (PRASA), with the rubber stamp of the EQB, always amended its projects for its own convenience regardless of environmental or structural consequences. This also became a recurring theme in my discussions with the Tipan community.

For others it appeared more sinister. Don Gabriel, who had gotten work driving some of the consulting engineers on the project around town, professed deep doubts about the true nature of the mixing zone. "They claimed the pipe was done. Then they put something, a red dye of some kind, into the system, to see where it came out. When it didn't arrive, they said that meant it was mixing really well, that it was good. Me, I think they have no idea where the pipe ends."

Available materials seem to document the stated location of the outfall pipe. However, several compelling pieces of evidence also support the concerns of Tipanecos about the interrelatedness of the dumping of waste, the saga of the pipe construction, and the decline of wildlife. First is a statement made by representatives of the Puerto Rico Water Environment Association, the professional organization to which most engineers working with water issues in Puerto Rico belong, including those associated with this treatment plant. In comments made in support of 301(h) waivers for secondary treatment for the treatment plants in Bayamón and Puerto Nuevo, the Association stated:

> Valid concerns have been voiced about the potential impacts of toxic and bioaccumulative pollutants from municipal discharges. Although secondary treatment may provide incidental removal of some of these compounds, not all such compounds can be managed by biological treatment. Some of these substances can actually have significant adverse effects on

biological treatment processes or seriously affect the quality of resulting biosolids. For these reasons, such compounds are best managed through pollution prevention programs, such as the existing PRASA industrial pretreatment program, and domestic toxic control programs. Pollution prevention and waste minimization should always take precedence over end-of-the-pipe treatment.[25]

While these comments were made in the current era of more stringent industrial pretreatment, they suggest that even if it were performed optimally (which evidence suggests it seldom has been), secondary treatment of toxic wastes may not have been sufficient for the Nocorá influent. Federal pretreatment regulation of pharmaceutical wastewater was not established until the late 1990s.

Additionally, a series of microbiological studies carried out in the 1980s found conclusively that the effluent being discharged into the ocean had high levels of biological pathogens, and that contrary to the design of the outfall, waste was collecting near the shore.[26] Furthermore, one of the studies observed, in spite of the wave action of the mixing zone, the effluent moving back toward the shore was accumulating in an area rich in mangroves and other wetland ecological systems. This study warned that there was a likelihood that both pathogenic bacteria and their necessary nutrients could likewise accumulate in the wetlands environment, creating a "disease reservoir."[27] The findings of these studies, which were designed to measure biological contaminants, suggest that the plant was not even capable of effectively processing the *domestic* waste it was receiving during this time. These studies did not evaluate the chemical quality of the effluent, but considering that the treatment of industrial wastes is generally agreed to be a more specialized process than that of domestic wastes, the data do not reflect well on the functioning of the plant overall. Finally, a study designed to evaluate waste dispersal methods through the detection of volatile organic compounds (VOCs) in ocean waters found that, although the effluent from the plant was significantly lower in VOCs than untreated waste, "the coastal environment is not readily flushed of the discharged waste, and waste contamination does impinge on the shoreline."[28] In spite of persistent doubts about the efficacy of the treatment of the water, PRASA regularly sought waivers of secondary treatment requirements for the Nocorá plant. These waivers allow plants that treat domestic waste to comply with a lower level of treatment when discharging into ocean waters, and have often been sought by PRASA for their coastal plants, due to the higher costs of complying with secondary treatment. In the case of the Nocorá plant, the waivers have been routinely denied. Given the plant's ongoing problems, the performance of the denial may have been intended to demonstrate the effectiveness of the permit system, in lieu of other regulatory action.

Bad Odors and the Problem of Defining a Problem

The secondary treatment phase of the plant was inaugurated in 1981, and within two years there was already evidence of severe problems—and evidence of the difficulty of getting those problems recognized. In a memo to the EPA–Caribbean field office in June 1983, an EPA engineer reported his communications with the earliest incarnation of the group CDAN, and his subsequent inspection of the treatment plant.[29] The primary complaint from the community was a phrase that would become ubiquitous in Nocorá for the next several decades, and that would recur repeatedly in my fieldwork: bad odors (*malos olores*).

This simple phrase has a way of sounding at times silly, at times quaint. A bad odor, in common parlance, is something that causes social discomfort more than physical. It is the result of a person nearby who is smoking a cigar, passing digestive gas, or driving an old car. A bad odor is, in the words of the EPA memo, a "nuisance." It is presumed by most people to be not a big deal, certainly not something around which an entire community can coalesce. It does not sound like the reasonable basis for a lawsuit, or a public health study.

In the wastewater treatment literature, however, the monitoring of both odors and corrosion is a constant and serious concern for treatment systems, and the two are in fact often correlated.[30] For the town of Nocorá, the subject of *malos olores* (also called *olores objetables*, or objectionable odors) is likewise a very serious one, whether the odors come from the treatment plant in Tipan, or directly from the factories. Because of the technical challenges involved in measuring environmental exposures and linking them directly to disease, I will not argue that the disposal of pharmaceutical waste is "killing" the neighbors of Tipan in a strict epidemiological sense (as implied by Francisco's words in the Introduction). Rather, I wish to consider the proposition that 20 years of pollution and of insufficient action on the part of the polluters has deprived Tipanecos of "*what matters most: life and the potential it holds when we are feeling our best*," to borrow a phrase from the public relations materials of a local pharmaceutical company (emphasis added).

In many examples of industrial pollution, it is typical for polluters to claim previous ignorance of the potential for harm from their products or by-products, and to earnestly display present-day environmental accomplishments as a counternarrative to criticism. One U.S.-based environmental engineer I interviewed even made this argument on behalf of the Nocorá pharmaceuticals, assuring me that "abuse in general [in the industry] was out of ignorance." However, the claim of 'we didn't know' in the case of the Nocorá Consortium and the treatment plant does not, as one might say, hold water. PRASA's now well-known track record of poor maintenance[31] was corroborated by the earliest reports from regulatory inspectors of the Nocorá treatment plant.

Signs of Structural Distress

The 12-page report to the EPA field office[32] is an impressive compendium of operational problems at the treatment plant in Tipan. It includes mention of machinery that is inoperable as a result of disrepair and/or severe corrosion, uncalibrated and/or nonfunctioning monitoring instruments, and significant inconsistencies in monitoring records. The inspector noted, "There is no way the plant can be run effectively if the instrumentation deficiencies are not corrected." One of the two primary settling tanks was completely out of operation and looked "corroded in most of its metal parts and [was] in very poor condition." He further observed that one of the two aerated grit chambers for the initial removal of sand and other solids appeared "not to have been in operation for weeks."[33]

The inspector also found what he considered to be evidence of several violations of the National Pollutant Discharge Elimination System (NPDES) permit, including to the effluent limitation, monitoring requirements, and special discharge conditions. According to the permit, only the seven original pharmaceutical partners were identified by PRASA as "major contributing industries authorized to discharge" at the plant. However, PRASA had failed to identify to the enforcement agencies nine other industrial users of the treatment plant. He noted that the color of the effluent exiting the plant, to be released by means of the ocean outfall, was sufficiently black to alter the color of the receiving water, in spite of the mixing zone. He also noted it had a "very offensive smell."

A significant finding of this 1983 inspection was that the use of the plant had substantially diverged from the intentions of the original design. There appeared to be little or no consideration by those who had planned the plant of the impact of increasing industrial usage, apart from an increased quantity of liquid. According to the inspection, the plant was receiving far below its capacity for the *volume* of influent, and yet utterly failing to treat the high concentration of wastes contained within that influent. For the majority of residents of Tipan, the consequences of these operating conditions were frequent clouds of noxious fumes floating into their homes, causing respiratory problems, nausea, severe eye irritation, and often severe lack of sleep.

Within several months of this inspection the community had experienced no substantial relief from the situation, causing the *Comité para Defender el Ambiente Nocoreño* to once again contact the EPA, this time at the regional level in New York. In October 1983, CDAN received a highly unsatisfactory response from that office. Admittedly, accession to CDAN's request that the facility be closed until the problems could be resolved was an unlikely outcome, and the EPA was justified in pointing out that without the plant, the industries in the area would have nowhere to dispose of waste, and would have to stop production.[34] In what was to become a familiar refrain from officials, the EPA administrator suggested that such changes would cause layoffs of local employees, an outcome she presumed no one wanted.

As representative of CDAN, Ricardo Solano had received both this October letter and the field inspection memo of a few months earlier. A comparison of both documents is instructive to understanding the pattern of contradiction that would characterize the community-government-industry interactions for the next 20 years. Notably, both documents addressed the question of possible violations of the NPDES permit. As mentioned, the field inspection memo[35] described several strongly suspected violations, evidenced particularly by the foul quality of the effluent discharge. In contrast, the regional administrator's letter states:

> The Environmental Protection Agency (EPA) has been closely monitoring the [Nocorá] facility with respect to compliance with its National Pollutant Discharge Elimination System (NPDES) permit. According to monthly sampling reports that are submitted to the EPA, the facility is consistently in compliance with its effluent limitations. Furthermore, a sampling survey conducted by EPA in April, 1983 also indicated compliance with effluent limitations for a wide range of parameters.[36]

Given the discrepancy between the poor operational functioning found by the inspector in June 1983, and the confidence expressed by the regional office with regard to self-reported compliance only a few months later, it is not surprising that the residents of Tipan were soon trying to gather their own evidence.

Regulations Catch Up—But the Damage Is Done

Sitting at Don Reynaldo's kitchen table, I found myself flipping through photographs, and came across one I recognized. "Look, it's Don Gabriel," I said, holding up the picture. "He's so young." This was a relative statement, since the Don Gabriel I knew, a fisherman and active member of CDAN, was a small, wiry man, of few words, with a head of pure white hair. The one staring out of the photograph, holding up a manhole cover so the camera could see the inside of the sewer, was far less wrinkled, with hair of iron gray. I flipped through and saw groups of men standing over a sewer pipe, pictures taken in Tipan, and in downtown Nocorá. An election poster marked the year as 1984.

Don Reynaldo leaned over to me when I asked what exactly they were doing. "That was before my time," he said, looking carefully. "But the one of Gabriel I think is meant to show the damage in the pipe. When the sewers are built they have metal ladders into them, you know, at the manholes. When the residents opened them up, they found the ladders had been eaten away, corroded completely."

The next time I saw him, I asked Don Gabriel about the manholes, and he laughed. "Didn't you hear about the manholes? Sometimes, whatever they were putting in the pipe, it would mix all up, and smell terrible. The air coming out of the manholes would make you choke. But even worse, sometimes the manhole covers would explode! Pow, clear into the air!"

The September 2003 report, "EPA's National Pretreatment Program, 1973–2003: Thirty Years of Protecting the Environment" gives credence to these fantastical sounding reports of explosions and other disaster-quality events from the Tipan activists, citing the following areas as arguments in favor of a rigorous pretreatment program:

> *Protecting the physical integrity of the sewer system.* Volatile organic compounds discharged to sewers may accumulate in the head space of sewer lines, increasing the potential for explosions that may cause significant damage. Discharge limitations and management practices required by the Pretreatment Program reduce the likelihood of such catastrophes.
>
> *Preventing the buildup of poisonous gases.* Discharges of toxic organics can generate poisonous gases, through various kinds of mixing and chemical reactions. Appropriate pretreatment discharge limits prevent this gas buildup.[37]

This same report lauds the achievements of the EPA's pretreatment program for industrial discharges into Publicly Owned Treatment Works (POTWs, such as the Tipan treatment plant), noting as an example a major drop-off in the transfer of toxic organic chemicals to POTWs across the country beginning in 1988. These nationwide numbers fell rapidly between 1988 and 1990, reaching a low-level plateau in 1994.

However, it was not until 1990 that EPA first published an "Effluent Guidelines Plan (55 FR 80), in which schedules were established for developing new and revised effluent guidelines for several industry categories," including the pharmaceuticals.[38] Charging that this plan did not sufficiently meet the requirements of the Clean Water Act, public interest groups quickly filed a lawsuit, and in 1992 a Consent Decree required that EPA begin developing a special rule specifically for the pharmaceutical industry. This process, which began in 1992, required that a rule be proposed by 1995, to go into effect in 1998, and require full compliance by 2001.[39]

Examining the Toxic Release Inventory(TRI) summaries for the year 2003, and comparing them to the years 1988–2002, the effect of the pretreatment rule on the release of toxins to public treatment plants is impressive. Between 1988 and 2002, when pharmaceutical industries were permitted to send wastewater into the Nocorá treatment plant, they released more than 47 million pounds of TRI-monitored chemicals. The most recent data indicate that they are now releasing primarily the less toxic pollutants for which reporting is required, and in much lower quantities. From the time the plant opened (1981) through 1987, there are no public data.

When asked about the pretreatment rule, one pharmaceutical environmental manager extolled the virtues, quite rightly, of their on-site pretreatment system, which, according to an independent environmental engineer who oversaw the project, was absolutely state-of-the-art. Praise of their technological achievements aside, however, the manager did express some resentment of the pretreatment regulations:

> Each company paid a percentage to build the [regional] plant, and still pays, by percentage, for its maintenance. This percentage gives each company rights to put a certain amount of BOD into the system. But now with the pretreatment required, we're putting almost zero BOD into the system. So pretreatment regulations have really taken away property rights that we bought and paid for. . . . That's another way of looking at it.[40]

While this argument might hold sway in an unregulated market system, under U.S. jurisdiction the property rights of corporations, as legally created entities, are only those that are granted by law. However, as entities with no natural lifespan, it is perhaps not surprising that the corporate view of law is more negotiable and flexible than it might otherwise be. Corporations, like their polluting by-products, may very well outlive the laws that regulate them.[41]

During my fieldwork, concerns about the outcome of a class action lawsuit (filed by a group of Tipanecos in 2000) were running high. It is therefore understandable that few managers volunteered their views on the case directly, or even on their relationship to Tipan in general. However, as in the quote above, their statements demonstrated that their perspectives on local pollution were not proactive. Rather they strongly reflected the idea that the interest of companies should be protected. This attitude toward the off-site waste management makes an interesting contrast to the views expressed by another environmental manager with regard to *on-site* pollution management: The SuperMed environmental engineer, who had been promoted to community relations work, generously praised his own company's preemptive stance on chemical leaks. "I have always been proud to work for a company like SuperMed. . . . Leaks happen," he continued with a shrug, explaining that it was always better to use above-ground pipes for toxic wastes, because then leaks could not cause as much damage.

> They were visionaries. The designers of these facilities in the 1970s saw that Puerto Rico was so beautiful, so pristine, even I was surprised when I started working here in the late 1980s, to see these facilities built above ground, in order to protect the underground water. . . . I would be lying if I said we'd been perfect. There have been situations in which you have to sit down and explain. For example, if a line breaks . . . you hope it doesn't, you work to prevent it, but these things happen.

Echoing the seeming inevitability of leaking pipes, the public relations officer for BigPharma also stated in an interview, "Accidents do happen."

Underground pipes, like those delivering the industrial influent to the treatment plant, are obviously more difficult to monitor, and are therefore more potentially hazardous. In the case of a waste stream that is composed of a highly variable, highly volatile mix of chemicals from multiple facilities, they would be all the more so. One might ask why they should not receive regular monitoring. But as informants consistently reported on this question, the companies had always taken pains to assert that once the wastes entered the shared portion of the pipe, they were no longer individually liable for the pipe maintenance, in part because it became impossible to identify which industry was the source of any individual chemical.

On the one occasion when a pharmaceutical representative did divulge his perspective on the Tipan legal case to me, it was equally revealing:

There is a group, down by the beach, that has a lawsuit [. . .] and they really might win, might get some money. But they're not really suffering. They didn't know they had problems until some big lawyers from San Juan and those environmentalists told them they were suffering. And now, they could really get some money for that.

This attitude recalls the analysis proposed by social theorists[42] that people inhabiting oppressive roles tend to see themselves as human, while seeing the groups they oppress as faceless masses, as somehow less than human.[43] In this case the manager, an environmental specialist expressing the corporate perspective, could not acknowledge that the Tipanecos had sufficient self-awareness to judge their own experience accurately. His words suggest that his environmental expertise had instead given *him* the ability to more accurately assess their suffering. And in his judgment, they were not really suffering.

Health and Quality of Life Concerns in Tipan

From the beginning of the treatment plant's operations, residents of Tipan reported health problems associated with the odors.[44] The acute symptoms they described were primarily respiratory, as well as burning of the eyes and nasal passages. They also frequently reported symptoms that are more difficult to define in strict clinical terms, but which are nevertheless indicative of disturbed health, particularly if they are chronic; e.g., the frequently occurring odors of both domestic waste and chemicals were reported by many residents to cause nausea so overwhelming that they could not eat. The sudden arrival of strong odors was credited with profoundly disturbing the sleep patterns of residents, preventing them from falling asleep as well as waking them in the middle of the night.

For residents of Tipan, antiquated notions of miasmic sickness, contamination produced by foul odors emanating from noxious waters, was not a public health fairy tale, but a reality.[45] When Don Reynaldo arrived in Tipan in 1995,[46] he began coordinating some of his neighbors to write daily reports of the experience of *la peste*. "We call it *la peste*, because it is more than just a bad smell," Don Reynaldo explained. "You see, the word *peste*, it's like *pestilencia*, it gives the idea of sickness." Recognizing that reports from members of CDAN could perhaps be dismissed as "troublemaking" or "the usual suspects," he recruited three women from the neighborhood to do reports on their own. "I had Beatriz [his wife] recruit women from her church, because they lived in houses that were somewhat apart from one another [and therefore respresentative], but also because of their religious dedication, no one would be able to accuse them of lying for me." He collected daily notes on their experience of *la peste* for several years in the mid- to late 1990s, and sent copies, with his own reports, at weekly intervals, to pharmaceutical managers, PRASA officials and managers of the treatment plant, and at one point, to the union representative of the local PRASA workers. Excerpts from these reports eloquently describe both the chronicity and the intensity of the impact of the treatment plant on barrio life.

> Friday: 5:00 am. It began. Very strong the kind of stink that leaves the eyes watery and burning. What is it going to take to make it stop? We are never going to be free! It began at 10:00 pm again!
>
> Sunday: 8:20 am, later 5:00 pm–11:59 pm. Today was horrible, an incredibly strong odor of gas, I have had a headache for three days, and the odor of gas is affecting me very much.
>
> Monday: This morning very early at 5:30 am the stink flooded my bedroom. Not only do we have to sleep with it, but now like an "alarm clock" it wakes us up! Who can eat breakfast like this!

Similarly compelling are the expressions of relief, gratitude, and even encouragement to the plant operators when the reporters have nothing to report: "Monday: Didn't feel the stink today! Not even at night. It's the way it should be."

In his cover letters for the reports, Don Reynaldo often expressed not only the frustration and ill health of his community, but also a sense that if only their experience could be compassionately understood, then those who had the knowledge, the resources, and the power to address the situation at the plant would do so. In mid-1996, Don Reynaldo informed those receiving the reports that they would now be sent in English, in hopes that this would facilitate understanding for any North Americans who held management positions. As most Puerto Ricans in high positions were likely to be able to at least read English, the reports remained accessible to them. On New Year's Eve of 1996, Don Reynaldo wrote:

> Last day of the year and the problems of the odors have not been solved. This is destroying our health, it is impossible for us to enjoy our life, because the odors come into our houses making us unhappy, making us sick, and not able to rest because of the gases that come from the Plant. What is causing all these problems? [. . .] This not only makes us sick, but it also contaminates our surroundings, and who knows, problems in other

areas. We hope that deep in your hearts you really want to do your best to help solve this problem. Something you have promised so many times that you will do.

Don Reynaldo continued to express his courteous, if desperate-sounding, hope that between the companies and PRASA a solution would be reached, through some combination of better maintenance and more attentive supervision of the treatment plant. Nevertheless, CDAN had begun considering other options, and they began sending information to an environmental lawyer. Nearly another four years would pass before CDAN would actually take the drastic step of naming not only PRASA, but the corporate pharmaceutical members of the Nocorá Consortium, in a lawsuit filed in February 2000. Shortly thereafter, residents began to notice a significant decrease in the frequency and intensity of odors, though periodic problems remained. CDAN members believed, and the ethnographic evidence supports the idea, that without the threat of a court order for oversight, the Consortium and PRASA would have had few incentives to keep the plant under control.

The Balance of Power and Control of Information

The lawsuit did not endear CDAN to the pharmaceuticals—nor to Nocoreño elected officials. But the official position of the Nocorá municipal government as it was expressed to me was that organized communities are a positive force in the life of the municipality. Speaking of CDAN and the community activism in Tipan, a high-ranking official familiar with environmental issues told me that "the plant has improved because it was *obligated* to by the community. The municipality, too, has supported the community's efforts, we've given them money to help their organization, brought in experts to work on the problems." Without prompting, he brought up the lawsuit himself, claiming that it had been an important part of the improvement process, providing a certain kind of pressure, because "bad publicity doesn't interest the industries."

The municipal administration had, however, also played a role in trying to destabilize CDAN's legal efforts. One of the "helping" actions promised through the municipally sponsored "Committee on Odors" was to arrange an epidemiological study. The study was supposed to establish whether the gaseous emissions from the treatment plant, particularly hydrogen sulfide and volatile organic compounds, were causing the widely reported respiratory ailments in the neighborhood. It was to be organized, on behalf of Tipanecos, through the alcalde's office by means of the regional health department. When it was arranged, the group's outside environmental advisors asked for a copy of the questionnaire in advance. It turned out to be a basic survey, "to show that health problems were from smoking, hygiene, etc., with *no attempt to measure air quality*," the environmental consultants stated.[47] Follow-up interviews in the Environmental Health Division, and my own review of the survey instrument, confirmed the intent of the study. Said one health worker: "When I found out they were going to use the survey to blame the community, I refused to work on it." When questioned, a supervisor familiar with the project gave me a confused look, saying, "A simple health survey was what was requested of us." The requested survey would not have answered whether an association existed between the gases coming from the treatment plant and respiratory disease. The point person for the alcalde in dealing with such arrangements, the environmental director, had a Master's degree in Public Health—it can only be assumed he would have known the difference between a sanitary survey and a more elaborate toxic impact study.

The officially sanctioned sanitary survey was halted by CDAN, but as part of the process of planning their lawsuit the group also made an effort to collect its own data, a classic example of what Phil Brown has called "popular epidemiology."[48] In 2000, the U.S. Census identified 359 households as comprising the urbanized areas of Tipan; in 1997, CDAN was able to collect the health data, shown in table 1.1, from 353 households in that area.

As an epidemiologist, I would never present data such as those in table 1.1 as definitive proof that there is a causal relationship between the wastewater treatment plant and the asthma and other respiratory ailments reported among Tipan's residents. However, given the available data (which sometimes list health issues as present in the household without identifying individual sufferers), the statistics shown here do suggest a qualitatively significant social suffering. The numbers also indicate a substantial burden of

Table 1.1. Households Reporting One or More Member(s) with Respiratory Complaints

Condition	Percent
Asthma or chronic "difficulty breathing" (undiagnosed)	75.1
Asthma alone	37.7
Non-asthma chronic respiratory infections (including chronic cold)	46.7
Total asthma and/or other chronic respiratory infection (defined separately from "difficulty breathing")	84.4

care and/or chronic symptom management that is distributed widely across households in Tipan—a measure of community health seldom addressed by traditional epidemiologic methods. I found that although they tried to be more active in CDAN, a number of local women had difficulty balancing activism, work, and the need to care for family members struggling with asthma and other chronic health problems. Furthermore, when viewed in light of two recent studies of asthma in Puerto Rico, the figures in table 1.1 represent a community health problem that merited serious investigation. A study of island Puerto Rican homes[49] suggests that traditional indoor exposures (e.g., mold and dust) are less relevant to asthma locally, in good part because the homes are so well ventilated, as is the case in Tipan. Another study[50] using Behavioral Risk Factor Surveillance Survey (BRFSS) data concluded that asthma prevalence among island-dwelling Puerto Ricans did not differ among age groups, people smoking at least 100 cigarettes in their entire life, or physical activity, some of the "usual suspects" of asthma.

Together, these two studies suggest that Tipan's data on asthma and chronic respiratory problems did indeed deserve the attention of a specially tailored study—a study taking into account not solely the usual individual behavioral variables, but external air quality as well (such as might freely blow into well-ventilated houses from nearby sources). Indeed, as one employee of the local health clinic stated, "The high incidence of bronchial asthma, bad odors, and environmental pollution worry us. Studies should be done to minimize these risks." Admittedly, the Department of Health does not always have the resources to conduct complex studies that focus on small groups of people. However, scarce resources were not the basis of the failure to accurately quantify Tipan's health. In an effort to avoid the bad publicity that "doesn't interest the industries," the evidence suggests that the municipal government intentionally requested a study that would collect only enough information to effectively blame the residents for any existing pattern of disease (by means of their behaviors). These findings would have ultimately exonerated their local corporate citizens.

While the *alcalde* [mayor] of Nocorá would most likely have supported or been neutral about a suit naming only PRASA as a defendant, he was much colder to the residents of Tipan after they threatened the pharmaceuticals. As the backbone of Nocorá's economy, they were an integral part of the alcalde's vision for its future growth and development. In spite of the widespread acknowledgment, including by municipal insiders, that the suit was an essential catalyst to improvements at the plant, Tipan became increasingly isolated and actively removed from participation in the sociopolitical life of Nocorá. During the period of the lawsuit, major development projects were being planned for Tipan, and the community was not kept well-informed, including regarding major land re-zoning and other changes. The alcalde's vision of Tipan's future would certainly have affected present and future residents, particularly those who would be living in a planned housing development near Barrio Tipan.[51]

The Companies Sometimes Work Together—For Their Own Benefit

Residents eventually became engaged in a variety of problem-solving efforts, both independent (prying up manhole covers) and cooperative (decades-old industry-government-resident committees). Given the persistent complaints, and the acknowledgment of a problem by representatives of PRASA, local government, and the pharmaceutical companies, it is hard to understand how the *malos olores* problem could remain unresolved. The abysmally poor track record of PRASA's environmental compliance[52] should have led "*los grandes*" (as Tipanecos sometimes referred to those with more power than they had) to be alert from the beginning to the need for more effective oversight of the plant. However, other documents suggest that the industry itself was most concerned with meeting the demands of technical compliance without sacrificing their competitive edge in production.

A 1994 memo from an industry environmental compliance specialist, once a high-ranking member of the Environmental Quality Board (EQB), makes this perspective clear.[53] The memo, outlining a request for an exception to the treatment plant permit, emphasized the high costs of requiring the plant to meet treatment specifications as its effluent exited the plant and entered the outfall pipe (the usual place to measure compliance). This was the point at which the 1983 inspection noted a foul-smelling black effluent, which the inspector believed had discolored the ocean water in spite of the mixing zone.[54] In order for the mixing zone to be effective, it was assumed that the plant was in good working order.

In the case of the Nocorá wastewater treatment plant, it was never just the destination of the treated waters that gave cause for concern, but the quality of influent into the plant, and the gases released during the treatment process. The better the treatment, the fewer locations in the process to release gases, and the higher the quality of the water being put into the ocean where local fishermen made their livelihoods. However, in the period during which the first organized threat of legal action was raised in the mid-1990s, the pharmaceuticals were making it clear that they preferred that water quality not be measured at either the influent site or the effluent site (as is typical), *but at the mixing zone itself.*[55] This strategy demonstrates that technical legal

compliance with Clean Water Act regulation was a concern for the companies, but their focus on the mixing zone does not suggest a system-wide perspective on the dangers of the wastestream. Furthermore, it does not line
up with the later sentiments expressed by local leaders in the field that "Pollution prevention and waste minimization should always take precedence
over end-of-the-pipe treatment."[56] This set of comments, also quoted earlier,
is one of the most direct examples of how technically accurate information
can be bent to the will of the expert, and how easily blame is shifted through
expert-based discourse. The memo appealing to the primacy of the mixing
zone sought to shift responsibility and cost away from the pharmaceuticals;
the later memo promoting pretreatment shifted responsibility and cost away
from PRASA (the Aqueduct and Sewer Authority, managers of the wastewater treatment plants).

If we consider the proposal to measure at the mixing zone to indicate
indifference to the realities of both air and water pollution from the Nocorá
wastewater treatment plant (NWTP), the following quote from the same
memo shows that minimizing costs was the main concern of the companies:

> Since it is in the interest of the Commonwealth of Puerto Rico to maintain
> and promote the selection of Puerto Rico as a suitable home for the phar-
> maceutical industry, the maximum operational flexibility of the [N]WTP
> should be made available.[57]

Other documentation from about a year later also indicates that although
the Consortium was involved in trying to make improvements to the treatment plant to minimize the odors reaching Tipan, its mandate was to "exe-
cute the best alternative at the least cost."[58] It is also important to note in
the block quote given earlier the thinly veiled threat that the pharmaceutical
industry *as a whole* would likely abandon Puerto Rico if the proposal was
not accepted. The threat of not just one factory abandoning the island, but an
entire industry upon which the island's economy relied substantially, was not
an idle one. By 1997, the pharmaceutical preparations industry had secured
its place as the largest manufacturing employer in Puerto Rico.[59]

While the industrial nature of the influent was largely resolved by the
pretreatment regulations, the problems of hydrogen sulfide production
and corrosion within the system remain constant problems for all treatment facilities. The literature on this issue, as noted above, agrees that only
high-quality maintenance will prevent such odor- and pollution-related difficulties. According to the general tenets of Corporate Social Responsibility
(CSR), with which the pharmaceutical companies willingly ally themselves,

as private partners with government in the business of the Nocorá treatment plant, they had an ethical, if perhaps not a legal, obligation to the
Tipan community. This obligation required that they move beyond their
traditional adversarial stance as the wastewater treatment plant's cost-
cutting banker, and demand higher quality return for their investment in
the plant. An audit by the island's Office of the Comptroller reported that
though improvements had been made by the time of my fieldwork, PRASA
continued to have serious management and maintenance problems with
their water treatment plants.[60] Perhaps such difficulties could be expected in
a large public system such as PRASA—but if, as the alcalde assured me, the
drug companies were immediately responsive to urgent needs of the Nocorá
plant, then surely Tipanecos should have been able to expect better than
average maintenance:

> They [the pharmaceutical companies] pay 80% of the operational costs of
> the plant, continuously. Whatever type of repair that needs to be made that
> is urgent, they come with their own people, in association with PRASA . . .
> wherever the necessary part is, in the world, by airplane or whatever, they
> bring it here . . . not for the protection or the health of the *pueblo*, you
> understand, but because it affects their production. But as a consequence,
> we have benefited, because the majority of Nocorá is now connected to a
> sewer system[61] . . . which has allowed the people to improve their health
> overall.

This quote suggests that Alcalde Martínez,[62] though he was an active partner
of the local industry, was more pragmatic than complimentary in his view
about the motives of the pharmaceuticals. It may well have been that their
purported commitment (which much of the evidence would contradict) was
merely one of mutually rewarding self-interest. However, if the pharmaceuticals had a commitment to more than just compliance, as they would have
liked the public to believe, they should certainly have been treating the complaints of residents with the respect, and the action, they deserved.

The Individual Face of Corporate Conduct

In our conversations around his kitchen table Don Reynaldo sometimes
spoke with thoughtful regret about suing the pharmaceuticals; at times he
said that he did not want to name them, as well as PRASA, but he had no
choice. "They always treated me politely, you know," he told me more than
once, a grave look always on his face.

The one from SuperMed, particularly, he was always very gentleman-like with me. I remember him telling me, 'Don Reynaldo, I think I see a light, it's a very small light, but I think there is a light at the end of the tunnel.' He always seemed like he wanted to help.

I asked Don Reynaldo when it was that the environmental engineer from SuperMed (whom I later interviewed) claimed to see this "light at the end of the tunnel." He guessed it was around 1998 or 1999, before the lawsuit, because they never spoke after the suit was filed. I observed that it was interesting that the pharmaceutical rep had predicted an end to the wastewater problems just around the time that the pretreatment regulation was handed down. I wondered aloud if the tiny light was 2001, when the industry was scheduled to require full compliance. He was quiet a moment, and then he said, "It could be. It could very well be."

The pharmaceutical representatives I worked with represented a range of attitudes toward the average citizens of the community of Nocorá. In considering the group as a whole, it is clear that although the cultural structures of the corporation limited the vision and actions of the managers working in community relations, their individual qualities can make a difference in some areas. One from AlphaPharm in particular gave a much more convincing demonstration of his commitment to his job in "Community Affairs" than was typical. During our interviews and in observing some of his outreach activities, this community affairs manager articulated very clearly that he viewed his role, as a manager and as a person, in terms of doing good in the world. He acknowledged to me once that there were limits to what one person could accomplish, but that in the distinct areas of responsibility in his life (e.g., in the home, as well as at work) he strove to improve the lot of those around him. Demonstrating his grounding in Human Resources, he spoke passionately about his efforts to help AlphaPharm's employees. "We always try to give the employees we already have the opportunity to get more training to move to a new, better job." Nevertheless, this industry manager was ultimately unwilling, or perhaps unable, to concede the obvious advantages his company had when dealing with residents' complaints: money, connections, organization, and arguably a better public image than some local environmentalists.

If someone in the neighborhood has a problem, they should come to me. Like the woman who called because she thought our construction had caused the flooding on her street. She called, and I investigated. What I don't like is when outsiders come in and get involved. I don't think that's right.

Even when the pharmaceutical managers expressed a more humane outlook, they shared a sense of entitlement to political and legal access, which they did not acknowledge as an important factor in the quest of grassroots groups for social justice. They were quick to label nonresident environmentalists or other advocates "outsiders," though none of the managers I spoke with lived in Nocorá. As Don Lirio demonstrated, this social distance did not go unnoticed by Tipanecos: "They don't come here," he fumed quietly one afternoon. "They don't know about our environment, they live somewhere else!" For the managers it was the residence of the company itself within the town's borders that gave them, or any corporate official, a claim to insider knowledge. And yet corporate community affairs representatives often claimed to "know the community" based on their own personal experiences, moving with remarkable fluidity between expressing their own feelings and expressing opinions that sounded more like a personal identification with corporate policy.

In presenting the corporate perspective on local environmental activism, managers tended to attribute most concerns to reactionary NIMBYism (Not in My Backyard activism),[63] and therefore ultimately to ignorance. In the case of Tipan, the wastewater treatment plant, and the Nocorá pharmaceutical industry community concerns were not based in ignorance. Rather, it exemplified the attempts of a small community, unified by more than 20 years of embodied physical experience and organized struggle, to have their right to well-being acknowledged and respected—to be free of the effects of poisonous by-products. Efforts to isolate and minimize the history of pollution in Tipan, using the narrative of economic progress for the rest of Nocorá and Puerto Rico as a supposedly self-evident trade-off, should not have been acceptable. Likewise, the suggestions that the environmental problem was not really that bad, that Tipanecos were "not really suffering," was a misappropriation of conventional epidemiological wisdom that "the dose makes the poison." In this perspective, low levels of toxic exposures were not presumed to constitute a "real" risk, barring an easily measureable negative outcome. However, a variety of evidence demonstrates that in light of the social responsibility claims made by these same companies, they must be held to a higher standard, one they espoused themselves.

While I have sought to critique the naturalized structures, roles, and other power dynamics that contribute to health (or in this case its lack), I began the research from the perspective that the corporations and their representatives, too, had a story to tell; I designed the project with the intention of taking the pharmaceutical corporations at their word with regard to their community-social behaviors, or at least to ethnographically understand their perspective. What I often found, as is evident in the quotes above, was that in seeking to explain their own perspectives, and to defend typically self-protective corporate stances, pharmaceutical managers inadvertently revealed many of the paradoxes of the practice of so-called corporate citizenship. With the assistance of government agencies and elected officials, the pharmaceutical companies of Nocorá created an environment in which the evaluation of "what matters most: life and the potential it holds when we are feeling our best," was, in fact, open to debate. As a consequence, the quality-of-life of Tipanecos was not, in practice, at the core of the pharmaceuticals' missions. Rather, the most central value remained to minimize the costs of production for the world's most profitable industry.[64]

Such obvious human suffering and apparent disinterest on the part of figures of authority often provokes the question, "How did things get so bad in the first place?" It would be easy to shake one's fist and blame the oppressive nature of an ever-expanding and dehumanizing capitalist system. However, in order to understand how such harmful social relationships and cultural patterns develop over time in a place like Nocorá, it is crucial to take a step back and look at the community through a historical lens.

Figure 2.1. Decaying structure of the old *Central* (sugar refinery). Photo by the author.

Progress

Benicia's neighbor, Lucia, took it upon herself to explain the local political dynamic to me. "Estrello and I, we go way back, and so people always ask me about him. I'm not in his party. But I know him, and he's always seen things the way he sees them. He's always had a vision for the town." She sighed. "The problem is, he's stubborn, and he doesn't let anyone say anything. He just does things his way. A lot of times he's had ideas I can understand, but then he takes it too far.

"Take the houses by the river. They would flood every year, twice a year sometimes. And people would just move back in and clean up. Collect their FEMA money. Not 'move to a safer place money,' but 'just do it all again the next time' money. So Estrello tears down those houses, builds the dam, and builds these new apartments. I understand building the dam, it was necessary. But once you had the dam, the houses would be safe. He tore them down because they were ugly.

"He did the same with the library. The library, did you notice it's named after [a famous boxer born in Nocorá]? That's where his house was, the house where he grew up, an old house. Estrello proposed to build a library on the site, using money from the pharmaceuticals, and to make it an 'electronic' library, with computers. Everyone was thrilled. We thought, the house will be preserved, or at least part of it, like a museum, and we'll get a new library. But when the time came, he knocked the house down completely, built a new structure, and there's a tiny room upstairs with a few of [the boxer]'s personal things. It's not a monument to him! But that's what he does, he knocks things down and builds new. Soon there won't be anything left of our *pueblo* except what he built. I'm not sure that's progress."

2

In the Beginning Was the Corporation

Progress, Pollution, and the Public Trust

[O]fficial statistics substantially overstate production of goods and services on the island. The problem arises from section 936 of the U.S. tax code [instituted in 1976 and repealed in 1995 with a 10-year phase-out], which provided strong incentives for U.S. corporations to use transfer pricing to shift reported income to Puerto Rico. . . . U.S. tax policy has done a disservice to Puerto Rico by providing U.S. corporations incentives for investments with few or no employment or local linkages.
    —Susan M. Collins et al. (2006, 3)

The history of Nocorá is to a large extent the history of the land and its uses.
    —Elena Padilla Seda (1966 [1956], 273)

As Puerto Rico entered the twenty-first century, a number of scholars undertook the difficult task of analyzing the island's economic struggles and recommending new pathways to development.[1] This is always a difficult task because traditionally the question of development has never been one solely of economic policy. It is necessarily the combined product of political, economic, and social policies, ultimately framing the health of individual bodies and the broader community. As a once-celebrated and then much-maligned development "project," Puerto Rico in fact has a significant place in the scholarly literature on development.[2] Export-led industrialization practices, known as Operation Bootstrap, were implemented in the context of a colonial possession inviting U.S. capital investment to industrialize,[3] and ultimately to bring modern infrastructure to the island to benefit the population as a whole. Thus, economic development strategies are nearly always bound up in the debate about the island's political status (as a Commonwealth or "Free Associated State" of the United States).

Like many scholars of the island, I take the view that the status of Puerto Rico since the invasion of the United States in 1898 has been essentially colonial. However, I also share a concern not only that the scholarship of Puerto Rico be attentive to the deep and lasting effects of the colonial condition on Puerto Rican society, but that a portion of the responsibility for the failures and successes of development also be placed on "responsible Puerto Ricans, from politicians to the universities to the private sector."[4] For development economist James Dietz, this squaring of responsibility in policy-making is not just about a historical perspective, but is crucial to a new era of positive growth, entrepreneurship, and economic sustainability. He laments,

> those in a position to structure the economy after the 1940s chose to believe, and then to act upon that belief, that Puerto Ricans themselves could not provide the dynamic for future growth and progress in their own economy.[5]

This negative outlook is presumed to have two fundamental policy outcomes: (1) the U.S.-based industrialization process provided no basis for the development of a strong entrepreneurial class, thus failing to create fertile ground for the growth of native intellectual capital related to Puerto Rican–owned business and the ownership of innovation; and (2) that the combination of capital-intensive (rather than labor-intensive) industry, with increases in government transfer payments as substitute for income created an environment in which unemployment could be a more viable means of supporting a family than seeking what few jobs were available.[6]

This second point is not meant (by me, or by the scholars I am citing) to reify the image of Puerto Ricans as lazy. For example, in 1995, *earned benefits* (such as Social Security, Medicare, and federal retirement income including, significantly, veterans' benefits) constituted about 71 percent of transfer payments to island residents, rather than what is generally thought of as "welfare" payments. Nevertheless, Dietz also concludes that as a whole, "transfer payments, not the U.S.-dominated manufacturing sector, have been the motor force for the progress in standard of living."[7] These data indicate two important issues: (1) economic policy created an environment in which companies *were not in fact lured to the island for labor* (cheap or otherwise), but rather for their own tax benefits; and (2) at the same time fewer and fewer jobs were being created at the labor and skills level attainable by most Puerto Ricans, and people were, in effect, increasingly being paid *not to work.*[8] From this angle, the continuing push to develop and expand capital-heavy industries like the pharmaceuticals is frankly perplexing.

This chapter presents a historic perspective on the relationships between ideologies, policies of development and modernization, health, and the environment in Puerto Rico, and specifically in Nocorá. Understanding the history of a place and a problem is crucial to understanding how the problem developed, and to thinking about possible solutions for the future. This understanding is also vital on a social level because it can help the people who bear the weight of the problem to see themselves not solely as victims, but as potential agents of change. In Nocorá, as in many industrialized settings, it is also necessary to examine the efficacy of government regulations meant to control the excesses of economic development, such as environmental and potential public health damage. By taking a closer look at the processes through which projects gain approval, it becomes clear how the history and ideology of development have created a fertile ground for practices that produce social suffering.

Industrialization: Appealing to a New Sense of Progress

By the 1970s, Puerto Rico's competitive advantages in traditional labor-intensive manufacturing (such as making shoes and textiles) were already running dry. The other advantages (e.g., common currency with and free access to the U.S. marketplace) were not enough to compensate for these changes.[9] Additionally, Puerto Rico had few natural resources that could benefit industrial production, and thus finding new draws for corporate investment required a strategic shift. Unemployment, which had peaked in 1950, and then plummeted to less than 6 percent by 1970, began climbing again almost immediately.

Many commentators have bemoaned the rationale of inviting capital-intensive industry (such as chemical manufacturers) to aid a floundering labor market. However, this "diversification in production" was initially part of a broader plan intended to integrate local industries, and thereby strengthen the production base.[10] For example, oil refining operations were lured in the hopes of bringing in other factories that could make use of oil-related products. The combination of capital-intensive production with the existing labor-intensive facilities was supposed to stabilize the overall island economy against market fluctuations. However, the labor-intensive industries were already beginning to move to cheaper labor markets, and the oil-induced recession in the mid-1970s had disastrous effects on Puerto Rico's foray into that sector.

Against this backdrop of struggle to maintain development standards, it is interesting to note discrepancies between overall economic history and the history put forth by the pharmaceutical industry itself. According to industry-related media,[11] the drug industry on the island is "40 Years Young!" Though the founding pharmaceutical plant goes unnamed, several sources date the first factory to 1957, with others following suit by 1960. While pharmaceutical manufacturing is unquestionably the industry that has gained the most from the implementation of the 1976 federal tax benefits (enshrined in Section 936 of the U.S. tax code[12]), their arrival predates those most well-known tax benefits. Broadcasting this fact fits well with the narrative that they have a long-term commitment to the island, and that, in effect, "it's not about the taxes." This narrative of commitment has not, however, caught hold with regular Puerto Ricans in daily discourse.

The first and most readily acknowledged factor in early founding of pharmaceutical plants on the island is the presence of preexisting tax benefits as part of the initial Operation Bootstrap philosophy. In addition, Puerto Rico was proven to be rich in the one natural resource vital to pharmaceutical chemical processing: untouched aquifers of extremely high-quality water.[13] The North Coast Province aquifer area, stretching from Aguadilla in the west to Río Grande, represents approximately 19 percent of Puerto Rico's land mass and more than 63 percent of its aquifers.[14] In the year 2000, pharmaceutical and other related chemical manufacturing processes (Standard Industrial Classification (SIC) code 28) accounted for 7.38 million gallons per day (Mg/d) of self-supplied groundwater withdrawals.[15] The total amount of industrial self-supplied groundwater was 9.00 Mg/d, across four main industry codes. The drug companies in the town of Nocorá, central to the story of this book, accounted for 37 percent of the total, by far the greatest percentage.

It is useful to consider why the local populace did not by and large object to the insertion of highly toxic industries[16] into their immediate environs, in spite of a certain level of awareness of the risks involved.[17] In historical perspective it would be simplest to assign the largely undereducated and disenfranchised residents the label of ignorant. The sheer magnitude of pollution caused by the chemical industries in their 40-plus year tenure could hardly have been predicted by anyone unfamiliar with industrial chemistry. However, simple ignorance does not sufficiently explain the persistent belief among many Puerto Ricans, even among residents of the northern industrial region, that their lives have been vastly improved by the presence of the pharmaceutical industry.[18]

Which leaves us with the question, Why? To some degree the answer is straightforward cost-benefit analysis, and the obvious embeddedness of the pharmaceutical industry in the process of economic development. However, given the stark reality that this capital-intensive industry as a whole has failed to provide jobs, we must then look into murkier waters, so to speak, for answers. As a high-technology industry associated with the health field, the drug industry has benefited from a widely held association with individual and community-level progress. The bases of this association are, however, subject to much contestation on the local level.

On my first visit to Puerto Rico I noted that politics tended to enter casual conversations within mere moments, and my first conversation with Don Felipe del Mogote was no exception. A retired lawyer living in La Cañita, the rural municipality that seceded from Nocorá in the late 1960s, Don Felipe had always been an ardent supporter of the PPD. I first met him over a friendly game of dominos on a Sunday afternoon family visit, and after listening for a while to the ongoing news of a public quarrel over the raising of the U.S. flag he informed me, quite suddenly, that people who criticized the PPD did not have a leg to stand on. "Before them, we had nothing. The hospitals were always full of sick people. Now we have all this, and people want to criticize." His granddaughter leaned across the table and said, "In case you couldn't tell, my grandparents are *populares.*"

In saying that the hospitals were always full of sick people, Don Felipe was referring to a population long burdened with the health consequences of severe poverty. In obtaining Puerto Rico as a prize of war, the U.S. government had an immediate interest in making the island and its population less vulnerable to debilitating diseases. Initial public health action against tropical disease began as a combined military-philanthropic effort, uniting U.S. needs to eliminate malaria and other endemic diseases in strategic "war areas" with the broader hygiene programs of the Rockefeller Foundation.[19] Having been invited to the island to deal with tuberculosis, the International Health Division (IHD) of the Rockefeller Foundation instead decided to focus on what they perceived to be the greatest need that matched their strengths: eradicating parasitic diseases such as malaria, hookworm, and dysentery. As historian Laura Briggs notes,

> The IHD was far more comfortable with altering geography—filling in places where water pooled, putting down tile in irrigation canals, building latrines—than with engaging in the politically fraught activity of trying to improve poor people's standard of living.[20]

Perhaps not surprisingly, the eugenic social philosophy[21] underlying these policies proved to be a contradictory force in public health and development on the island. On the one hand, it provided a liberal logic through which social welfare monies could be directed to improving the economic situation of Puerto Ricans,[22] and supported the idea that Puerto Ricans as a group could become a modern nation. On the other hand, eugenics also carried with it a mandate to aggressively limit population growth, an outlook which was to have dramatic consequences for women's health and well-being. When these programs arrived in Nocorá they did so with particular force, becoming part of an already established pattern of paternalistic social relationships between citizens and local elites.

The negative aspects of the U.S.-driven public health campaigns have been aptly discussed by Briggs and others, and still form an important, if limited, part of the present-day discourse about modernization and health for everyday Puerto Ricans. What I wish to emphasize here is that in my own research, particularly my ethnographic experience in Nocorá and outside of the activist-intelligentsia, the collective memory of life *before*—life when "the hospitals were full of sick people"—was still powerful enough to mediate many people's potential bad feelings about invasive public health practices. People I spoke with about the transition from the 1940s to the present are equally likely to remember, as Briggs puts it, that the eugenics paradigm also carried with it

> programs like supplementary feeding for infants and young children, "milk stations" to provide fresh and unadulterated milk for infants and new mothers, child nursing and dental clinics, visiting nurses and child welfare social workers, and a tuberculosis sanitarium that could minimize contagion and provide wholesome food, rest, and respite from labor and overcrowding living conditions.[23]

As Eduardo Seda Bonilla noted in his follow-up to the *People of Puerto Rico* study, the "showcase for democracy" had achieved advancements in many aspects of social welfare, especially health:

> The health of the people has become an object of careful attention by means of programs to provide potable water. . . . The health of the people is protected by means of regulations in the sale of food, environmental drainage [presumably referring to the management of sources of mosquitoes, etc.], vaccination against contagious diseases . . . and all sorts of preventative programs tending to reduce mortality and increase life expectancies.[24]

Many people I spoke with were also likely to either remember, or refer to the previous generation's experience in, receiving *parcelas* of land and assistance in building new concrete houses. In contrast to the wood and thatch- or zinc-roofed structures which could not withstand hurricane-force winds, and could expose residents to parasites through dirt floors, a concrete house and a small area of one's own land made even limited land reform a great success among many of the previously landless population. In a comment typical of this point of view, Benicia, whose father had managed a section of the local sugar plantations, said to me on several occasions, "It was a hard life. Cutting cane is very hard work. People do not want to go back to that, and that is what they see if the industries leave."

The influence of Operation Bootstrap on the cultural politics of Puerto Rico is well-documented.[25] Less familiar to many readers is the legacy of Bootstrap's sister social program, "Operation Serenity." Aptly named, the goal of Serenity can be described as creating a social environment that promoted the culture and community ideals of the traditional "rural lifestyle that Operation Bootstrap had set up to eradicate."[26] Operation Serenity rescued, and reasserted in a systematic and value-laden manner, the cultural symbolics of the *jíbaro* peasant (hard work and Christian religion), as well as the indigenous Taíno (noble heritage, which no modernizing force can erase), and in a more limited way, African culture (usually represented by music). Blending these three "races" or "roots" of Puerto Rican culture into a seemingly harmonious spiritual whole, the Institute of Puerto Rican Culture (ICP) created a system that valorized a unique cultural identity. It also took education as one of its core concerns, maintaining a strong role for the modernizing influence overall.[27]

The separation of cultural politics from political nationalism has been a rich source for social science research on Puerto Rican identities.[28] As such it is highly relevant to the formation of communities and therefore to the environment. Together, Operations Bootstrap and Serenity created a new context in which poverty was mitigated, cultural identity celebrated, and rebellion diffused. The overall public perception, that the benefits of development were worth any potential risks, is helpful in thinking about why many Puerto Ricans accepted without much protest what amounted to an assault on their environment, even as evidence of harm began to accumulate.[29] However, over time policies more explicitly aimed at minimizing critical public participation in development planning also became part of the process.

Politics and the Environment: Status, Pollution, and Paperwork

Though the industrial policies of Operation Bootstrap created a boom in the island's economy in the early 1970s, the success was short-lived. Unemployment among Puerto Rican ages sixteen and over skyrocketed after a 5.5

percent nadir in 1970, reaching nearly 15 percent in 1980 and surpassing 20 percent in 1990.[30] Coinciding with the increase of unemployment in Puerto Rico was a crystallization of environmental concerns in the United States and on the island. These concerns had been building since the 1960s, and culminated in the establishment of the federal Environmental Protection Agency (EPA) in 1970. The governor of Puerto Rico at that time, Luis A. Ferré (PNP), anticipated the federal agency by six months, calling for the establishment of the Environmental Quality Board (EQB) or Junta de Calidad Ambiental (JCA). According to EQB's official history, the agency was charged with the task of "establishing the socioeconomic development of our [sic] island, in accord with the optimal environmental quality."[31] Astute readers will note not only which concern is listed first, but the choice of the word "optimal" to describe the environment vis-à-vis socioeconomic development. Optimal implies that the environment will be at a high standard *relative* to development, a conditional relationship that has always dogged efforts of the EQB and other actors concerned with the environment.

In the intricate history and practice of development and environmental public policies in Puerto Rico, research has amply demonstrated how even the best intentions of regulatory actors can be circumvented. A comparison of the use of the Environmental Impact Statement (EIS) and the less rigorous Environmental Assessment (EA) in regulating development projects demonstrates how development ideologies have continually taken precedence over ecological concerns. The very structure of the development discourse places human well-being and ecological preservation in opposition to one another. From this perspective the environment is worth sacrificing in order to relieve human suffering brought on by poverty. However, policies enacted in Puerto Rico have failed to recognize the subtle, cumulative, and longer-term human suffering that is caused by environmental degradation. These policies have ultimately promoted corporate interests over those of local communities, and "private interests became public."[32]

In Puerto Rico, industry insiders, ideologically representing the interests of private corporations, have often taken turns as heads or subheads of regulatory agencies.[33] Many environmental engineers who have worked for the Puerto Rico Aqueduct and Sewer Authority (PRASA) have also worked for the pharmaceutical companies in the area of compliance, and have often taken turns in the upper ranks of the EQB and the local outposts of the EPA. Even when the EQB has not been led by those aligned with industrial interests, these same interests have typically held more influence in the halls of government than have the regulatory agencies. As one former EQB official stated, "The Board [EQB] was, and still is, the accused in *La Forteleza* [the

Governor's office]: it has the burden of proof" when it comes to making recommendations against projects.[34] However, the creation of and access to scientific knowledge (and therefore "proof") is not distributed equally among
those to whom it matters most. To give an example in Nocorá, I found
that documents pertaining to new construction or infrastructure projects,
required to be made available for public comment, were placed in different
locations, depending on the perceived level of existing community criticism.
I found proposals for shopping sites and other less controversial projects
housed in the municipal public library. However, I found documentation
(within copies of the proposal itself) that plans for expansion of the water
treatment plant had only been held in offices to which the public had significantly more limited access.

The Effects of Policy on Participation

In the 1970s the EQB was instrumental in the Puerto Rican government's
attempts to gain autonomy in environmental affairs, arguing that the newly
established EPA was not equipped to understand the unique situation of the
island. In a resolution presented to the governor in 1973, the chairman of
the EQB advocated environmental autonomy from the federal government.
He argued that while the laws of the United States applied to Puerto Rico,
and the goals with respect to the environment were essentially the same, the
imposition of external priorities and timetables would "interfere with the
prompt and most adequate solution to our [sic] problems."[35] The resolution
went on to recommend,

> to the Honorable Governor of Puerto Rico to take those actions he judges
> pertinent to the ends of achieving those legal changes necessary such that
> Puerto Rico may resolve its environmental problems locally, in harmony[36]
> with the prevailing realities on the Island.

At the heart of the development approach was a process through which
the founding regulatory document of the Environmental Quality Board,
the Environmental Impact Statement (EIS), came to effectively be replaced
by the weaker Environmental Assessment (EA) (in which public participation and input are not required).[37] The EA was initially envisioned as a
preliminary bureaucratic step in Puerto Rico, to be used as the EQB further
refined its protocols; however, by 1984 the EQB had formally instituted the
EA option as a permanently acceptable alternative to the EIS. The requirement to engage in the full EIS process was reduced to the discretion of the

agency to request follow-up information or the full EIS process when additional information was deemed necessary.[38] For many projects, the determination of "necessary" was subject to a variety of industry and government influences. And even in cases where environmental studies are done, as with health studies sponsored by those seeking to prove no negative effect, there is significant risk that the study itself can be biased. As one well-known epidemiologist who often works with communities told me,

> I think that if you can you need to train the communities how to answer these questionnaires so they don't fall into the trap—because often times the establishment will want to be able to show that the community is mistaken.

In current practice, one finds both the EIS and EA in use in the evaluation of development and other building projects on the island, often depending on the level of existing public scrutiny of any given project. Whether or not a project receives the public interest and inquiry indicated by an EIS is often subject to political and economic pressures, both from industry and from other governmental bodies. An EIS, furthermore, is not a guarantee of disapproval or alteration of any project: as one informant, an environmental planner working for the government, told me, "I have piles of negative reports for projects on my desk. . . . Most of them will wind up getting approved in spite of all the evidence that they should not be, or should not be in their current form." Looking around my living room he waved his arm and continued.

> This [recently built] urbanization is in an obvious violation of zoning laws—it's within the buffer zone that is now supposed to exist between residential buildings and industrial. But if the Planning Board approves a project it can go ahead, *even* if it's technically against the law.

The performance of the participation process itself, in many contexts, creates a sense of inevitability for a project more significantly than it functions to solicit community-based input.[39]

Even giving the benefit of the doubt to developers, the Planning Board, and the EQB, there is a serious addendum necessary to the use of the supposedly powerful and participatory planning document, the Environmental Impact Statement. Most Environmental Impact Assessment (EIA) procedures (referring to the whole group of such processes) worldwide include the consideration of human health, but in practice the assessment of health impacts is very weak. A comprehensive review of the literature as well as 42 examples of U.S.-based EIS documents from years 1979 to 1996[40] demonstrated convincingly that 62 percent of the studies addressed no health impact at all, and those that do are so narrow in scope as to be virtually useless. We have only to look back to the previous chapter to see how a carefully constructed investigation can create the illusion of no harm.

Among those studies that did assess direct health impact, they tended to work from a strict perspective of epidemiological risk, focusing on the quantitative probabilities of people developing cancer from exposure to a single toxin.[41] This approach, of focusing on a single source in a direct causal relationship, has come under greater scrutiny within the field of epidemiology,[42] and new methodological approaches continue to emerge on the cutting edge of the discipline. As the community epidemiologist noted:

> I believe that in epidemiology we need to be able to separate statistical significance from clinical significance. I'm very clear on this. Statistics are tools that work when they work. When they don't work, we need to look elsewhere. A lot of times with a group that's small, [the p-value] doesn't mean a thing. Health problems, some of them you can quantify, but not all. You can never quantify the impact of a health problem in all its dimensions.

However, the linear statistical approach is still dominant in the field as it is practiced in the often resource-poor world of public health. And it remains dominant in the area of environmental assessment as well, where developers and local governments seek to cut as many costs as possible to bring a project into being. As one of the EIA experts interviewed by Steinemann says, "Sure, my instincts tell me this [project] is going to have all sorts of health impacts. But how do I figure them out? If I can't measure them, I can't put them in the EIS."[43] These methodological and financial limitations contribute to the structural violence that can be caused by industrial development in poorer countries, such that even if no one is making a decision with the direct wish to harm people, the existing system makes it hard not to harm them. It becomes difficult to measure health impacts of new projects, even with the best intentions, and the intentions of government and industry may not always reflect the long-term health of communities as their core concern. Unfortunately, new research methods are costly to develop, and they create new realms of uncertainty for government agencies with interests in approving projects, as well as for industries looking to cover their legal bases at the least cost. As uncertainty is what is seeking to be managed in the first place,[44] the incentives to change the practice are few.

Concerns over legal and political liability (or perceived responsibility) are at the core of many environmental conflicts, and it is the case in Puerto Rico, as elsewhere, that the ability to claim ignorance has long served corporate and governmental interests in development. Again, Steinemann's professional informants are quote-worthy:

> Another EIA analyst indicated that public concern could prompt an agency to conduct a human health impact assessment, but that "if the public is not aware of a particular hazard, the lead agency probably won't address human health concerns."[45]

Environmental professionals I interviewed presented different views on the role of ignorance in the causal chain of environmental problems, with those whose ties more closely represented corporate interests more willing to give the benefit of the doubt. This perspective states that industry used to be more ignorant than it is now, and failing that excuse, that a few "bad apples" are the cause of most environmental problems.[46] I interviewed one environmental engineer who had worked on many waste treatment projects for the pharmaceuticals in Nocorá as well as on the mainland. He mused that abuses to the environment had generally been caused by a "lack of vision" among the middle managers responsible for day-to-day operations. By focusing the blame on a few individuals, this type of discourse is fundamentally corporate: it seeks to minimize liability for the greatest number of individuals by making it the fault of a few (potentially disposable) people. Likewise the expressed belief that, as this engineer continued, "now managers aspire to something better" ignores the structural disincentives for companies to change by emphasizing individual good will brought about by an almost spiritual new environmental awareness. It also strongly parallels the feel-good rhetoric of corporate volunteerism, a theme that arose often in my research on corporate social responsibility.

Having gained an understanding of the broader structures within which the economic development of Puerto Rico emerged, we can now narrow the focus of these concerns directly onto Nocorá. It is under this local historical magnifying glass that we can see exactly how the ideologies and practices of economic development have created a society in which pollution becomes an accepted part of everyday life. We will first step back into the era of early economic development, then follow the trail of cultural change into Nocoreño society today.

Nocorá's Land and History

Situated on the northern central coast of Puerto Rico, the municipality of Nocorá runs from the limestone foothills down to the coastal plains and the shore of the Atlantic Ocean. Like most northern municipalities it is twice bisected by insular highways, one old (Route 4) and one new (the AutoExpreso). And, like many of its neighbors, Nocorá boasts a rich landscape that includes the ecological treasure troves of mangroves and karstic (limestone) outcroppings (hills of which are known as *mogotes*). However, these natural resources have been seriously depleted or otherwise damaged by both residential and commercial building practices.

The filling in of swampier areas near the coast, as well as the mining of *mogotes* for construction fill, has been in practice since before large-scale development began. However, these practices have now become an established aspect of the building process, rather than something individuals did in order to build their own houses, make some extra money, or address local mosquito problems. In the early 2000s, the Army Corps of Engineers emerged as the greatest *tumba-mogotes* (leveler of hills) in Nocorá, taking out a large stone hill in its entirety to construct a dam around the town center. This new dam, and the re-channeling of the Río Grande de Bajas on the town's eastern bank, has greatly reduced the characteristic flooding of the *pueblo* (town center). Still, in other parts of Nocorá, flooding from the periodic overflowing of the river has remained a severe problem. In Tipan, where a system of canals once operated by the Land Authority strategically flooded and drained sugarcane fields, natural and man-made debris often caused a variety of water-related difficulties for residents. Much of the area once dedicated to sugarcane cultivation lay fallow, or was indifferently harvested for weed-like grasses used for feeding livestock. In some higher-lying areas cattle was grazed on the land, while the fields nearest the shore were increasingly being used to "recycle" the sludge produced by the wastewater treatment plant.[47]

Though considered by many Puerto Ricans, including *sanjuanero* acquaintances of mine, to be something of a backwater, Nocorá has always had qualities that have drawn anthropologists to its northern coast. Previously studied twice, both times prior to heavy industrialization, Nocorá has provided significant insight for students of cultural ecology and culture change.

Nocorá and the Cultural Ecology of Sugar

Elena Padilla Seda and the *People of Puerto Rico* (PPR) research team arrived in 1949, hypothesizing that the culture[48] of Nocorá would be different not

only from those that produced tobacco and coffee, but also from the southern coastal sugar town of Cañamelar. They believed this mainly because
Nocorá's sugar production was

> [a] government-owned, proportional profit project which has the social
> objective of distributing work and dividing profits among as many per-
> sons as possible; and second because its culture has changed in response
> to modernized productive arrangements more slowly and less completely
> than that of Cañamelar.[49]

The researchers found that Nocoreños, under the less-obviously capitalistic
system of the Land Authority, nevertheless "referred to the Land Authority
[an arm of the insular government] as the 'corporation' or 'capital.'"[50] This most
likely stemmed from the fact that when the Land Authority purchased the
means of sugar production in 1944, it did so from the Nocorá Corporation, a
local association of familial landowners. But in spite of the use of these terms,
these labor relationships translated into a weaker working-class identity—not
to say the cane workers were not in fact working class, but they did not see
themselves as a group potentially opposed to their managers. Although there
were socialist threads running through some layers of Nocoreño society, they
never really cohered as a political force against local elites. The slow pace of
cultural change meant that Nocoreños as a group tended to maintain the cultural relations typical of the workers to earlier *hacendados*. In other words,
the face-to-face, paternalistic relationships of the *hacienda* took precedence
over the more industrial, systematized corporate style.

One of the reasons these relationships continued in Nocorá was because of
the melding of certain expectations of government and industry. As local residents had a tendency to think of their paternalistic benefactors as "the corporation," it seems that the various industries (such as food processing, the making
of shoes, and eventually pharmaceuticals) benefited from the remarkably non-
oppositional, and even positive, set of meanings placed on this term by Nocoreños. In the time period represented by the *People of Puerto Rico* study and Seda
Bonilla's follow-up study of Nocorá,[51] the perceived obligations of government
and corporation to local residents and workers were to become substantially
intertwined. The overall pattern of these relationships has proven persistent.

Social Relations in the Land Authority Era

In Nocorá in the Land Authority years, the expectation was that the corporation would provide work to the "maximum number of people," even if that

work did not produce an adequate wage to support a family. Increases in mechanization were resisted by managers because they would have posed "a very serious political and social problem."[52] Although some elites recognized that there might have been a benefit to raising the standard of living for fewer numbers of workers, local managers did not ultimately have the power to change the organization of labor. The poor laborers tended to be less politically volatile as long as they had work (even if their standard of living was very low). As such, maintaining voter complacency was the practical goal of the project, although the higher-minded goal of proportional profit-sharing had been its organizing principle.

Organized labor was moderately active in Nocorá prior to the establishment of the government-owned sugar industry, but the effectiveness of strikes and collective bargaining had been effectively minimized. "By giving concessions and privileges to certain workers upon whose loyalties the employers could count, the landowners undermined the class solidarity of the workers," notes Padilla Seda.[53] The union's goal was likewise to have as many workers as possible, rather than advocate for higher wages for established workers. In a pattern that a number of my informants claimed continued to characterize existing union activity in Puerto Rico, "labor leadership had become so centralized and autocratic that it often failed to recognize local needs and made agreements with local employers that thwarted the aims of the local employees."[54]

The Puerto Rican Federation of Labor did succeed in creating active voter support for the Socialist Party (PS) in Nocorá.[55] In 1924, the Socialist Party entered into a coalition with the pro-statehood Republican Party, and collectively dominated electoral politics until the rise of the populares in the mid-1940s. In fact, the Socialist/Republican coalition retained a great deal of support in Nocorá, even in the years leading up to the establishment of the Constitution. In what might seem an unlikely alliance with the professional classes and supporters of big sugar, local workers also tended to support the idea of statehood based on the assumption that it would ultimately benefit workers. When the PPD formulated the Free Associated State, they gained votes from the pro-statehood socialists, while the Puerto Rican Independence Party split off into more or less its present form. In the mid-1960s, when the Commonwealth status had become status quo as opposed to a process of transition, pro-statehood advocates formed the New Progressive Party (PNP). Residents of Nocorá who had once supported the Socialist/Republican coalition and a pro-statehood agenda had never become very strongly identified with a revolutionary identity, either in terms of political-economic class or political status.[56] It is these working-class *estadistas* who formed the core of pro-statehood support in Nocorá, particularly in Tipan, and have always been skeptical of the PPD-dominated local government.

However, local residents initially identified Nocorá's relative poverty in the early transition to industrialization as a consequence of insufficient patronage of the populares. In the late 1940s, locals described Nocorá as having no opportunity (*ambiente*), making no progress, compared to other municipalities where government favoritism resulted in greater industrial prosperity. By this time younger people had also begun to migrate to the mainland to work in agriculture. In these early years, the circular migratory pattern was still more regular (in this case annual) than it would later become for migrant farm laborers; during the northern winters Nocoreños could return home to harvest cane.

It is interesting to note that, because of the seasonal nature of work in the cane fields and at the mill, residents of Nocorá turned to many of the part-time economic activities with which many still supported themselves. Several of my informants who once worked in the fields as young men supplemented their incomes by fishing and carpentry: when the *Central* (sugar mill) was closed they turned to these activities full time. For this generation industrialization brought some increased economic stability, not from the factory jobs themselves, but from the massive, if episodic, construction work necessary to create a substantial industrial infrastructure.

Padilla Seda also notes that Tipan, like others of its size established via the 1942 Land Law, was located, by statute, in a locale "near sources of employment, schools, health units, and other public services."[57] Although space in the settlement area was then provided for other institutions and activities (chapels, recreation), one can see how discursively employment was continually linked with other government services. At the same time, Nocorá was a small enough place that its residents needed to go to neighboring municipalities for any large commercial purchase, and some even did their regular weekly shopping outside of their own town. Thus, while government was linked to the production or income side of the market, it did not at first have as clearly defined a relationship to the consumption side.

Consumption and *Confianza* at the End of the Sugar-based Economy

When Padilla Seda's research associate returned to Nocorá in 1959 (ten years after the conclusion of the PPR studies), rumors were flying that the Land Authority was intent on selling the sugar enterprise. There was a conflicting attitude toward the Land Authority projects by local workers: government influence in the organization of these projects had led to notable inefficiencies and political cronyism, leading many to seek scarce employment in the private sector. Likewise, young people seen as scorning the work of cutting cane were described as "hanging around looking nice until someone sends them passage to the United States."[58]

There was nevertheless a concern that the familiar source of municipal employment would be sold to private interests, and would be shut down. This fear was being addressed by amplified public announcement cars (still a ubiquitous form of public communication in the less urbanized areas of Puerto Rico today) to the effect:

> Dear companions of Nocorá: the *Central* is not for sale and I assure you of it myself, as your mayor and friend . . . Do not believe those who wish to mislead you with the calls of sirens. The *Central* is not for sale. This is propaganda of the *pipiolos* [independence party].[59]

The Central was sold to private investors a scant two years later, and closed operations completely in 1963.

In the wake of this dramatic economic shift, new enterprises were appearing, and new consumer goods soon followed. Small-scale clothing manufacturing marked the slow movement of Nocorá toward economic development,[60] and radios, televisions, refrigerators, and other amenities were becoming more common. Informants from Tipan commented on the higher costs of living, the overall lack of work, and the need for the government to build better roads. The car fare from the town center to the beach had tripled.[61] The older men and women talked about the large numbers of young people going to work in the States (ironically many still in agriculture, via the government-sponsored Migration Program).[62]

In Tipan many of the houses were made of cement, rather than wood or thatch, with windows covered with Miami blinds. However, local residents seemed unimpressed by the improvement in their lodgings, as it held little relationship to improved personal economic conditions. "'The government,' [Don Andrés] comments resignedly, 'gave us this little house so that poverty does not leave us without protection when those seasons come.'"[63] But in addition to the houses themselves, Seda Bonilla saw that even beachside Tipan had electrical cables draping across balconies, and a television antenna on the roof of a local political leader's house.

Walking through Tipan, he also noticed the stark absence of young people. His survey of Tipan revealed almost a complete dearth of residents of childbearing age, as many had begun to migrate to the mainland for work on a quasi-permanent basis (in contrast to the earlier circular migration patterns). For those who remained there were few if any viable options, especially for men. Some residents were hopeful that the findings of his research might encourage the government to do something to improve the local economy—but pessimism was the order of the day.

> Things are bad here, everyone is going to the States. . . . If the government were to put a little factory here, the young people wouldn't have to leave; but here, what future is there? [Working in the] Cane, and that's work for the uneducated. For my children that go to school, where can they end up?[64]

Nocoreños continued to complain that their town held little opportunity for employment. As the quote above illustrates, while education had improved, many saw little chance to apply that learning to well-paying jobs. This type of organized underemployment can create an atmosphere in which severe economic dependency on local political actors will flourish.[65] Those who remained were drawn inexorably into a local political economy that placed the alcalde, as chief economic coordinator and negotiator, at the center of all social relationships. This convergence of old and new clientelisms helped sustain expectations that "*el gobierno*" would provide economically, in one form or another.[66]

In the personalistic relationships still dominant in Nocorá in the late 1950s and early 1960s, the uncertainty of dependence was linked to the perceived need for reliance on the figure of a gatekeeper, a natural leader and problem-solver. While *confianza*, or trust, may have existed between a personalistic leader and his constituency, it was conditional, and often unidirectional. The services of government could be granted as favors to individuals, but could also be taken away with equal ease. As long as the leader maintained his electoral majority, there were no consequences for abandoning the disenfranchised. There were rewards for loyalty, but ultimately voters, like workers in a factory setting, were replaceable. This system united a feeling of small community, familial-type relationships with the worst elements of a market economy. Services, as favors, like votes, were bought and sold, making the democratic process "a histrionic display empty of substantive content."[67]

Seda Bonilla was particularly concerned with the degree to which these "histrionic displays," as well as blatant rumor-mongering and discursive sleights-of-hand, took the place of informed debate of policy and ideas. He relates the girlish enthusiasm of one normally sedate acquaintance of his at the victory of the alcalde "Sebastiancito," a politician supremely skilled, by all accounts, at "creating for himself an image of benefactor managing municipal funds like one who is taking money out of his own pocket." Other residents observed his actions of charity, such as the traditional giving of gifts around the Christmas holidays, with greater skepticism, noting "Out of a budget of around $136,000, $49,000 is assigned for Charity."[68]

Overall, the atmosphere of political patronage described in Nocorá consisted of two types of loyalty: one, of the kind of personal loyalty described above. Indeed, such personalism might be linked with skepticism, an understandable concern that favors can be retracted, as well as that political leaders are benefiting personally even as they serve. However, an underlying skepticism, as well as doubts expressed by longtime residents as to whether "*los grandes*" (the big ones) really cared at all about workers and other everyday people, had a way of reinforcing loyalty as well. When politicians or other elites delivered on promises, even a skeptic could feel personally satisfied.

The other type of loyalty gaining traction in Puerto Rico was that of political parties, and the easy melding of "the party in power" with "the government" in people's minds. By the early 1960s the PPD had consolidated its power, and particularly so in Nocorá. Residents, Seda Bonilla observed, had a tendency to blindly commit themselves to the party, under the belief that the party was controlling all the mechanisms of government—and ultimately all the services required for survival. For those who were most dependent, either for work, or the increasing levels of other types of economic support, the incentive to question government leadership was dwindling. From this perspective true *confianza* was at a minimum—it was being replaced by dependent personalism, either in politics or in religious healing practices.[69] Networks of *confianza*, the heart of any community, and of centrality to Puerto Rican social relations,[70] were being misplaced and manipulated.

Local Politics and Government Institutions, Past and Present

The *alcaldía*, or mayor's office, of Nocorá was overwhelmingly held by the Popular Democratic Party (PPD) beginning in 1941, only three years after the founding of the party by Luis Muñoz Marín. The exception was two terms in the late 1970s and early 1980s, during which a member of the New Progressive Party (PNP, pro-statehood) held the office. However, I was assured by many of my informants that this was not only an oddity, but in fact, the PNP mayor had long been PPD, but changed parties due to some internal party squabbling. In the election of 1984 Nocorá's only PNP mayor was replaced by yet another PPD candidate. Estrello Martínez (still the alcalde in early 2012) came to power when the newly minted PPD alcalde died after only two years in office in 1986. As is the method for replacing elected officials who resign or die in office in Puerto Rico, Martínez was chosen by his party leadership to take the office. He was re-elected in 1988, and in every election until 2012 by substantial majorities over a variety of PNP opponents. And while the political status preferences of the alcaldes may not bear directly on their behavior toward industry, the development ideologies of the PPD have had a clear influence.

The political status of Free Associated State, if not perhaps in its original formulation, became firmly wedded to a development strategy based on its continued liminal status. As I have outlined above, the island's betwixt-and-between condition has been a constant tool used to leverage competitive economic advantages when attracting industry. The development plans advocated by the Puerto Rican government called for manufacturing plants needing low-wage laborers, such as textiles. Unfortunately, this strategy also had the undesirable effect of being "ineffective in alleviating male unemployment."[71]

Industrialization: Implications for Gender and Culture

Nocorá provides a fascinating microcosm of the role of a "progressive," rapidly modernizing ideology, not the least of which as a notable site of the sterilization movement, which has been the focus of much research and debate.[72] It is this particular ideology of development that sets the stage for the continued development of the pharmaceutical industry, and that underlies the conflict between Tipan and that same industry (and its allies). Likewise, the belief that high-technology (and therefore non-labor-intensive) industries, are axiomatically progressive or more modernizing, and provide well-paying jobs, is pervasive among the people of Nocorá. As many informants told me repeatedly, recalling the words of Seda Bonilla's informant, "cutting cane was hard work . . . pineapple was worse. People don't want to do that kind of work anymore."

During one of my several interviews with Alcalde Martínez, he surprised me by referring to the fact that in spite of its small size, the town had been one of several locations on the island where women had access to the now infamous sterilization operation (tubal ligation). In fact, he proclaimed proudly, his uncle had been one of the men who, with an eye toward progress, had been responsible for making the tiny hospital on the hill the regional sterilization capital. Echoing the long-held development ideologies of his PPD cohorts, Martínez unquestioningly viewed a lack of family planning as a barrier to progress, to industrialization, to development.

For all its failure as a source of economic vitality, the sale and subsequent closing of the government-run sugar mill and its associated plantations in 1963 had a devastating effect on the economy and daily life of
Nocorá. Then-alcalde Sebastian Robles acted quickly to mobilize the Commonwealth government to create powerful incentives for industrial development, but his vision of an aggressive modernity went beyond economic
change. Robles had a driving vision of the future of his town, and was
eager to create not just the economy, but the local family itself, in his
desired image.

In an interview recorded with Robles after his 20-year reign as alcalde, he
coupled his vision of progress directly with the need to limit the number of
children born in the municipality, thereby allowing women to work outside
the home.[73] It is instructive to hear a description of the situation in Robles'
own words (*translation mine*):

> Thanks to God, the female sterilization program had magnificent results.
> We had the proof in the 1970 Census. The local population had not
> increased, owing to the success of the female sterilization program here
> in [Nocorá]; They closed schools in several sectors [including Tipan,
> La Planchita, and other poorer areas] because there were not enough
> children. . . .
>
> [*walking through the center of town*] You might notice many men in the
> streets. The women are in the factories. [The men] are in other activities,
> they finish their work early, and then they socialize in the streets. . . .
>
> The mothers are not so preoccupied now, because the children of
> a marriage have been limited to three. This was my great endeavor, that
> which I have achieved as alcalde of this municipality after 20 long years.

Nocorá was one of three municipalities particularly named (of 77 at that
time) which "maintained their local hospitals under municipal auspices
exclusively."[74] In a town such as Nocorá, "under municipal auspices" meant
that the alcalde set the policies for the hospital.[75]

In a documentary film addressing the sterilization debate,[76] a woman
recounts her experience of seeking the sterilization operation at the Nocorá
municipal hospital. After watching women going into the hospital and wondering what they were having done, she inquired of the nurse in charge.
Upon receiving the information about the operation, she responded eagerly,
asking if she, too, could undergo the surgery. The nurse instructed her to go
see the alcalde. She was able to get the operation within four days of their
meeting.

From the earliest stages of industrialization, the type of work being offered was most likely to be taken up by women. New industries like home-based needlework, as well as low-skill assembly manufacturing, allowed women to work from home, or drew them to more urban areas on the island. Men primarily went to the States for agriculture work.[77] With the decline of agriculture, Sebastian Robles could not hope to re-make Nocorá as a sugar-, or even pineapple-based,[78] economic center. But he took his substantial political capital directly to the Commonwealth legislature, and set the stage for massive industrial development.

The Arrival of the Pharmaceutical Industry

The dedication plaque that bears his name on the Nocorá municipal health clinic describes Sebastian Robles as "an excellent educator and visionary *alcalde* of this municipality," and "the architect of industrial Nocorá, the largest pharmaceutical complex in the world." At what point Robles decided that the drug industry was the most appropriate to bring Nocorá out of its long economic slumber is not known. But historical documents suggest that he was well aware of the precarious nature of the town's reliance on sugar, and when the closure of the Central became imminent he wasted no time.

A 1963 session of the island's Chamber of Representatives' subcommittees on Work, Agriculture, Commerce and Industry was held the day after the Central closed, specifically to address the "zone of emergency" in Nocorá. Initial plans included a works program of $1 million funded by the Commonwealth government. Among these projects were the building of schools, houses, roads, bridges, and aqueducts, and at least three factories that were to house government-sponsored industries, such as textiles and shoe manufacture. This first phase of Operation Bootstrap had limited success in providing jobs for local workers, and while women were able to begin work in the factories, the economic contribution of men was largely limited to the construction of facilities.

By 1970, the next phase of industrialization had already begun, and Nocorá was on the forefront of attracting the technology- and capital-heavy pharmaceuticals. However, there remained two discrepancies in the ability of this new industry to provide the jobs Nocoreños so desperately needed: (1) as described earlier, the numbers of jobs available in these factories were not many, and (2) the educational level of the average Nocoreño, albeit higher than his or her cane-cutting predecessors, was not sufficient to become employed at any but the most menial tasks in pharmaceutical production.

Nocorá Today

The population of Nocorá remained fairly stable from the time the *People of Puerto Rico* study was undertaken. Population control measures and substantial out-migration were significant, and until the early 2000s Nocorá was not the sort of town to which people were drawn as new residents. According to the 2000 Census, 84.5 percent of the Nocoreño population (ages five and up) had lived in the municipality for at least five years. Many people I spoke with had lived there most, if not all, their lives. This trend had begun to shift in the years following the Census, and new urbanizations were being built to attract new residents, such as the neighborhood in Salvador la Cruz in which I lived. In developing and selling these new homes, the municipal government relied on the perception that the various pollution problems had largely been solved. Promotional materials suggested that Nocorá was a place where people could enjoy the recently built amenities of good shopping and entertainment in a more bucolic setting. This sentiment was supported by Nocoreños themselves. Overall they tended to be grateful for the benefits of modern life, such as better nutrition, easier access to goods and services. However, the quality of life benefits most often described in Nocorá had as much to do with tranquility, something not typically associated with industrialization. Regardless of neighborhood, Nocoreños time and again expressed to me that their greatest desire was to live their small-town lives in peace, with progress a secondary concern for most.

The active labor pool was growing in the early 2000s, owing to a recent influx of new residents fleeing the increasing violence and chaos of the San Juan metropolitan area. But growth was accompanied by rising unemployment. According to data from the island's Department of Labor and Human Resources, of the population 16 years of age and over, 43 percent of Nocorá residents participated in the labor force in 2000. Unemployment in Nocorá consistently averages 4 percent higher than the rest of Puerto Rico. In a report to the alcalde presented during my fieldwork, it was noted that Nocorá boasted a unique municipal industry profile (fully half the jobs available there were in manufacturing). However, nearly half of Nocoreños worked in other municipalities.[79]

The report also presented an important element of the dismal reality behind Nocoreño underemployment: among those 18 and older, 45 percent had not graduated from high school. Twenty-seven percent had achieved their "four year" (high school) diploma and had no further schooling. While a certain number of jobs in the chemical plants did not require an advanced degree in chemistry, adherence to many of the quite-elaborate safety measures for even the most menial jobs required a high level of literacy. And though I was able to view a number of safety instruction manuals that were readily available in Spanish, bilingualism in English remained, and will likely continue to be, an extremely desirable trait within the corporate structure of the multinationals.

This town was not, of course, simply a series of labor and other economic statistics. Nocorá remained characteristic of many small towns, where people often lived in the same neighborhoods in which they were raised and attended elementary school. Social relations were a mixture of the traditional respect often associated with more rural environments and the skepticism of knowing everyone else's dirty laundry. The pace of life was often slower than in the more densely populated metropolitan areas, and broad stretches of grazing pasture surrounded the industrial core of the municipality. Still, at the turn of the twenty-first century, Nocorá was becoming more susceptible to the loud cars, petty corner drug-dealing, and other signs of urban life. Although my informants did not directly blame the pharmaceuticals for the rise of these social problems, there was a general consensus that underemployment was a major contributing factor. Given the imperfect fit of the polluting industries as economic benefactors, it remains something of a puzzle as to how they remained so effectively integrated into Nocorá's social fabric.

Victor Turner wrote that all societies are composed of structure and antistructure. That is, while there are institutions, levels of organization in social groups, and they are often physically located in "areas of common living,"[80] there is something besides organization and commonly shared physical environment that holds groups of people together. Turner referred to this "modality of social relationships" as *communitas*, the Latin word for community, another way of describing the unfulfilled social needs that concerned Seda Bonilla so much.[81] For Turner, the maintenance of society is a dialectical process, in which relationships of differential power must be maintained through ritual. These rituals require that during some periods of time even the most powerful are seen to be, at least symbolically, vulnerable, common, or subject to the scrutiny of those less powerful.

In democratic societies, such as Puerto Rico, cyclical elections can help serve this function.[82] However, as Seda Bonilla suggests, the personalistic nature of politics on the island[83] has the effect of imitating the ritual process, while the electorate has become increasingly disenchanted with the political-economic realities they face. Additionally, as the Puerto Rican election cycle for all offices is only once every four years, the electorate requires other additional social rituals, and looks to the participation of other social actors, in order to create a sense of connection to political and cultural elites that are paradoxically both paternalistic and increasingly socially distant.

Combining the observations from the two quotes at the opening of the chapter, it is apparent that the "uses" to which the land and water have primarily been put are to produce goods and profits for consumption in places that are not Nocorá. It can therefore be argued from a purely economic standpoint that it made the most sense for corporations to focus their economic and political capital in supporting government figures. These relationships "between equals" created leverage through which they could use their influence to achieve their goals, such as getting new construction approved easily, or getting permits to dispose of waste. They had a direct line of communication through which to reinforce the long-standing culturally received, and politically enshrined, wisdom that they are necessary to Puerto Rico. However, from the perspective of benefiting the broader community, the pure economic perspective begins to weaken. The next chapter explores the importance of ritual and *confianza* in modern Nocorá, assessing how a broader swathe of the community perceived its relationships with its pharmaceutical neighbors, and how these corporations acted to fulfill their role as self-described members of that community.

Figure 3.1. Ruins of an abandoned hotel built on a limestone outcrop in Tipan. Referred to by a local legislator as an "ecological disaster," the ruins call into question the decision to aggressively redevelop the site. Photo by the author.

Playing Politics

I was uncharacteristically nervous that afternoon as I drove toward the beach for the regular monthly meeting of CDAN. Over the course of the year I had become an accepted and visible fixture at the meetings, something less than a full participant, but certainly more than a regular observer of their activities. The group's leaders had insisted that I always sit near the table from which the vice president ran the meetings so I could hear well, but in a way it made my position seem more active, even to those who had placed me there. Today, however, I had decided I was officially moving out of the position of observer, and was taking a deliberate step to influence the events surrounding me.

I had become aware that the parts of Tipan closest to the beach were soon to be the target of the administrative process known as expropriation—the taking of property by the government, supposedly for the public good. I had in fact seen the plans during a visit to the alcalde's office. I was also fairly certain that CDAN had little knowledge of this impending threat, due to their intense focus on the wastewater plant, and their orchestrated isolation from the municipal administration. I wasn't sure if they were aware that other environmental and community groups were mobilizing around the issue up and down the northern coast. Given the severity of the changes planned, I was determined to do the one thing I felt could really give something back to CDAN before I left the field. I would attempt to connect them with the larger movement by bringing an organizer from *La Vida Cristiana*, an NGO helping to coordinate the regional anti-expropriation campaign. I was hopeful that they could at least learn about the issue and decide if they wanted to address it as an organization. I had no clue, however, how I was going to introduce the topic.

I needn't have worried—Don Lirio began the meeting by presenting a newspaper article that mentioned the growing linkages between community and environmental organizations, including those focused on expropriation. "We need to get connected to them," he said with his characteristic passion. "They are also struggling for their communities, and they could help us!"

I was taking notes on their discussion and generally feeling confident that things were going in a good direction when suddenly the usually soft-spoken Don Leonardo jumped out of his chair, raising his voice. "This is not what we are about!" he shouted. "We are not struggling for our community! We are struggling to clean up the environment! Once we start talking about the community, we're playing politics, and we don't do politics!"

Doña Carina, usually low-key though she chaired the meetings, reached out her hand to calm him down, while other voices started to rise. The carefully controlled allegiances of party politics were beginning to bubble up among the CDAN members, and Don Leonardo and others who were members of the alcalde's PPD party were clearly uncomfortable with the direction Don Lirio, an *independentista*, was headed. Don Reynaldo, an *estadista* like Doña Carina, also tried to defuse the argument, but tempers were flaring like I'd never seen. Who would have thought that struggling for "the community" would be so taboo?

3

The Rituals and Consequences
of Community Politics and Dissent

Communitas breaks in through the interstices of structure, in lim-
inality; at the edges of structure, in marginality; and from beneath
structure, in inferiority.
  —Victor Turner (1969, 128)

Donde manda capitán no manda marinero. [Where the captain is in
charge the sailor does not give orders.]
  —Puerto Rican *refrán* (proverb)

The history of Nocorá, as in all of Puerto Rico, is replete with stories of decisions "made based on health, family economies, or *beliefs about modernity.*"[1]
Residents of Nocorá have long struggled to balance their own notions of
modernity and progress, highly influenced as they are by both development
ideologies and their own, often difficult, life experiences. The quote above
is referring specifically to sterilization choices. However, the observation
is broadly applicable to many decisions that influence both individual and
community health. In the case of Nocorá, making choices about health was
likely to mean choosing to be agnostic about the relationship between health
and the environment. The overall benefits of their everyday actions played
more into immediate conformity with the body politic, and the shorter-term
maintenance of the social body. However, the trade-off has been the health
of both their individual bodies and the longer-term health of the community,
beyond the structure of social institutions, and the performance of social
relationships.

In anthropological studies of social cohesion[2] it becomes clear that, contrary to what we might expect, conflicted societies such as Nocorá do not have a tendency to fall apart. This chapter focuses on the role of municipal and corporate rituals in maintaining social harmony in spite of pervasive doubts about the quality-of-life impact of pharmaceutical manufacturing. Through analyses of public opinion and discourses around trust, or *confianza*, the symbolic importance of the drug industry in Nocoreño society becomes clear, especially through their highly orchestrated relationships to institutions of power such as the *alcaldía*. Residents often chose to minimize their concerns about the environment and the potential for health problems, enacting choices through the lens of several Puerto Rican cultural idioms: the verb *bregar*,[3] which is a way of thinking about non-confrontational struggles in impossible situations; and *jaibería*, a similar idea used to describe the metaphorical tactic of evasively walking sideways in order to eventually get where you want to go (like a crab does).[4] These tactics, born in a cultural context of colonialism and neocolonialism, can provide potential for Nocoreños (like other Puerto Ricans) to resolve "the specific 'small problems' that erode our [sic] enjoyment of life—" producing "more enabling narratives of self and community."[5] However, the union of corporate interests and resources with largely unchecked governmental authority has created an increasingly narrow field for such activities that might otherwise have given voice to environmental health concerns.

Ideals of Progress and the Presence of Industry

While those who lived and worked in industrial Nocorá had concerns about both their economic and ecological well-being, several factors limited their abilities to express these concerns. As one of the municipal secretaries noted, "If the industry left, our quality of life would improve 100%, but this would greatly affect us in our economy." These factors were embedded in the municipal government's longstanding visions of both community and progress, the history of which we saw in the last chapter. These visions are linked by the presence of the pharmaceutical companies, creating an equation in which, I will argue, the alcalde was one of the most defining figures. It was through him that community needs were constructed for public consumption (such as the perspective that environmental issues were subservient to economic ones). The path for meeting those needs (e.g., such that development should emphasize increased pharmaceutical and biotechnological investment), was decided by him without much public participation, and community concerns over that path were marginalized through the management of public forums and the media. The success of these methods of governing required that the alcalde fulfilled certain aspects of community ritual function, which ultimately affirmed his right to then speak for the community to the exclusion of most others.

The municipal administration held a tight rein over development planning, whether related to the pharmaceutical industry or otherwise. The alcalde was unquestionably at the center of the decision-making process, if not the sole architect of Nocorá's path into the future. Observational experience, as well as the alcalde's own descriptions of his role, supports the conclusion that while the municipal assembly had recently gained the status of "legislature," and therefore had a more direct decision-making authority with regard to budgets and legal matters, the legislature still functioned largely to give approval to the alcalde's plans. A two-term representative of Tipan described the system this way:

> Our function is to study, with at least 24 hours notice, and approve, or disapprove the projects that the alcalde brings us. We may make amendments, changes. We have to approve them by a two thirds vote. We can also bring forward our own projects or proposals. And we negotiate these with him because at the end of the day he is the one who says whether a project is going to move forward or not.

While monthly meetings of the legislature were, in theory, public, they were not well publicized. When I stated my intention to attend the meetings, several of my acquaintances expressed surprise. Those from Tipan particularly warned me that I should be cautious, as they were skeptical that observers would be welcomed unless personally invited. During one particular meeting that I attended, the alcalde had asked permission of the legislature to personally present several expensive budgetary items. The format in that case functioned very much as Schwartzman has described the enactment of many meetings: as a distinctive type of communicative event, rather than a vehicle for problem-solving or decision-making.[6] Approval of projects was sought pro forma, and at times critical questions were asked. However, at the municipal level in Nocorá, there was no divided government, and as the local leader of his party, the alcalde was assured of the majority's support for even his most ambitious ideas.

During a later meeting, at which a development project was being approved, I walked into a mostly empty meeting room, and was greeted by the alcalde. He motioned to a jumpy looking man standing to the side, and introduced him as the municipal planner, and we shook hands. As the alcalde walked toward the table to begin the meeting, Fernando, the planner, questioned me a bit about my project, and then stated with a tone of pride, "I am responsible for making all the decisions about what gets closed down, what gets expropriated."[7] It was clear that he viewed himself as instrumental in the alcalde's campaign for a new, modern Nocorá, and like many of his compatriots, described the alcalde as a man of "vision." "My office is right over there," he pointed to a building around the corner. "You can come speak to me and I will tell you more about the plans for the pueblo, all the things we are doing. Speak to my secretary to make an appointment."

In spite of his seemingly enthusiastic offer, I was never able to meet Fernando for an interview. I discovered that he was not only very busy, but he did not live in Nocorá, and came to his local office from San Juan only rarely. Sitting in the waiting area several times over the course of many weeks, his secretary did give me a view into the functioning of the office overall, particularly when he called in to speak with her on the phone. Hanging up one day after he forgot our second appointment she commented, "he is always very, very busy," and rolled her eyes. "There is always paperwork we are needing to do, to file with offices. . . . Half the time he is calling to ask if I can find a file, and I don't know where he's put it." She sighed, with a look that clearly said, *I just work here.* "Whenever the priority comes down, we all rush around trying to make it happen."

There has long been a tendency toward this type of municipal governance in Nocorá, and indeed, in much of Puerto Rico. However, the stakes had risen in the time that Martínez had been alcalde. In 1992, the Commonwealth government took the first steps toward increasing the level of local control in the island's 78 municipalities, providing that the local government had the capacity to do so. Some of the explicit purposes of the Law of Autonomous Municipalities include:

> to provide for the modernization of systems and procedures and the establishment of better accounting and operational controls; to increase the range of capabilities and functions of the municipalities, transferring to them the responsibilities of planning and regulation of their territories and authorize the delegation to them of other responsibilities of the Central Government; to establish means for the participation of citizens in the development of their communities.

In spite of its small size, Nocorá had already succeeded in earning the right to call itself a "*municipio autónomo.*" It was among a select group that had met certain organizational and budgetary benchmarks, undoubtedly assisted by the substantial budget brought it by pharmaceutical payments. As evidenced by the separate office of planning, it had been allowed to take a good deal of control over development in general, and land use specifically.

The motto of Alcalde Martínez's office was "For a good government, a good administration," and any observer would be hard pressed to have found anything appearing organizationally amiss in the halls of the Casa Alcaldía or the Legislature. However, the degree of control exercised was sometimes viewed negatively by more skeptical longtime residents. *"Él tiene sus manos en muchos calderos"* [He has his hands in many pots], one woman told me. And while she meant that Martínez was able to exercise a great deal of influence over many local issues, there was, among his detractors, a suspicion that he, like many other politicians, had managed to benefit economically from his power. This issue was brought into relief when, just before the elections of 2004, Martínez announced that he was renouncing his salary, and received some positive press for the act. A flattering cartoon appeared in the local press, and his campaign was quick to capitalize—in my newly built urbanization I received a copy of the cartoon stapled to a full-color cardstock flyer of the alcalde's face, his name and party prominently displayed for the benefit of any new residents who might have registered to vote in Nocorá. His supporters took it as a sign of his generosity. His critics were quick to point out that he could afford it because, at the very least, he was already drawing a retirement pension from his years of working in public education and government.[8] "So all he's really doing is not getting paid twice!" several informants grumbled. While Martínez was generally considered, by both supporters and detractors, to be the heir of the legacy of Sebastián Robles, this comment recalls several of the more unflattering observations made by Seda Bonilla's[9] informants in earlier decades.

Whether or not they approved of his politics or his activities, most Nocoreños agreed that Estrello, as he was generally known in the town, was in charge. While I had heard reports of his brusque treatment of those he considered opponents, and saw some of his terse written correspondence with the Tipan activists, I had several opportunities to witness his powerful charisma as well. There was no doubt that he was a leader who could accomplish much when he wanted to, and who had a distinct vision. Among his more measured critics, I found that it was not so much his overall integrity that they questioned, but rather his obstinacy. Once he had an idea in his head, there seemed to be little to prevent him from carrying out his plan, and in our interviews he acknowledged this tendency. In the service of his impressive development plans (e.g., channeling[10] the Rió Grande de Bajas to prevent flooding in the urban center of town,[11] re-zoning to

Figure 3.2. Commemorative plaque created by local artisans on the completion of major stages of channeling the Río Grande de Bajas. The shield carries the coat of arms of Nocorá. The dam prevented heavy flooding of the main part of the urbanized center of Nocorá. Whether it worsened flooding in other areas is a subject of contention. Photo by the author.

create more industrialized areas, building new shopping centers for both local and distant potential shoppers, re-peopling the decaying urban center of town), Martínez had an enviable talent for bringing together human and economic resources from far and wide. Funding for the river project was obtained at the federal level, a result of his use of a Washington lobbying firm. His vision and dedication have drawn comparisons (see figure 3.2) to Don Quixote, a popular figure in the Hispanic imagination, and particularly so in Puerto Rico.

Here particularly I wish to draw the reader's attention to the symbolic linking of the famously futile crusader's image with alcalde Martínez and his flagship infrastructure project, channeling the river that forms the eastern border of the municipality and the construction of a dam around the town's urban center. Martínez presented one of the plaques to me as a gift, in effect commemorating our first interview. Though not dwelling too deeply on the choice of Don Quixote, a favorite figure for the statuettes typical of Puerto Rican folk art, when asked, Martínez allowed that it had been selected because people thought of him as Quixotic. Grinning widely at the thought, he explained in a rising voice that it was because he had vision, and sometimes people thought his ideas too big, too expensive, or simply "crazy." But he exuded a vibrant confidence that in his case, his record of accomplishment would speak for itself, and that he would be remembered as an idealist with chivalrous intentions.

Martínez's confidence could be read all over Nocorá, on the large wooden billboards that were used to announce municipal projects already under way. Typically in Puerto Rico these signs declared the description of the project, the budget, the number of jobs created (if the number was impressive enough), and the government sponsors. In Nocorá there was an additional message. Earlier in his career Martínez used the billboards as a testimonial to his goals, and a desire to fulfill promises, asking: "That God enlighten our mind in order to continue the development of our *pueblo*." The word *pueblo* can be interpreted as "people," and also as "town." In the framework of this study, the use of *pueblo* as opposed to, for example, *municipio*, is a publicly stated appeal to an emotional sense of community. As time moved on, however, Martínez's language expressed increasing confidence that continued success was a given. Signage in use during 2004–2005 declared: "With the favor of God, completing what is promised."

None of these observations is meant to imply that Nocorá had not benefited from at least some of the projects he championed so forcefully. However, it is perhaps the open question of *what was getting left behind* in the vision of this otherwise "good administration" that was at the root of discontent in Nocorá. In Martínez's own words,

> the transference of all the powers has permitted that each municipio, each with its own idiosyncrasies, can pursue its own development, its own potential, and attend to its own particular needs, given the space provided through the Law of Autonomous Municipalities. . . . In other words it gives us the capacity to execute, through our own initiative, responding to the needs of our own co-citizens.

This statement directly parallels the arguments for autonomy sought by Puerto Rican policymakers to gain exceptions to federal environmental regulations. And in order to quell any disagreements with Martínez's administrative priorities, defined by him as progress, he made substantial efforts to ritualistically cement his image as the person responsible for the modernizing changes in Nocorá.

The Role of Ritual in Nocorá

The ritual process[12] is integral to the annual cycle of Nocoreño life, particu-larly as it pertains to the reinforcement of the power establishment. It has been persuasively argued that cultural identity in Puerto Rico has become "sponsored" by outside economic interests, such as Winston tobacco, Bud-weiser beer, and of course, the pharmaceuticals.[13] As such, corporate spon-sorship has effectively been encouraged as official policy of both PNP and PPD administrations, with the result of diffusing the impulse toward politi-cal (and effectively economic) independence. In Nocorá, I would argue, the role of sponsorship and ritualized consumerism was not so much about anx-iety over political partyism and independence. Rather, the ritualized forms, such as the *fiestas patronales*, Three Kings Day, and other opportunities for town-wide parties, were tightly choreographed by the municipal govern-ment for the purpose of shoring up the administration's paternal relationship with residents. A secondary outcome of this process was that opposition to the development strategies of the alcalde were minimized, and criticism of his corporate partners was carefully controlled.

The sponsorship present in this case was corporate in two senses: Most explicitly, there was direct corporate sponsorship of municipal activities, particularly if costly musical entertainment was provided, or if the activity was in some way related to health promotion. In these public settings Mar-tínez was often the pharmaceutical industry's most eloquent public relations promoter. Still, the most prominently displayed sponsor of any activity was always the municipality of Nocorá.[14] When the municipality was the *official* sponsor, as was the case at the *fiestas patronales* I observed in the summers of 2004 and 2011, a photograph of the alcalde himself was the most frequently flashed image on the increasingly common multimedia screen, project-ing images of the entertainment and other announcements to the crowd. The municipal celebration of Noche de San Juan Bautista, held at the public beach in Tipan in late June, was likewise an event in which the municipal-ity itself was celebrated. Gratitude to the alcalde was frequently expressed through the projection of images, and by performers and MCs over the pub-lic address system. In these contexts, that is, celebrations of the identity and culture of Nocorá itself, corporate sponsorship was not usually emphasized. But the size of the activities[15] and the quality of entertainment provided[16] would not have been possible without a substantial municipal budget, fully half of which was provided to Nocorá through municipal taxation of local industries.

Three Kings Day, the final act of the traditional Christmas season in much of Latin America, is celebrated in a number of municipalities on the island by gift giving on a monumental scale, from alcaldes to local children. Nocorá was no exception, and one acquaintance assured me that Martínez's generosity was gaining him a regional reputation. "I know people who've come from several towns over," she told me. Thousands of children lined up in a well-cordoned-off and tightly managed enclosure to receive one of several options, including dolls, balls, and other such small but worthwhile toys. Passing through a well-monitored gauntlet to receive their gift and to shake hands with the alcalde, children and their parents passed into one of the town's parks where the ubiquitous food vendors and *casas de brinca* [inflatable jumping houses] awaited them. I stood chatting with Martínez a few moments, as he grinned at the lines of people, telling me that this practice was a long-standing cultural tradition that he took particular pleasure in fulfilling. As I passed into the park, however, even I was surprised to see an elaborate stage area set up for local performers, and in front of the stage, waiting until the first round of giving was complete, were more than 300 bicycles of various sizes, waiting to be raffled off to the children in the crowd.[17]

Figure 3.3. The great bicycle giveaway. Photo by the author.

Not every child in the crowd would win a bicycle, but every child had a good chance at it. Based on population estimates from the 2000 Census and suggesting, for the sake of argument, that all the children in Nocorá between the ages of 5 and 14 were eligible to win, approximately 8 percent of children in town received a bike from the alcalde in that single year.[18] It is logical to think that those most appreciative of the gifts, and perhaps of even the opportunity to win them, were likely to be among the poorest of Martínez's constituents. Even allowing that some recipients may have been from other municipalities, the mere *performance* of such generosity fit squarely into the traditions not only of the Puerto Rican Christmas celebration, but of the personalistic politics of what Seda Bonilla called in Nocorá a market-like pseudo-*communitas*.[19] In twenty-first-century Nocorá, Seda Bonilla's concern with this inexplicable glue that makes a community of people hold together was more relevant than ever before. A focus on communitas points to the consequences of merging significant corporate financial resources with the concentration of local governance in the hands of a *cacique*. Martínez perfectly fit the description of a political strongman in the Spanish colonial tradition, an "active and skilled manipulator who is very adept in presenting himself as an indispensable mediator between the people and the centre of power."[20] The result was that the alcalde could almost literally purchase the goodwill of his constituents. By cloaking this market transaction in the traditional rituals of Puerto Rican culture, he was able to satisfy the social demands for community cohesion, if in a way that rang hollowly at times.

An interesting set of exceptions to this pattern of municipal sponsorship were the activities organized by the Centro Cultural of Nocorá. These offices of culture, affiliated with the Commonwealth government's Institute of Puerto Rican Culture (ICP), have long been the local means by which the tenets of Operation Serenity were practiced. In this aggregate sense they can be seen as complicit supporters of the prevailing development ideologies of both the PPD and PNP. Indeed, on the local level the Centros have often functioned as the mouthpiece of a powerful alcalde.[21] In Nocorá, however, where this subservient relationship might be most expected, it was in fact the opposite. The Centro Cultural, though led for many years by a member of the alcalde's PPD party, nevertheless maintained an independent voice in Nocoreño society. Its programming, including an annual Fiesta Folklórica showcase of traditional Puerto Rican music, lessons in the traditional *cuatro* instrument for all ages, and a *velorio cantado*[22] for the Christmas holidays, was as rich as any municipality could boast. Though they received a certain amount of funding from the municipality, the alcalde was often conspicuously absent from these events.

The pharmaceuticals, too, provided some sponsorship for Centro Cultural activities and services, notably donating the resources to print a variety of publications, including a quarterly cultural magazine and occasional monographs of local interest. However, the leadership of the Centro was careful to maintain a calculated neutrality: the president, Don Teodoro, had long been associated with the community struggle over the wastewater treatment plant.[23] When I asked him about his relationship with the pharmaceuticals, he smiled, saying wryly, "I have a very good relationship with *them*. But they do not have a good relationship with *me*." This statement was indicative of the carefully constructed balance many Nocoreños strive to maintain, effectively drawing a boundary between their social and individual bodies.

The Centro's leaders also saw its mission much as the ICP originally envisioned it: their goals were to promote civic engagement with the cultural traditions of Puerto Rico without being *partidista*, without getting involved in issues that could be judged as being explicitly political in nature. Achieving this balance of community representation had been tricky. At times during CDAN's history, they had used some of the administrative resources of the Centro to pursue less confrontational means of bringing their complaints to light. For this reason, perhaps, a pharmaceutical company can be excused if it sent its annual invitation to a meeting about "environmental achievements" to the Centro Cultural, and in doing so believed it had done its part in communicating with "the community." Similar notices were sent to a regional, officially recognized, non-confrontational, environmental NGO (which I call "GUIA").[24] GUIA also purported to represent the "community" of Nocorá, in spite of the fact that the NGO's headquarters are located in Bajas, the neighboring municipio. When I asked the president of the Centro, as well as the leader of GUIA, whether they would be attending (and whether I could attend with them), they gave nearly identical answers: (1) the guest list was very strict, only those explicitly invited could attend,[25] and (2) no, they would not be attending, because in their experience such meetings were just bragging sessions by the companies to tout their so-called environmental achievements. The meeting would not be worth their time. Underlying this response by the Centro leadership was also a concern that by participating in a communication act such as this annual "report of environmental successes," they could be seen as validating the industry's version of its environmental record. Thus, it may be that as a neutrality-seeking repository of community information in the context of Nocorá, the Centro inadvertently represented an unfortunate missing link in the direct chain of communication between corporate elites and residents.

Communication Breakdowns Damage *Confianza*

"*La comunicación es pésima* [dreadful]," Don Reynaldo replied when, after several months of participant observation, I observed to him that poor communication seemed to be a major issue in Nocorá. Different methods, styles, and levels of access to communication had significant effects on the structure and function of community relationships. Although Don Reynaldo lamented problems with communication, I observed that when the municipality, i.e., the alcalde, wanted to get information out to the public, he had a number of effective tools. As with the full-color flyer slipped under my door praising the mayor for renouncing his salary, when necessary he could mobilize a contingent of supporters to distribute printed materials as broadly as he liked. Also, as in every other part of the island, any news item that was wanted to reach as wide an audience as possible was audio-recorded and blared through neighborhoods on the announcement trucks that had been ubiquitous in the less urban areas of Puerto Rico since Seda Bonilla did his fieldwork. Public hearings about development projects or planning issues were not announced by these means, although the municipality had several such announcement trucks at its disposal, and made regular use of them to advertise a wide range of sponsored activities.

Seda Bonilla noted that in 1959 relationships of *confianza*, or trust, were already eroding in Nocorá, particularly in Tipan. My fieldwork suggests that with regard to *confianza*, Tipanecos were deeply conflicted: they would have liked to have had more trust in those they saw as more powerful, "*los grandes.*" But they had been let down time and time again, and they believed their health and well-being were being sacrificed for the financial gains of others. As one neighbor offered when he handed back my survey:

> Here there are no community services—*supposedly* they're coming to clean the beach. The EPA is *supposedly* working on [the environmental problems], but when there's money involved . . . [he sighed]. Then again, it's not an easy thing to deal with the environment.

Residents who were directly critical nevertheless tended to shy away from saying that other Nocoreños did not benefit, particularly those who worked in the factories, or those who could benefit from industry sponsorship of activities or services. When asked whether they felt the pharmaceuticals had a relationship of good faith and good communication with the community, several Tipanecos not affiliated with CDAN remarked that the companies had good relations with the municipal government. The terms they used drew a clear distinction between *el municipio* and *la comunidad*. Some accepted this as the order of things, or at least were resigned to it. Others said it with scorn, implying that the business people would hardly lower themselves to speak directly with people like those from Tipan. As another noted,

> They work with the municipalities, not with the communities. I don't have any experience with any community services here. Those that benefit are the municipalities, and they help protect them [the companies] from those who criticize too much.

In fact, the alcalde and his administration described with pride the level of openness that existed between the corporations and the government in Nocorá. From the perspective of making corporations more accountable, however, a relative openness between elite-level players, such as the municipality and the corporations, did not reflect practical transparency with residents. The municipality itself operated decidedly with what is sometimes called a "trust me"[26] model of transparency,[27] in which most key decisions are made behind closed doors. The words of high-ranking municipal officers strongly made the counterpoint that was so evident in the everyday experiences of the not-so-privileged. The lieutenant alcalde, in one of our conversations, asked me to what degree I was familiar with the Puerto Rican press. "Puerto Rico has a lot of news coverage," he said. "They're opinionated, they're not really objective. I'm not saying that it's good or bad—it just is." The alcalde, he explained, had removed the distorting interference of the press as an issue. He liked to resolve problems through negotiation, in the offices of the pharmaceuticals, or in his own offices, not "in the street. If there is some kind of disagreement going on, and the press comes to me, I tell them we're negotiating."

Removing the press from the process, however, can have dire consequences for a relatively small or disenfranchised group of residents. Without regular, open access to the negotiating tables, they often had little choice but to try their case in the so-called court of public opinion. Many activists, including those more professionalized, who sometimes offered advisory support to groups like CDAN, spoke often of the importance for activists to be media-savvy. In Nocorá, however, the government and corporations disapproved of creating what they described as a media circus. These elite actors had been very successful at diminishing the impact of CDAN's efforts to reach the press in two ways since the filing of the "big news" lawsuit against the pharmaceutical companies and the water company in 2000:

1. Though during my fieldwork there still officially existed a "committee on odors" made up of residents, government, and corporate members, the lawsuit had been used as an excuse to cease communications between residents and the corporations. During 2004–2005 some progress was made in reconnecting local legislators with CDAN, and some of those officials had a meeting with the operators of the water treatment plant (which I was able to attend). However, meetings of that sort had not happened for several years.

2. The lawsuit was drawn out through an excessive discovery process and other commonly practiced delay tactics, such that the suit was in court for nearly eight years. This delay made the activist momentum among Tipanecos decrease sharply, even as they still suffered from the treatment plant's pollution.

While the residents of Tipan continued to have problems with the air quality from the treatment plant, and they had many concerns about their nearby water quality, their environmental complaints were not generally considered newsworthy. I discovered this one afternoon when I received a phone call from Don Cesar, whose home in Tipan backed up to a canal bordering the fields where the sludge from the treatment plant was deposited. The residents spent several days trying to discover why the canal had suddenly begun to run the color of green antifreeze, and through a well-connected outside advisor eventually succeeded in bringing in a field agent of the Environmental Quality Board. However, no media, local or island-wide, ever returned their calls. Furthermore, it was apparent through my interactions with the field agent (who preferred to speak to me, a well-educated, if non-native-speaking outsider) that local communities were not generally considered to be the most reliable sources of information, even about their own backyards.

"It's difficult," she told me. "The communities always think it's some sort of chemical. And they want immediate answers. There aren't always immediate answers." As we walked along the edge of the canal I could understand how she might have trouble imagining that there could be a chemical spill in the middle of what otherwise appeared to be a landscape of mangroves and hayfields. She didn't realize, as the residents were only too well aware, that whenever rain drained into the canal, it carried material from the wastewater sludge. After attempting to collect a sample of the discolored water the agent left, leaving behind a distinct impression that the investigation would go nowhere. Don Cesar watched her walk away and shook his head.

> I grew up here, lived in the States for 45 years, and now live here again. People here now don't know what it was like then—they only think of work, without knowing the consequences. I'll tell you, there aren't any wild animals [here anymore]. For me they, they haven't done anything. I suppose the workers might say something different.

The Quandaries of Nocoreño Public Opinion

Understanding public opinion of the pharmaceutical industry among residents of Nocorá, particularly as it related to the environment and to quality of life, was of utmost importance as I conducted the research for this book. It was therefore necessary to supplement my extensive participant observation and qualitative interview data, collected among a broad swathe of people knowledgeable about the role of the pharmaceutical companies, and about life in Nocorá. I conducted a brief quantitative survey (see appendix) among people who lived and worked in the pharmaceutical sphere of influence. My sampling strategy was not intended to represent the municipality as a whole, but rather to gain a sense of the attitudes toward the pharmaceutical companies among a representative group of those reasonably considered to be "stakeholders."[28] I conceptualized the survey as a "stakeholder snapshot," from which I would not necessarily draw any absolute conclusions, but which would hopefully give statistical weight and some demographic specificity to the overall sense of ambivalence I was gleaning from my more qualitative research. My research, by combining a variety of qualitative and quantitative data about everyday quality of life, seeks to "combine measurements with assessments of what the measures mean to the people being measured."[29]

In Tipan, home to the only tangible grassroots environmental organization in Nocorá, and the regional wastewater treatment plant, I went door-to-door to survey residents who were not explicitly involved in the struggle. This approach represented an attempt to measure the variation that might exist in this sector of the municipality. To gain access to other views, I sampled in locations where people were likely to have had some more explicit experience with, and therefore opinion about, the pharmaceuticals:[30] (1) employees of the local health center; (2) employees of the municipal government; (3) visitors to and staff of the library and cultural center, which both receive funds from the companies; and (4) the local schools, where the companies claim to focus much of their community-oriented work.

My sample included 222 people, which I further screened so that the final group represented those who either lived or worked in Nocorá or who had family members who worked or had worked for the pharmaceuticals. The final sample used for further analysis was 207 people. The descriptive statistics with regard to the key variables discussed in this chapter are given in table 3.1.

In simple terms among this sample of Nocoreños, and those who can legitimately be considered "stakeholders" in the future of the municipality, a modest, though statistically significant, majority (58%) viewed the

Table 3.1. Overall Distribution of Demographics and Responses to Survey Questions

	N	Percent
Gender		
Men	63	31
Women	135	8
Ages		
18–29	30	15
30–39	61	30
40–49	49	24
50–59	33	16
60 or older	31	15
Residence		
Tipan	61	29
Other, Nocorá	88	43
Other, northern	58	28
Self or family member ever worked for pharmaceutical company:		
Yes [of this group 24 (12%) had personally worked for pharmaceuticals]	145	73
No	55	28

pharmaceutical companies in their midst as acting "in good faith." They also overwhelmingly (94%) expressed concerns about the quality of their physical environment as a result of the production activities of those same companies. Finally, a majority (62%) also agreed that their "quality of life" would be worse if the pharmaceutical industry were to leave Puerto Rico, as was so feared after the ending of the 936 tax benefits. These data unquestionably present a picture of community sentiment that is complex, and perhaps internally contradictory.

It is particularly instructive to note that among a small group of respondents, the pharmaceutical companies might be simultaneously considered "good neighbors" (66%) while not acting in good faith or practicing good communication. This was a conflicted sentiment I noted particularly in Tipan, where residents were often willing to credit the companies with having an overall positive economic impact, and yet were utterly

Table 3.1. (continued)

	N	Percent
1. Our quality of life would be worse if the pharmaceutical industry leaves Puerto Rico.		
Agree	126	62
Disagree	76	38
2. There is a great concern with issues related to the pollution from the pharmaceuticals.		
Agree	194	94
Disagree	13	6
3. The pharmaceuticals maintain a relationship of good faith and good communication with the community.		
Agree	119	58
Disagree	86	42
4. The pharmaceuticals are good neighbors, like part of our community.		
Agree	134	66
Disagree	69	34
5. Between the good and the bad things that the pharmaceuticals bring to our community, there is:		
more of the bad	45	23
equal proportion	118	59
more of the good	36	18

Note: Totals out of N=207. Some categories may not sum to 207 due to nonresponse.

untrusting as regards issues of communication and their concern about the environment. It is also particularly noteworthy that while majorities in both cases agreed with the "Good neighbor" and "Good faith/good communication," another majority also felt that "Between the good and the bad things the pharmaceuticals bring to our community," they were "in equal proportion."

Respondents were also asked to rank five items (education, sports, environment, health, and community activities) in terms of (1) the best services the pharmaceuticals provide to the community, and (2) areas in which they need to improve. If a respondent ranked any item either a 1 or a 2, they were coded as priorities for that respondent. With the most votes (44%), respondents ranked education as the best area, while the environment was, predictably, a top choice in the areas needing improvement (77%). For those who lived and worked near the factories in Salvador la Cruz, air quality continued to be a concern. For those in Tipan, both air and water quality were of concern, in terms of human health, *and* in terms of the health of wildlife in the delicate mangrove ecology. Further research is undoubtedly needed to further identify precisely *how* the pharmaceutical industry should be "doing more" in the context of each sector's local environment, but clearly they were not considered to be doing enough in general.

Walking through the residential neighborhood near the road that leads out of the *pueblo* toward Tipan, I noticed that a laminated sign with the logo of one of the local factories on it had been glued to a lamppost. Upon closer inspection I noted that the sign pointed the way toward the Actividad Limpieza de Playa, with the English translation underneath: Helps Clean-Up Barco de Caña Beach. The sign was posted presumably for the benefit of factory workers who were not familiar with the local geography, but it is difficult to imagine why the purpose of the activity would need to be translated into English.[31] This is not to make light of the fact that the beaches in Puerto Rico are often a disturbing repository of trash. Rather, it is to point out that it is unlikely that picking up trash on the beach, while admittedly a feel-good group "pro-environment" activity, is the best way to address the most pressing environmental concerns of Nocorá, and particularly of Tipan. Local residents clearly had heard about the activity—as quoted earlier, the rumor had been cause for some skepticism about follow-through as well as the activity itself. Also of significance is that the beach clean-up was not an activity coordinated with the existing pro-environment activists in that same neighborhood. In fact, since 2008 an environmental movement in the neighborhood Barco de Caña has gained strength over concerns about severe flooding and the desire of the alcalde to use the damage as a rationale to expropriate private lands. These problems are of a much more urgent nature than beach litter. The activity was, in CSR terms, a "win-win," but primarily from the company's perspective: It was a harmless activity that appears to help the community and costs the corporation little or nothing. As CSR analyst David Vogel has noted, this combination of qualities is the most desirable for corporations.[32]

Services related to health were a close second as an area needing improvement (63%), suggesting that while the pharmaceuticals have increased their sponsorship of such activities as mobile clinics, and are a ubiquitous presence at every health-related walk-a-thon (raising money for cancer, heart, stroke, and other medical research and services), people would like to see more concerted efforts at providing much needed services. Walk-a-thons, like beach clean-ups, are feel-good activities[33] that bring together groups of people of varying social statuses (here employees of the pharmaceuticals) to achieve a general goal that is hard to fault. As Victor Turner observed,

> there are those who, in the exercise of daily authority or as representatives of major structural groupings, have little opportunity to deal with their fellow men as concrete individuals and equals. . . . They might find an opportunity to . . . be symbolically at least regarded as the servants of the masses.[34]

A group of such employees is made equal within their group through the performance of a manual task, and the symbolism of wearing a company t-shirt. With that same t-shirt they are also identified as being part of a high-status, giving entity, and as such are certainly creating communitas *within* their work environment. Yet raising money for a national nonprofit, such as the American Cancer Society, while building team spirit among workers, and raising the profile of the company (they provide the team t-shirts, which are worn long after the event is over), so often fails to meet the specific and immediate needs of a locally grounded community. In an interview with one CSR manager, in which he described the donations his company made to local health causes, he named the Heart Walk, a once-a-year fund-raising walk-a-thon for the American Heart Association. This example is ironic for two distinct reasons. First, a substantial portion of the money raised through walk-a-thons (and similar events) is from donations collected by participants from friends and family, not corporate philanthropy.[35] Second, describing the Heart Walk, and similar events, as an effort the company made toward "prevention" of heart disease is misleading. Raising money for health research in the current system is often raising money for research into drug-related cures—and thus is self-serving for pharmaceutical companies.[36] Likewise, although drug research is important, the use of the term "prevention" to describe most drug research and development could very well be considered disingenuous.[37] The perspective expressed by the manager was likely not meant to be purposely inaccurate. Rather, it is through the institutionalized process of glossing over the important distinction between concepts like "prevention" and "cure" that the drug companies benefit from a vague sense that they are doing good in the world, while concentrating the benefits of their activities behind the factory gates. Their beneficent reach seldom addressed deeper quality-of-life concerns in the broader reaches of Nocoreño society.

Quality of Life and *Confianza*

What impact do Nocoreños perceive the pharmaceuticals to have on their everyday quality of life, and what do those perceptions tell us about the foundations of community, such as communitas and *confianza*? I drew upon two survey items to shed light on Nocoreños' views:[38]

> Our quality of life would be worse if the pharmaceutical industry leaves Puerto Rico (*Agree or Disagree*); and
> The pharmaceutical companies maintain a relationship of good faith and good communication with the community (*Agree or Disagree*).

The first item directly addressed the direct relationship between quality of life, as defined by the respondent, and the pharmaceutical industry. The nonparametric response (62% agree), as discussed above, is reflective of a basic sentiment. Using demographic and other responses, a multivariate analysis was performed to evaluate whether any of the other survey data might shed some light on how the respondents were assessing quality of life in their answers. Based on the significance of raw associations between other variables and the quality-of-life question, it was decided that the following variables should be evaluated for a multivariate model:

- Age
- Gender
- School employee?
- Resident of Tipan?
- Pharmaceuticals bring mostly bad/equal/good to the community
- Do they act in good faith / with good communication?

Table 3.2 Multivariate (Logistic) Statistics for Quality-of-Life Survey Question

Variable	Odds Ratio	Confidence Limits
Ages		
18–29	2.843	(0.966 - 8.368)
30–39	4.599	(1.744 -11.913)*
40–49	1.408	(0.550 - 3.601)
50–59	1.510	(0.548 - 4.163)
60 and up	Referent	
"Confianza"		
Agree	2.505	(1.356 - 4.629)*
Disagree	Referent	

* indicates statistical significance at α = 0.05.

Following standard procedures, a logistic regression analysis[39] was performed, assessing the relationship between these variables and the belief that quality of life would be worse if the pharmaceuticals were to leave Puerto Rico. The final model revealed that of the original group, only two variables were significantly associated with the quality-of-life statement: Age; and Good faith/Good communication, which I believe to be a reasonable measure of *confianza*, or trust, between the community and the drug companies. The model statistics appear in table 3.2.

Statistical analyses based on this survey cannot, of course, fully explain the complex relationships between demographic and attitudinal independent variables and concerns about quality of life. However, this model is suggestive of some very interesting patterns. First, there was no association between believing that quality of life would decline if the industry left and having either personally worked, or being related to someone, who worked for the industry. Equally interesting is that most of the other "common sense" associations, significant as individual cross-tabulations, drop out in the multivariate model. In this population, which represented a reasonable, if not strictly random, sample of people living and working in Nocorá, being between 30 and 39 years of age was significantly associated with the equation, pharmaceuticals = good quality of life, when controlling for gender, residence in Tipan, balance of "good vs. bad," and employment in the local schools (where the industry focuses much of its public beneficence).

Based on qualitative ethnographic data, as well as historic and other contextualizing information, this result suggests that for this age group, whose childhood occurred during the peak of Puerto Rico's capital-intensive industrial phase, the pharmaceuticals represented economic security *irrespective* of personal employment experience. The marginal significance of the same association among those in the 18–29 age group supports this conclusion, although other data suggest that this younger group also had some skepticism, and a greater awareness of environmental issues may modify its perception of this security.

The relationship between what I am defining as *confianza*, or trust (the belief that the pharmaceutical industry maintains a relationship of good faith and good communication with the community) and the conviction that quality of life would decrease if the industry left the island is perhaps the most instructive. Those who expressed trust in the industry were 2.5 times more likely to link the collective quality of life of their community to that industry, *controlling for other variables that would logically seem to influence this point of view*. This, too, suggests that, more important than personal, direct experience with the economic benefits of the pharmaceutical companies (as measured by this survey), belief in the goodness of the companies, in their motives, and other "feel-good" qualities influenced the value Nocoreños placed on having the pharmaceutical factories and members of their community. In other words, performance, in the ritual sense, matters.

As important as the role of the elected executive remains in Puerto Rico, the social role of the non-elected power players in Nocorá cannot be overemphasized. I argue that the drug companies, too, participate in the ritual process in an attempt to cement their relations with those they perceive, and help construct, as representing the community. As one resident noted in the margins of the survey she responded to, "In terms of good communication, yes—between equals." Effectively the benefactors of the alcalde, who then used his substantial budget to do as he saw fit, they have helped create a social environment in which cultural identities can have corporate sponsors, and authenticity can have a price tag.[40] Further, they support a system in which residents and those with less power are actively excluded from participation in community decision-making. In practical terms for Nocoreños, there is a fluidity between seemingly contradictory positions, allowing them to criticize the pharmaceuticals as polluters and question their contributions to the community, while strongly believing that they are now necessary, and sometimes even good.

Good Neighbors versus *Confianza*

That a majority of respondents, including residents of Tipan, should reply yes to the question of whether the pharmaceuticals are "good neighbors" is not surprising: it is consistent with the modernizing outlook of Operation Bootstrap and traditional development ideas about industry. The expectation in Nocorá is that factories provide jobs, and boost the economy. While only 12 percent of the respondents to the survey reported having personally worked for the pharmaceuticals, 61 percent had family members who had had these enviable jobs. Thus, it seems that Nocoreños were willing to accept the idea that the factories provide jobs much because they know people who have worked there. And while the capital-intensive factories of the pharmaceuticals may not have perfectly met the expectations of many as regards jobs themselves, the process of industrialization has appeared to improve the local economy overall.[41] Furthermore, neither philanthropic charity nor Corporate Social Responsibility (CSR) has a long history in Puerto Rico, and the expectation that corporations would do more than "their jobs," providing as economic patrons, was only just beginning to gain traction in the late 1990s and early 2000s.

I have argued that the question about "good faith and good communication," on the other hand, represents *confianza*. *Confianza* was the word always used by Corporate Social Responsibility advocates in Puerto Rico (and other parts of Latin America) to describe the most necessary foundation of a stable civil society.[42] For this group of respondents who have tied their well-being to the drug factories, it appears that the industry has, in this respect, met its CSR mandate of "creating *confianza*." We are now left to grapple with a fundamentally qualitative question: How did the pharmaceutical companies view themselves in relation to the "community"? Considering that these statistics draw a picture that is by no means unanimous in its approval of the industry, how was this relationship contested on the ground, in the everyday lives of Nocoreños?

It is instructive to look at how the pharmaceutical representatives themselves answered the question: "how do you define the community?" The answers varied, but fell into four distinct areas of emphasis, all companies expressing each to greater and lesser degrees: (1) Geographical proximity to the factory itself; (2) First, our workers; (3) All of Nocorá; and (4) All of Puerto Rico. Here I will address responses 2 and 3 specifically, and will return to responses 1 and 4 (as well as to the here-unspoken community of shareholders[43]) in my later discussion of Corporate Social Responsibility.

The response that "community" for a corporation is first and foremost its workers is, from one perspective, admirable. As the Corporate Social

Responsibility literature is quick to point out, responsibility for the well-being of workers signaled the earliest shift among industrialists toward concern for something beyond profits. Current thinking tends to qualify programs such as health benefits, safety compliance, family leave, and others as "win-wins," arguing that happy, healthy workers are more productive and more likely to stay with the company, and therefore save the company money both in lost work and training of new employees.[44] Business research also shows that there are corporate benefits to company-organized volunteerism,[45] including high morale among employees. This supports the idea that the positive group feelings of the beach cleaning activity in Tipan, for example, were just as important to the company's self-defined "sense of community" as the benefit to the noncorporate community environment.

This example may explain, in part, how the companies can legitimately claim to be fulfilling their role as community members, helping to care for the social body, as it were, while leaving many Nocoreños unsatisfied, and unhealthy. Nevertheless, I would argue that they fulfill the old role of economic patron (though not necessarily employer) most effectively, and the role of true local partner-participant the least. In one conversation with the Community Relations director of AlphaPharm, I noted how easily he slid between talking about the lives of the workers and the well-being of the company, though in a manner more suggestive of pragmatism than perhaps compassion:

> Around 1984 we began a project to have our own powerplants, because at that time there was a crisis of regular failures of the power supply. When you're brewing microorganisms, the temperature needs to be constant. For example, when Hurricane Georges came through in 1998, and destroyed so much, we didn't have an interruption of work. Of course there were people who couldn't come to work, there were people who were affected very seriously, and those who didn't come were excused, we understood there was a problem, but for those who were here, our doors were open, and our operations continued to run.

Using the phrase "our doors were open" merges a feeling of welcoming support with the sense that workers, like the company itself, placed productivity as a high personal priority, even in times of unquestionable crisis.

Confronting "la brega" in Nocorá

It is evident by the number of "Agree" responses (94%) to the survey statement "There is great concern over issues related to pollution from the pharmaceuticals," that Nocoreños view the chemical contamination of their environment as part of everyday life. As Doña Graciela, an older woman who worked in the local library, told me with a pronounced shrug, "Well, yes, of course people are worried. But this is our life. There are always things we have to deal with in life. *Bregamos con todo eso.*"

According to cultural critic Arcadio Díaz Quiñones, "Between Puerto Ricans to speak of *bregar* is to speak of that which is most obvious," and likewise most specifically Puerto Rican.[46] He observes, "There is a vocation of harmony in *bregar*, to harmonize necessities and interests."[47] For most Spanish-speakers, *bregar* is a synonym for *luchar*, and both verbs mean "to struggle." An apt example in the Latin American context is one of revolution: one may hear a particular cause, something worth really fighting for, referred to as "*la lucha*." Across the wide variety of activists I encountered who were working in environmental protection, the cause of improving and protecting the environment was always referred to as "*la lucha*."[48]

For most Puerto Ricans, *la brega* is a very different space to inhabit than *la lucha*. As the observations of Doña Graciela suggest, la brega, or the space inhabited by Puerto Ricans in their daily lives, is very much a place in which one deals with things, gets along, chooses one's battles. It can be said that la brega retains some of its earlier significance of action—it is not passive. But it refuses the intensity of a frontal attack. I encountered a quite pedestrian example of this one evening after a day of nearly unbearable heat, visiting with my friend Benicia. She had been listening to one of her favorite radio commentators during the regular traffic jam coming back from San Juan that afternoon, and he had had a caller asking him if it was correct to refer to the heat, which any dictionary will tell you is masculine (*el calor*), as *la calor*. The commentator explained that at least in Puerto Rico, based on usage, he would say that both were equally acceptable. For example, he knew that in places like Nocorá people often said "la calor." Benicia, laughing, said that she had been very gratified by his answer—because indeed, in her experience the people of Nocorá referred to the heat as feminine. "It's softer. And there is a sense of resignation about it, I think," she said. I asked her if the heat was something that everyone just had to *bregar*, or deal with. "Exactly," she said. "What use would there be in fighting it?" In my most recent visit to Nocorá in 2011, following the student demonstrations over fee increases at the University of Puerto Rico, I heard a related objection to the more destructive, confrontational actions of some of the protesters—"Yes, things need to change, but that's not the way to do it." Samuel's reflection on getting through life "little by little" continued to resonate strongly with many people.

The difficulty is that in Nocorá it was unclear whether the compromising resistance of *jaiberia*, or walking sideways, could be leveraged as a tactic for solving problems of the magnitude of corporate pollution, arguably as dif-fuse in its power[49] as the effects of climate. It has been precisely the diffuse-ness of this power that makes it difficult to counter, as we will see in the next chapter. Frances Negrón-Muntaner has argued that in the struggle to cause the removal of the U.S. Navy from the island of Vieques, the emphasis of the broad-based movement on the "small problems" of the local environment and local-level harms was what made the movement ultimately successful.[50] Echoing the concern of residents who initially saw environmental activism as "*cosa de independentistas*," the Vieques movement required the sidestep-ping of the question of political independence that some activists saw as cen-tral to the struggle. Unfortunately, the complex aftermath of the expulsion of the navy has made it increasingly difficult to tell if, in the final analysis, the activist victory will win quality-of-life improvements as significant as origi-nally hoped.[51]

Bregar can also be interpreted to mean "work" in a positive sense, as when politicians or other public figures *bregan bien* [work well, or for the public good].[52] On the other hand, as Don Lirio, a founding member of CDAN, explained it to me on my first visit to the group, with reference to the failed oversight of the water treatment plant in Tipan, "*Esta no brega*" [this is not working]. *Bregar* is the expression of the burdens of the everyday. I once saw two men greet one another in the checkout line at the supermarket. As they clasped hands one asked "*¿Como estás?*" [How are you?] The other replied with a sigh, "*Aqui, en la brega.*" [Here, in the "brega"]. *Bregar* is going to work, coming home, cooking dinner. It is the chronicity of life. Some resi-dents, such as the members of CDAN, saw themselves as being "*en la lucha,*" combining an everyday concern about the environment with a more forceful willingness to protest, and a longer-term concern about the future of their families. The rest of Nocorá continued more decidedly in *la brega*, making their trade-offs, managing their worries, asking worried health questions of themselves, but not of the powers that be. In this sense, la brega represented the broader context of ambivalence that pervades Puerto Rican society. In cases like that of Nocorá as a whole, it describes the conflict inherent in con-fronting what experience labels as risk, but culture acts to smooth over.

In the following chapter I present a case study of the interplay between la lucha and la brega in Nocorá, in which the struggle of the grassroots group CDAN is contrasted with that of the regional NGO, GUIA. This comparison illustrates that, according to the narrative promoted by the pharmaceutical industry, the members of CDAN had, in a sense, forfeited their participation in the broader community because they had chosen to fight, while most Nocoreños were more ambivalent about the relationship between industrial pollution and quality of life. This ambivalence, strengthened by the belief that the pharmaceuticals are in some general sense trustworthy, worked to minimize direct opposition, and created a new and disturbing definition of community.

Figure 4.1. Parade for environmental awareness, April 2005. Photo by the author.

"Fresh Minds" on Parade

The day was notable for a few reasons, the most important of which (so I thought at the time) was that I met the head of EPA–Caribbean. It was a typically beautiful afternoon, and the many youth organizations were lining up around the block for the GUIA-sponsored parade. There were marching bands, boy scouts, and girls that looked like miniature beauty queens. I noticed that a number of school groups were with their teachers, and unlike many of the kids who just seemed happy to have a parade, the school groups carried posters and crafts representing particular environmental themes.

I approached one group with a poster of an animal that seemed out of place in the usual pantheon of protected creatures in Puerto Rico's natural habitat. The teacher and students were eager to explain their project—they had won for their grade, and that was how they got to participate. "We are learning about conservation," their teacher explained.

"What is your poster about?" I asked the girl in the lead who, on being questioned directly, suddenly seemed shy. I leaned closer for her answer.

"We have to protect the environment," she said, "because otherwise the animals will die."

"That's right," I replied. "How do you do that?"

"Well," said her nearest friend, wanting some of the spotlight, "we have to keep the beaches clean, not litter. That's really important."

"Right, right." I said. Looking closer at the poster, I found myself still confused about what animal was painted there. Did the endangered sea turtles we heard so much about have big teeth? No, that was a turtle next to it. "Is that a crocodile?" I asked.

"It's a caiman," the first girl replied, seemingly happy to tell me something I didn't know.

I stared at her and her classmates, so excited to feel they were making a difference, so excited to be in the parade. I didn't have the heart to tell them that far from needing their protection, caimans were a threat to virtually every other species in the waters of Puerto Rico, invaders that threaten biodiversity and are dangerous to people.

Don Gerald's voice sounded behind me and I turned to greet him. "Aren't the children wonderful?" he asked. I agreed that they were, and I decided in that moment that I was unwilling to debate the ecological value (or threat) represented by the caimans on their posters. But I found myself wondering, what does it mean to educate young people about conservation? Who is (or who should be) setting the information standard for what ecological priorities matter?

4

Environmental Justice Is Not Always Just

We are transforming through this evolution the role of public relations, but it's more than a question of resources; we have to be organized in order to see how we can be most effective with our donations. I believe that organizations need to assume some community
values, and that the organization needs to be [present] in the mission we wish to support.
　　　—Director of Corporate Social Responsibility, PharmaGigante

We in the bank are trying to start to change the mentality of philanthropy to a mentality of partnership, and our priority is to invest in
the non-profit organizations, in their development and infrastructure, by which they will be able to assume a responsibility that neither the government nor private industry can fulfill, and for which
the demand is extremely high.
　　　—Vice President of Community Reinvestment, BancoGrande

In late January 2005, I received a phone call: it was Don Reynaldo, a representative of the citizens group *Comité para Defender el Ambiente Nocoreño*
(CDAN), requesting that I attend a hearing in San Juan. The judge, he
informed me, was to hear arguments in a lawsuit that CDAN members
had filed against the locally operated multinational pharmaceutical companies and the Puerto Rico Aqueduct and Sewer Authority (PRASA).
Hopes were running high that the judge would finally declare the case a
class action, and that a settlement of some kind would be forthcoming. I
agreed to attend and to take notes for the committee, feeling that providing an accurate summary of the proceedings to this grassroots organization (GRO)[1] would help create a more equitable distribution of information
about the case, as many CDAN members had little experience in law and
other highly orchestrated forms of public debate and discourse. I also felt it
enhanced my opportunity as an ethnographer, as witnessing the proceedings would give me an opportunity to watch the lawyers for both sides
in action, and therefore get a better sense of how the pharmaceuticals in

particular framed their argument in the case. I was not disappointed with the perspective I gained that morning.

There were a significant number of Tipanecos in the courtroom (about 40 were able to make the hour-long trip to the capital). In spite of their presence, the lawyer for the other side did not hesitate to directly question their suffering, in effect putting CDAN itself on trial. Indicating the group directly with his hand, he went further, questioning whether the collected neighbors of Tipan could even be considered a "community." This move attempted to shed doubt not only on the seriousness of their shared health problems, but on any collective identity beyond a desire to wrest a financial gain from the defendants. Despite their lack of experience with legal proceedings, the group plainly felt that the lawyer was not only trying to dismiss their case, but to dismiss the legitimacy of their experience. In discussions with them afterward it was clear that, after many years of feeling ignored, they now felt as if they were being erased.

The irony of the defense's claim struck me as particularly disingenuous, though it was in line with the official public relations framework under which the companies operated. Like many other corporations operating in disparate global locations,[2] the pharmaceuticals have employed a variety of strategies to ingratiate themselves with local communities, even going so far at times as to claim community membership equal to (or more valuable than) that of residents. Weaving together public relations messages like "Disease is our enemy. Working to save lives is our job,"[3] with targeted philanthropy to health and educational causes, drug companies have been successful in reducing criticism of their production by-products. This has been no small task in Nocorá, and their efforts have clearly been enhanced by their ritualized associations with people in powerful places, such as the alcalde. This chapter explores in greater depth some of the unexpected dynamics that existed *between* non-profit groups that are supposedly working toward the same goal (in this case environmental protection). These interactions further illustrate the cultural and political influence of the pharmaceutical companies in and around Nocorá, showing how successful they have been in creating an environmental focus that serves their own interests in civil society, as well as in government and the marketplace.

Harmonizing Environmental Injustice

In the context of profound concerns over environmental health, who speaks for the community? As industrialization has placed residential communities in increasingly close proximity to potential sources of contamination, social relationships between those residents and their corporate neighbors have grown more complex.[4] The emergence of CSR[5] has further confused the issue, creating a language through which corporations are not only able, but encouraged, to identify with local residents as potentially equal "stakeholders." As we have seen, the alcalde, as elected executive of Nocorá, was often presumed by corporate managers to be the best representative of all of Nocorá's interests, and other locally elected officials seldom if ever exercised what autonomy they had in putting a check on his actions. Indeed, the local legislative representative for Tipan told me:

> The reality is, in terms of daily necessities we're doing well. We're not lacking investment by the government. This is one reason why concerns about the environment come forward, because with the necessities taken care of, the way society is now, we can worry about the environment. In fact, one thing people have worried about is that with the question of the [wastewater treatment] plant, the bad odors, property values have gone down, and people don't like that. . . . In terms of development, we have sewers, we have telephones, cable, we have parks, ballcourts, community centers. In terms of development we're in good shape. I mean, we're looking ahead, we want to keep moving forward. . . . I'd say more or less we have 80–85% of the kinds of resources we might want as a community.

His comments underscored the notion that not only are people's lives generally good, but that the underlying reason for complaint is not driven by health concerns, but by fear of diminishing economic value.

Through this framework it has become more difficult for local residents to protest chronic contamination, as they are frequently accused of attacking their high-status "neighbors," the pharmaceutical companies. "Dispute resolution ideologies have long been used for the transmission of hegemonic ideas,"[6] certainly the case when individuals and GROs are encouraged (and arguably coerced) into resolving their complaints through the process known as "stakeholder dialogues." The naturalized value given to the companies and their allies also helps explain how the larger regional NGO (GUIA) has come to dominate the environmental justice scene in northern Puerto Rico.[7] By taking up the limited space available for environmental groups in the Nocorá region, GUIA provides a disruptive counterpoint to the efforts of smaller groups such as CDAN.

The role of "harmony ideology" is particularly important in "limiting the playing field to a recurrent dialectic between legality and its alternatives."[8] In this context, recourse to court-based dispute resolution may be successfully framed as inauthentic, excessively antagonistic, or simply unacceptable within current cultural norms. The questioning of CDAN as representative of a community of Nocoreños by the pharmaceutical lawyer, and the implication that they were driven by greed for economic gain, was just such an attempt to question their legitimacy within ideas being positioned as local values. Likewise, key decisions in the case turned on the competing testimony of each side's expert witnesses, environmental engineers called to evaluate not so much the damage itself, but whether or not the damage was caused by negligence. While some scholars have observed that in many cases people "have learned to mistrust expert knowledge,"[9] here it is not the knowledge of experts that is in question. If anything, members of CDAN were very likely to show respect for high levels of education and experience in their opponents, especially if those opponents had shown them courtesy. The larger problem was that CDAN had difficulty keeping an expert witness committed to their case. The pharmaceutical companies and the water company, who shared responsibility for the management and maintenance of the treatment plant, have long supplied the majority of jobs to environmental engineers in Puerto Rico.[10] Even engineers working within the university system had become reluctant to alienate these industries. The result is the "suppression of dissent in science,"[11] and therefore in the deployment of scientific expertise in support of communities of suffering.

Research that critically analyzes the hegemonic role of corporations reveals the extent of negligence on the part of corporations with regard to public safety. With regard to the hidden harm of commonly purchased commercial products, consumers can be considered to be, to an extent, complicit in their consumption of such products by not demanding better protections. This analysis raises the crucial question, however, as to what degree this complicity can be overcome when those designated to monitor risk are "all members of the same social class with similar values and commitments."[12] Here I wish to explore the dynamics of risk negotiation between the pharmaceutical companies and local Puerto Rican actors, as well as the broader context in which those dynamics take place. I suggest that some of these relationships are more thoroughly understood through the process of "capture," rather than solely through class status or membership.

Understanding Regulatory Capture

Throughout this research project I struggled to find a language with which I could articulate the concerns of anthropology (such as community and culture) in a manner that would be relevant for other disciplines concerned with pollution regulation and control (in this case business and law). When working (and at times identifying politically) with "the people," it can become easy for government and corporate representatives to dismiss the concerns of anthropological research as naïve, much as they dismiss the concerns expressed by the communities themselves. It also became important to think critically about the vocabulary used by proponents of CSR, as companies have rapidly embraced terms such as "stakeholders" in order to broadcast their interest in what others might call "the community." The difference between the sentiments of words like "stakeholder" and "community," however, was palpable even among those who thought the pharmaceuticals held the key to the island's future. As one local health worker stated, "There must be a way to maintain the pharmaceuticals in our territory, employing Puerto Ricans and creating a sense of belonging." In CSR terms she was blending the goals of a stakeholder with the desires typically voiced by a member of a community in need.

Ironically, even when they showed an interest in the ideas of culture and community, it was often difficult to discuss the application of these concepts with corporate managers or government agents. The operational definitions they used for these concepts tended to be too narrow and excessively functional, terms designed to be used in quickly deployed public relations programs, not nuanced academic analyses. In light of these challenges, I found the notion of "deep capture"[13] to be the most useful way of understanding not only the broader politics of pollution and protest in Nocorá, but the micropolitics as well. It is a particularly useful concept for unraveling the complex dynamics through which people and organizations can otherwise be simplistically labeled "sellouts," "troublemakers," "traitors," or ignored altogether.

The notion of regulatory capture is not new, described most succinctly in the 1960s and '70s by the economist George Stigler.[14] A free-market economist, Stigler demonstrated through numerous examples the problematic relationship between regulatory agencies and the industries they purport to regulate. Given the powerful incentives and capacity that corporations have to influence their regulators, it is not surprising that they often succeed. In the words of an article from the politically conservative *Wall Street Journal*, "[t]he people who filled regulatory jobs in past administrations were asleep at the switch because they were supposed to be."[15] In Stigler's analysis, regulators do not exist to fulfill some kind of idealized public good, but to serve themselves and their affiliated industries. Ultimately, Stigler asserts that the market will succeed where politics fails; that consumers voting with their wallets will have greater control for the public good, than will power-hungry, or power-enmeshed political actors.[16] Stigler's concluding emphasis on rational individual actors does not place enough weight on the collective momentum of human behavior, and the influence of ideologies. But his critique of the social nature of regulatory relationships helps to shed light on the long-term failure of Puerto Rico to protect its fragile environment.

Thinking Culture with "Deep" Capture

The process of "deep" capture[17] goes beyond the bounded realm of regulatory agencies and similar institutions. It describes the degree to which pro-industry (and pro-corporate) ways of thinking are so pervasive in seemingly neutral contexts, such as academia, that they are essentially invisible. They have become part of culture. And a variety of data suggest that corporations actively pursue this endpoint: "the corporation's most effective techniques of influence may have been provided not by overt pressure, but by encouraging scientists to continue thinking of themselves as independent and impartial."[18] Even research by scientists as eminent as epidemiologist Sir Richard Doll[19] may have at times been influenced, falsely exonerating chemical companies from harm their products caused.[20] In anthropological terms we might say that "seeing like a corporation," to paraphrase James Scott,[21] has become the naturalized perspective, even among those that favor environmental sustainability or protection. Through the perspective of deep capture we can see how these apparently contradictory positions are effectively harmonized, as corporations are viewed simultaneously as people with rights and needs, and yet in some cases so powerful as to be even omnipotent. It has been argued that the legal personhood of corporations is necessary in order for them to have standing in the courts and to create enforceable contracts.[22] And although there have always been limits on this brand of personhood,[23] in the case of Nocorá the connections between corporations and the government have a long cultural history. As early as the 1940s they were already nearly indistinguishable for most local residents.

When questioned directly about the problem of pollution, government actors, from the alcalde of Nocorá to the head of EPA–Caribbean, were fond of explaining that while pollution was a concern, *"hay que armonizar"* (it is necessary to harmonize) the demands of the economy (in this case the pharmaceuticals) with that of the environment. The compromising requirement of harmony,[24] regardless of who espouses it, is coercive to those "stakeholders" with less power. Even activist residents, such as Don Teodoro of the Centro Cultural, used the language of harmony to describe their understanding of economic realities and the local role of industry. Thus, they demonstrated that in spite of claims by the companies that protesters desired to cause trouble, the most powerful desire most of my informants expressed was to have sociopolitical as well as environmental peace restored to their daily lives.

In the Puerto Rican context, the will to harmony is not so much an appeal to religion or tradition (as is the case for many of the examples given by Nader), but rather it is grounded in the economic and development ideologies of the island.[25] As described in chapter 2, these ideologies are intimately intertwined with beliefs about material benefits, notably health as well as economic. The notion of harmonizing damage to the environment with economic "progress" is particularly powerful among those Puerto Ricans who believe that they literally owe their lives to the economic and public health initiatives, if not the political dominance, of the United States and Operation Bootstrap. The social body as a whole was arguably healthier in the earlier industrial era, and more recent evidence to the contrary cannot withstand the comparison to, as Don Felipe recalled, "hospitals full of sick people."

The pharmaceuticals entered the Puerto Rican economy as part of a development strategy that could, in theory, provide higher-wage jobs to local workers. But, in practice, the capital-intensive nature of chemical production has contributed substantially to the creation of what has been called a "post-work" society.[26] Through federal transfer payments[27] and other forms of economic support from the United States, the standard of living has risen sharply. Still, while unemployment on the island remained high, the pharmaceutical/biotechnology sector continued to be promoted by the Commonwealth government and industry interest groups "as a key development area . . . offer[ing] important incentives and support."[28] In a political environment in which cynicism dominates the public discourse, there is a strong tendency for people to feel disempowered in the face of corporations. Peter Benson and Stuart Kirsch[29] have suggested that corporations are allowed to produce significant levels of harm due to the resulting "politics of resignation." The regulatory capture concept elucidates the underlying mechanism through which those institutions charged with oversight become worthy of public skepticism. Deep capture broadens the scope of shared sentiment through which even those who are not outwardly cynical nevertheless participate in creating the sense of inevitability that so benefits the corporate mission.

A Tale of Two Environmental Groups

Like many environmental GROs, the *Comité para Defender el Ambiente Nocoreño* (CDAN) has one primary agenda, and they resist being drawn into any others. After 20 years of protest and patient "stakeholder dialogue," the group's members reached their limit and sued the Puerto Rico Aqueduct and

Sewer Authority (PRASA) and the pharmaceutical companies who had built the local wastewater treatment plant. In 2008, after years of legal maneuvering, hearings, and expert testimony, the class action lawsuit was finally settled. In all that time CDAN maintained their stance that their only desire was for the plant to operate without polluting the air and water of Tipan, regardless of whether that pollution was consistent with technical legal compliance or not. Founded with the explicit prohibition on any discussion of religion or politics, CDAN members for the most part studiously avoided reaching beyond the boundaries of their known problem. Some members were outright suspicious of too much involvement in other activities, even when linked to the environment.

In contrast, *Grupo Uniendo Iniciativa Ambiental* (GUIA) claimed to represent the whole northern region, describing itself as a steering committee with a broad base of membership. In practice, much of the day-to-day functioning, as well as the setting of the agenda, was carried out by an elderly gentleman named Gerald Velázquez. A former Commonwealth party (PPD) legislator, Velázquez demonstrated a strong penchant for what has arguably been the trademark practice of his lifelong political identity: compromise.

GUIA's claim to status and singularity among environmental organizations stemmed from the fact that it counted representatives of industry, government, and community groups as *members*. These representatives sat as "volunteers" on the steering committee. GUIA also acted as an umbrella for smaller local community groups, through which they could communicate their concerns to a wider and more powerful audience. For example, GUIA claimed the head of the U.S. EPA–Caribbean region as a member, and could therefore improve the visibility of smaller group problems through a fiction of equal "membership." There were undoubtedly benefits to this in fact hierarchical structure, once they had become formal members. However, the spokesman of GUIA always presumed to speak for these lower status community members. In the words of Velázquez himself,

> Many people don't have the knowledge in technical areas. . . . They are working many years in the fields, in agriculture, they don't have the education. We provide the knowledge, the experience. But you always have to invite the government, industry, those with economic influence. . . . The community doesn't have the power to convoke these influential people— but if they are invited by someone who has their respect, they will come listen. The community has to integrate. They don't have the knowledge, and they don't understand that they can be part of the process, part of the creation of policies, but they have to integrate.

The language of integration implies that community residents were de facto outsiders compared to industry and regulatory agencies.

The very structure of groups such as GUIA means that they "have complex political, religious, social and environmental agendas and ideologies, which are often intertwined in an undifferentiated manner."[30] The result is twofold: (1) the structure gave Velazquez legitimacy as a representative of a supposedly unified "community," and (2) important regulatory players were shielded from direct confrontation over actual complaints, even as they benefited from the illusion of "membership."

In many ways Velázquez, and thus GUIA, was a study in apparent contradictions. He articulated a number of trenchant critiques of the state of the environment, government, and industry in Puerto Rico. He was not especially an apologist for wrongs perpetrated by the industry, though he was painted that way by his detractors. He maintained a defiantly independent stance in his discourse with individuals (like me), and even in regular public meetings. However, in his most publicized speeches, such as those that received more extensive media coverage, he tended to speak very graciously about the pharmaceuticals as partners in his endeavors. And no wonder—as he acknowledged (at times), various 990 tax forms showed, and his critics trumpeted, he received a good portion of his operating budget from the industry's donations.[31]

It was precisely because GUIA was perceived as working harmoniously with industry groups and government agents that when they called attention to a problem, it was considered newsworthy. This stood in contrast to habitual complainers like CDAN, who have the same issue for far too many news cycles. By the time I was living in Nocorá, as mentioned before, even a canal running through a Tipan backyard that turned the color of antifreeze was not considered as newsworthy. However, a regularly scheduled GUIA meeting, to plan their annual scholastic environmental fair and parade, was attended by a local reporter.

A Long Line of Pro-Industry Government Actors

Although the pro-statehood PNP is most closely aligned with the Republican Party in the United States, and sometimes believed to be more pro-business, at the local level in Nocorá it is the PPD that has consistently been the ally of the pharmaceuticals. The sole PNP alcalde, elected in 1976, was the only government official who outwardly campaigned against the levels of pollution created by the pharmaceutical factories, even joining in resident protests outside the factory gates. When discussing corporate-community relationships, one corporate manager I interviewed referred to this instance of difficulty by emphasizing the ignorance of the antagonist, and the relative brevity of his influence: "He just didn't understand. . . . But now we've got someone we can work with again."

As noted earlier, the present alcalde, Estrello Martínez, came to power in 1986, and was re-elected until 2012 by substantial majorities. Martínez had always been a strong advocate for a "modernizing" (i.e., industrial) development strategy. In addition to forming close alliances with the pharmaceuticals, he aggressively renovated the *casco urbano* (urban center) of Nocorá, taking on the management of public housing projects, expropriating and tearing down decrepit free-standing housing stock, and planning modern apartments and public park areas. Though his constituency was tiny, Martínez's alcaldía boasted a standing relationship with Washington lobbyists. They successfully secured funds for these major projects, as well as commitments from the Army Corps of Engineers to build a dam around the urban center, preventing a chronic and severe flooding problem.

Functioning as a cacique, Martínez had become particularly adept at creating an illusion of being irreplaceable to Nocoreños—at the time of this writing he was the longest-serving alcalde on the island. He was able to achieve this because the municipal budget of Nocorá had been proportionally one of the largest on the island, due to the *patentes* paid by the resident industries. This budget allowed Martínez a great deal of flexibility, not only to create Nocorá in the image he desired, but to sit down at the negotiation tables with multinational companies as a comparative equal. It is very instructive to hear Martínez's own perspective on the importance of municipal autonomy, and to note the connection he made between that political status and the status of Puerto Rico in relation to the United States:

> We're still not satisfied, the municipios, with the Law of Autonomous Municipalities, it was a first step . . . but it needs to move ahead in a continuous process of development. In other words, we need something like [the status of] the Free Associated State, the law of Free Association, accepted by the United States and Puerto Rico. Free Association wasn't meant to be a permanent status, it was meant to evolve with the needs and particularities, with the mentality of the Puerto Rican—in collaboration, and with the government of the United States.

Recalling the potential for compromising the environment that has been abused in the course of pursuing economic development, it is not difficult to perceive Martínez's vision for how he wanted to manage the government of Nocorá. And while the development projects pursued by Martínez had benefits to the municipality overall, in pursuing them the alcalde demonstrated time and again his disinterest in (and at times contempt toward) the opposing wishes, and even the rights, of individual constituents. In acting as the representative of the neighborhood Tipan with regard to the treatment plant, he convened meetings and assigned various municipal functionaries to the problem, resulting in a great deal of talk and very little action or improvement. This willingness to engage as intermediary between CDAN and the pharmaceuticals ended abruptly when the Tipaneco neighbors sued the companies for their responsibility in the ongoing pollution. His office routinely ignored any petition or communication from known CDAN members, whether related to the environment, transportation, or any other issue that should fall into his purview. As the case was drawing to a close, he made arrangements to knock down the group's headquarters, in order to build a pumping station for PRASA on that site. While presumably a mechanical necessity for the system, residents considered the move to be in classic Martínez style, using a needed infrastructural improvement as a bulletproof excuse to pay back the group that had caused him so much irritation.

The Corporate Citizens

In her study of a French community located near a nuclear facility, Francoise Zonabend observed that people "draw on what, if you like, their society has *always known*, on the enduring facts and cultural messages buried in the social practices that get handed down from generation to generation."[32] In Nocorá the pharmaceutical companies, while relatively recent arrivals, fit so well into the familiar political and social structure that it is perhaps more surprising that they found any resistance at all, than that there was so little.

For several reasons I do not call the companies in question by their actual names, the most important of which is that in many ways relevant to the residents of Tipan and Nocorá, the pharmaceuticals work in concert with one another. Scholars of industrial ecology have argued that while their level of intra-company cooperation has not always been consistent, it has been significant, especially with regard to the operation of the wastewater treatment plant.[33] Furthermore, to name them as individuals would play into their competition for public trust and favor. Given that drug producers must be seen as trustworthy to successfully market many of their products,[34] this competition is fierce. As previously noted, Nocorá at the time of my study (2004–2005) boasted the world's highest factory per-capita concentration in the world, serving as the production site for a number of blockbuster drugs, including those used to treat high cholesterol and erectile dysfunction. And unlike other industries known for high levels of environmental contamination, such as oil and mining,[35] the public perception of the pharmaceuticals was strongly influenced by the fact that they were said to, in a sense, *produce* health.

The Harmony of Deep Capture

An analysis of deep capture[36] offers a powerful critique of the overuse of "rational actor" frameworks in both economics and legal theory. In practical terms, corporations use media and other discursive avenues to promote the idea of the rational actor, while simultaneously exploiting the reality of decision-making as being grounded in shifting and complex situations. Anthropologists working with grassroots environmental groups have increasingly noted the situated nature not only of the ecological commitments of residents and advocates,[37] but even of the environment itself.[38] Tsing, Brosius, and Zerner further note the "critical need to form new languages of advocacy and for discussion between advocates, donors, and scholars, based on real histories" of situated environmental conflicts.[39] In the context of Nocorá, the situation was significantly informed by the competing narratives of what pollution meant, who was an expert, and especially whose membership and participation in the "community" was deemed to be the most valuable.

Needless to say, in a context in which the pharmaceutical industry had been cast as the key to the island's modernizing economy, enforcement of existing regulations has been lax, and outspoken criticism of the industry discouraged by local governments and agencies. I quickly lost track of the number of conversations in which people from all walks of life would shrug and say that in spite of the pollution (which no one denied), they were better off than they had been before the industry arrived. As one university student who had several family members employed with the drug makers put it,

> We need to try to make a balance and harmony where the pharmaceuticals continue to support opportunities for employment and quality of life [while] trying not to do damage to the environment.

CDAN members, though some have worked in the drug industry, or have otherwise benefited economically from it, are a qualified exception—they acknowledged the trade-offs, but on balance do not feel it has been worth it.

Fighting to Be Heard

In spite of their criticisms, CDAN's approach to activism had not been characterized by aggressive or confrontational tactics. In fact, until 2000 the group emphasized letter writing, phone calls, arranged meetings with local politicians and corporate managers, and of course, attendance at public hearings in an attempt to get their complaints heard. Far from simply stating their concerns and grievances, CDAN had painstakingly documented (to the degree possible) their environmental harm, hoping that "evidence" would speak for itself. However, after being told for nearly 20 years that the problem was "being worked on," the members of the group felt they had no choice but to sue the pharmaceutical companies.

CDAN was once associated with GUIA as one of their satellite community groups, but the relationship quickly became strained. Though the precise timeline is unclear, reasons given for the breakup were agreed upon by group members: discussing the viability of new tactics after years of inaction and suffering, Velázquez lectured Don Reynaldo, then CDAN president, that suing the pharmaceutical industry for monetary damages presented a "conflict of interest." Velázquez himself often claimed loudly that he "would sue!" if he did not get results by his usual methods, by which he meant he was willing to use a lawsuit to force changes in behavior or pay for cleanup. But for a small, resident-based group like CDAN, whose experience amounted to a string of broken regulatory and maintenance promises, it made sense to try to make a lawsuit as costly as possible. As Don Cesar put it, "money is the language they understand."

This disagreement capped a growing dissatisfaction with the ways in which Velázquez represented the residents' problems with the treatment plant. In public hearings and similar forums participation is often limited, as time may only be allotted to one person to "represent the community." On more than one occasion other environmentally concerned residents found that the GUIA spokesman, already a familiar face to local authorities, was always presumed to be that representative, even if he knew little or nothing about their specific issues. Given his standing among governmental and other elites, Velázquez tended to assume likewise that he was the best and most knowledgeable spokesman for all. Furthermore, he was reluctant to cede the floor to someone who might pull the meeting off his message, or distract from his group's current priorities.

It is important to consider GUIA's major accomplishments in order to understand its broader role in the environmental scene. Many of the achievements in favor of communities fell under the broad category of consciousness- or awareness-raising about a serious environmental problem that ultimately had tangible results. An example of this would be when, in 2005, GUIA successfully lobbied the Bajas municipal government to allocate $700,000 to connect one of its outlying neighborhoods to the sanitary sewer system.[40] Other examples followed a similar trajectory: Neighbors complained about dumping in local sinkholes or waterways, and GUIA succeeded in bringing local media attention and encouraging the municipal government to take action. Velázquez, on behalf of GUIA, has been named an "Environmental Champion" by the EPA multiple times, recognizing his efforts. From EPA's standpoint, the work done by environmental activists in Puerto Rico is generally considered to be environmental justice work because Puerto Ricans as a whole are considered to be minorities, regardless of socioeconomic class. This fact complicates the legal and social status of socially marginal groups like the Tipanecos, and makes direct comparisons between Puerto Rican activists and other environmental justice groups[41] likewise more complicated to evaluate.

What sets these events apart from the struggles of CDAN and the wastewater treatment plant is twofold: (1) GUIA's signature successes often came when the source of a negative environmental circumstance was either easily identified (e.g., a local builder whose actions cause flooding), or impossible to identify (e.g., waste dumped in a sinkhole). Easily identified sources were more easily held accountable, especially by an organization with powerful friends. Unknowable sources created a circumstance in which local authorities needed to, of necessity, step forward to initiate cleanup, or place the problem on a priority list for future allocation of funds; (2) The identifiable sources of pollution tended not to be as powerful players as the pharmaceuticals, nor did they hold as ambivalent a place in the imagination of the people.[42] Although the drug industry had long been cause for environmental concern on the part of nearby residents, this concern was nearly always tempered with the fear that too much complaining would cause the industry to leave the island. In the case of the treatment plant, the power inherent in the local pharmaceutical dynamic was further complicated by the obfuscation of the point source by means of the combined effluent stream. From this perspective it becomes obvious that CDAN was never a good candidate to be one of GUIA's satellite groups, nor would their struggle be an appropriately bounded opportunity to showcase the legitimate public goods offered by GUIA.

GUIA claimed to represent the community-based environmental interests of the whole northern region. While many activists working in the grassroots saw GUIA (specifically Velázquez) as a tool of the industries, my ethnographic experience suggests the situation was more complex than a simple dichotomy between "activist" and "sellout" can illustrate. GUIA had an unquestionably positive impact in that it was working to create a broad environmental consciousness, particularly through activities with school age children. This is an area where GUIA could work directly with the pharmaceuticals who also liked to emphasize, as one manager put it, "fresh minds," looking to the future of a cleaner environment. The corporations could appear to be ahead of the curve, promoting projects that simultaneously drew attention away from the factories by emphasizing individual responsibility, such as for recycling. In describing these programs to me, the manager continued, "We emphasize the protection of the environment through education."

In light of its collaboration with the industry, several local activists I worked with considered GUIA to be what has been termed an "Astroturf" or fake grassroots group, driven exclusively by corporate interests.[43] However, "Deep capture makes clear that people's intentions and beliefs may have little to do with their behavior and that, insofar as they do, those intentions and beliefs are part of what interests compete to capture."[44] Velázquez and his organization have championed legitimate environmental causes. But even with good intentions toward the environment, a group such as GUIA could do great damage to a more localized environmental cause. A struggling community such as Nocorá could gain theoretical access to the negotiating tables with regulatory agencies and corporations through affiliation with GUIA, as long as they accepted the structural or social limits placed on expression of their problems. Equally troubling, cooperation with a group like GUIA, winner of EPA awards for environmental justice, lent legitimacy to industry, while making groups like CDAN look simply like rabble rousers unwilling to "unite" with a legitimated champion of the environment. Finally, in a context in which more formally organized groups controlled the public discourse about the environment, it became easy to label grassroots activists as ignorant, or, at a minimum, under-informed.[45]

For many grassroots leaders, activism is not a profession, but one aspect of a multifaceted daily life. CDAN's Don Reynaldo struggled against exclusion from the discourses of the more powerful, and particularly fought to gain both the attention and respect that his suffering and that of his neighbors deserved. As former president and spokesperson for the group, he had years of experience trying to obtain a great deal of complex information from government and corporate entities, and to disseminate that information among local residents. Likewise, he worked tirelessly to collect and make comprehensive the experiences of his neighbors, and to communicate those experiences to those institutions. Those members of CDAN who had assumed leadership roles at various times in their 20-year history expressed frustration with a consistent restraint on their access to a public forum, even within a structure designed for residents to express themselves.

Prior to the initiation of the lawsuit there had been what could be called, in CSR terms, a "joint stakeholder" committee "about the odors" emanating from the treatment plant (*Comité de Olores*). The name itself worked to minimize the health and environmental effects of the pollution from the treatment plant, and the meetings served primarily as an outlet for CDAN's complaints. It was also a showcase for the alcaldía and the industries to explain all the complex and costly actions they were supposedly taking to fix the problem. This committee's activities were further hampered when the role of Tipan's local legislator was taken by a man who was an employee of one of the pharmaceuticals, and coincidentally worked on Sundays, the day CDAN had long established as their regular meeting day. His distance from the concerns of CDAN was manifest in his assertion, stated earlier, that the community's needs were well met.

CDAN members also described many instances of being actively silenced in supposedly public meetings: Don Reynaldo in particular expressed not only frustration, but a sense of offended propriety, at being told abruptly to "sit down and be quiet" by the alcalde himself. And while CDAN first brought to my attention the poor efforts made to advertise public hearings on building projects or other potential environmental issues, I was to learn that all of these tactics, which marginalize similar grassroots groups, were endemic.

"Citizen participation in the local planning process is the biggest problem we have," a local university professor and environmental activist told me. To illustrate her point she described one of many public hearings, for which people had to call in sick to their jobs in order to attend because the meeting was held during business hours. Observers in support of the project identified a number of the attendees, reported them to their workplaces, and they subsequently lost their jobs for their truancy. Public hearings were required to be advertised, but the requirement was very broad, saying only that the municipality should employ "those means of information [media] that they consider adequate." Such advertisements were easily missed by locals who might not take a certain paper, or if the advertisement was buried. Unfortunately, as noted in the previous chapter, the performance of participation is usually sufficient to comply with the law, and is also helpful in convincing those who attend such meetings that they at least have a voice. As Lynn Morgan noted in her study of community participatory health care in Costa Rica,[46] participation was not so much a gauge of democracy, but rather a symbol to be manipulated.

Ironically, it was Don Reynaldo who, having only a third grade education, was the most successful spokesman for the movement over time. This was due mainly to persistence, and an impressive dedication to studying the available information, supported by the conviction that his cause was just. But self-education does not alter the claim by officials that "these people simply do not understand," implying that the science of pollution and its regulation is technically beyond the reach of the average person's understanding. For example, when discussing neighborhood complaints about bad-smelling emissions, one manager told me, "They don't realize that just because something smells bad, doesn't mean it's toxic." Velázquez strongly echoed the sentiment that groups of residents with environmental problems do not typically have sufficient knowledge to advocate effectively for their own causes. In fact, what is often being smelled is hydrogen sulfide, which is in fact toxic, though in technical terms it is unlikely to be present in concentrations high enough to merit legal action. Nevertheless, the smell of this chemical is extremely strong even in low concentrations, and even low-level exposures can result in symptoms[47] characteristic of those consistently reported by Tipanecos.

What the manager meant was that no one had consistently proven *legal noncompliance*, and that their critics were making a big deal out of something that is merely considered legally to be a "nuisance"—in other words the definition of "toxic" from the corporate perspective was strictly legal, not clinical. Velázquez may have been correct, that under certain circumstances these groups could only gain a voice through their affiliation with GUIA. But the example of CDAN illustrates the powerful manner in which his perspective at the same time reinforced his own deeply captured status.

In fact, education and professional experience were no guarantee of respect or attention in the corporate-community interaction. Ricardo Solano, a chemist and founding member of CDAN, found that his expertise gained him standing among his neighbors as someone who could help them understand the causes and consequence of the pollution. However, his social standing as a resident allowed him to be labeled as a troublemaker by company managers and local cooperating politicians, and he was lumped in with the so-called ignorant. By the time of my fieldwork, Don Ricardo had become a much less active member of the group, in part because of his frustration at having his own professional, as well as personal, experience effectively erased.

These examples illustrate how "expertise" is a complicated social status, with many shifting, flexible variables. In this context, "expert" was as much an ascribed status as an achieved one. Association with the socially or politically "correct" group (in this case, non-agitators) conferred the status of "one who understands," by implication understanding not only of the social and economic importance of the pharmaceutical factories, but of the technically benign quality of their various emissions. Activism is frequently *about* communication[48] and therefore about the work of creating the world through performative acts.[49] In this sense, Velázquez can be seen as having fought to maintain control of the terrain of expertise on behalf of those he represents—however, his gains generally came at the expense of CDAN, not regulators or industry.

In fact it can be argued that GUIA's approach was an example of how "harmony [. . .] models are also used as an attempt by those colonized to regain sovereignty,"[50] melding with the broader harmony strategy used to balance environmental damage with industrialization in the name of development. The uniqueness of Puerto Rico within the dominion of the United States (as a tropical island, and therefore a unique ecosystem, as well as a unique cultural and economic history) has long been leveraged by the Commonwealth government to subvert federal environmental regulations.[51] Ironically, this resistance to regulate on the part of the Puerto Rican government played directly into the desires of the multinationals to minimize the financial costs of waste management. These strategies could ultimately be considered a failing, short-term "war of position,"[52] in which the environment (and those who live in it) was harmed, and economic gains were at best unsustainable, and at worst, illusory.

Is This the Economic Protection Agency?

In an interview in 2005, I questioned the head of U.S. EPA–Caribbean about the balancing act required by Puerto Rico's industrial development model. He adamantly maintained that pollution and the environment could only be considered within that context. Acknowledging that the island existed in an overall state of unsustainability, he was quick to remind me that in comparison to other industries, the pharmaceuticals had a positive history of technical and legal compliance with both federal and local pollution laws. He emphasized that their strategy was to anticipate changes in the law and to become compliant by given deadlines, skirting the fact that they used every means at their disposal to prevent laws that harm their profit margins from being enacted.[53] Additionally, he took pains to explain to me the success of the pharmaceuticals' participation in public-private partnerships bringing potable water to communities not connected to PRASA's system, and the companies' willingness to provide technical support for such good works. Drawing attention to their beneficence toward non-PRASA water systems, this regulator-in-chief promoted the discursive shell game in which the listener is encouraged to disregard the damage done by the drug companies to PRASA's own system in Nocorá. At the conclusion of our interview, as I walked toward the exit, he called after me. "Thank you for working with Gerald Velázquez," he said. "His work with GUIA is very important."

Returning to the courtroom, it is also important to note the reticence of the judge to sanction PRASA, as a government agency with strong ties to industry, in two specific instances. First, in an example not unusual for the water company, the judge raised the point that there was an outstanding fine related to the case that had not been paid. The lawyer for PRASA, who was young, and appeared flustered, attempted to convince the judge that he was working to convince the agency to pay the fine, and in so doing to secure her good will. She agreed to allow them 15 additional days to pay, *after* which time they would begin to pay interest.

More significantly, CDAN's lawyer expressed concern that in spite of a lengthy discovery process, and the obligation of PRASA to deliver such documents, an important Environmental Impact Statement had never been sent, and her office had obtained it incidentally.[54] In response, PRASA's lawyer, again looking flustered, responded that he was new to the case and did not know much about the issue. The judge replied that each side must then request whatever documents they required in writing, and that five months hence would be the final deadline for all documentation to be submitted to the court to decide whether or not to declare a class action. The judge then stated for the record that both the lawyers for the pharmaceuticals and PRASA were employing tactics to postpone the decision to declare the suit a class action (a decision that would certainly place a greater burden on the defendants). In practice she gave them little incentive to alter their strategy.

Analyzing time itself is crucial to understanding the lived experience of contamination, because in a context of "toxic uncertainty," time moves differently for different actors.[55] Most significantly, time can seem to stand still for people who are waiting for answers to their questions about why they are sick, whether they can move to a new home, or, as in the case of Tipan, whether the corporate entity responsible for their suffering will make any restitution for the harm caused. However, corporate time is not the same as mortal time, in part because corporate time is counted in financial terms.[56] For polluted communities engaged in a court case where the opposition has seemingly endless resources, time can, as the expression goes, draw out like a blade. And while it seems obvious that the side with the most resources can pay their attorneys longer, the more fundamental reason that time matters in these cases is because the corporate litigants are, for all intents and purposes, immortal. They have all the time in the world because they will outlive all the flesh and blood persons involved in the case.[57]

Corporate influence is becoming increasingly pervasive in global society. Looking at culture through the lens of deep capture shows the degree to which, particularly in U.S. society, actors in every arena have begun to see like a corporation.[58] In Puerto Rico, a possession of the United States, the example of deep capture is not simply an outgrowth of an increasingly capitalistic society, fed by advertising and consumption. The development process itself, with its historic emphasis on the 936 companies, and its more recent mutation into a biotechnology research and development corridor, has created cultural pressure to view the pharmaceuticals themselves as a necessary and integral component of everyday life. It has been argued that in order for large bureaucratic institutions to function, they need to quantify, and effectively smooth over, the individual characteristics of citizens and localities.[59] State processes like Environmental Assessment accomplish this "smoothing" through statistical methods that can obscure negative local environmental and health impacts of development projects. Likewise, social and cultural processes support a discourse of local-level control that nevertheless augments the social status, political power, and economic success of large-scale corporate institutions. The conversion of this status into both social and political capital has allowed them to effectively dominate many of the institutions of civil society dedicated to the environment and other areas of concern to community health.

For anthropological researchers encountering conflict over health and the environment, it can be tempting to act as translators or messengers for grassroots groups with pollution problems. We may be thrust into that role while in the field, as we try to help less enfranchised activists get their message to regulatory agencies, the media, or to NGOs whose mission it is to help resolve these problems.[60] However, the premise of these harmonizing negotiations themselves is so often skewed in favor of governments, corporations, and even powerful NGOs, that it may be more significant to expose and critique the frequently false premise that "stakeholder dialogue" is a negotiation between relative equals. Collecting and compiling these examples, through which a narrow pro-industry perspective is created and supported, is an important contribution to counter the extent to which our cultural perspective is captured by corporate interests.

In describing the cultural context of Nocorá, the theme of Corporate Social Responsibility (CSR) has already been raised at several points, in conjunction with particular examples (such as employee volunteerism and environmental compliance). The following chapter takes up again the question of "stakeholders" and social responsibility from a different angle, bringing into consideration the role of the CSR itself as a social movement, and of those who seek to promote it.

Figure 5.1. Earth Day "symbolic planting," sponsored by one of the local factories. Local schoolchildren and neighbors from Barrio La Planchita pose with shovels and plants on the site of a planned garden installation in the shape of the recycling logo. Photo by the author.

Good Neighbors (A Conversation)

The night was unusually cool and Julia and I were outside while Félix and a friend watched the Cotto boxing match on Pay-Per-View. She was catching me up on the latest drama with the couple across the street and on her further plans for decorating for Christmas. She paused to take a drag on her cigarette and then looked at me with a hesitant smile. "I hope if you write these things in your book you'll change all the names."

I laughed, knowing my research didn't generally include the kind of neighborhood gossip that anthropologists might call "open secrets" about people's personal lives. "Don't worry, I'll change all the names," I told her. "Besides, I'm not really writing about this kind of stuff. . . ." I paused. "Now some of your work gossip, I might want to use . . . But I'll check with you to make sure it's not too incriminating."

We started chatting then about her work as a security guard at Mega-Pharm, which she loathed. The work paid reasonably well, but unlike Félix's job as the crew chief of a team of tank cleaners, she worked for an outsourcer, and had fewer benefits. However, the part she hated most was that in spite of being bilingual, and therefore arguably skilled, the security guards got little respect. Fortunately for me, this meant they shared their views freely, in contrast to some of the regular employees.

I described to her where my research was heading. "You know, I was thinking I might want to write some about you specifically, and a few other folks from around here."

"Really? I get to be in your book?" She tipped her head as if getting ready for her close-up.

"Well, you know, the pharmas, they talk a lot about being good neighbors."

"Oh yes, they certainly do."

"Which I always thought was funny because the United States used to talk about being 'good neighbors' to Latin America. . . ." She snorted. "And that was pretty much about doing what they wanted to in other countries. We'll help protect you if you do what we tell you, that sort of thing."

Julia rolled her eyes. "Yes . . . I always figured the companies knew exactly what they meant when they said that . . . they meant the same as the U.S. government . . . they are the neighbors who build the house next to yours, that cut down trees, destroy your view . . . and the rain running off their roof floods your house," she finished for good measure.

I smiled. "That's not really what I think of when I think of good neighbors."

Another eye roll. "No. They're not good neighbors. *Mira*, Ale, they have people who supposedly do these 'community relations.'" She let the cigarette burning down between her fingers punctuate the air quotes in the darkness. "The man who does it for MegaPharm, I see him every day because he comes in like everyone else and I have to check his briefcase and everything." She shook her head. "He's a real dog. There never was that position before and they made it for him. He was an engineer."

I admitted that I knew his name, and she continued. "Yes, that's him. And I know he personally does very little of the actual contact with the 'community.' I think he thinks it's beneath him. You can tell by the way he treats everyone who works in the factory who he thinks is beneath him. When he walks in he looks around to see who is there, and if there's someone wearing a tie, and that little tie that I wear on my uniform doesn't count, if someone looks important, he greets them. His secretary is a very elegant, polite woman, who arranges a lot of the activities, or community relations. She also gets his paper in the morning, rain or shine, and every time I see her do it, I think, 'that's what he thinks her job really is.' Going out and collecting his mail."

I told her that he used to be an environmental manager and was assigned to deal with a number of the environmental issues in the community—his background was not in relating to people. Julia suggested that it was only by circumstance they decided to create the position.

He just happened to have had the most experience of anyone with the "community," having been the one to try to clean up the public relations messes of the '80s and '90s. "But he really seems like he could care less," she concluded.

The phrase "good neighbors" was really nagging at me. "Remember the night I lost my house keys? And I was so hysterical, I just didn't know what to do? I walked into your kitchen, and when you saw my face you told me to come in, sit down, asked me if I'd had anything to eat. And you and Daniela [neighbor on the other side] told me not to worry, we'd figure out what to do. And we concluded that we'd have to break into the house.

"I realized then that even though I was desperate not to have to call the owner of the house, if I hadn't trusted you, and Daniela, and Félix, and

Héctor . . . I wouldn't have been there having that conversation with you. I was willing to let Héctor and Félix break into my house, knowing that after that they could have done it again, but trusting that they wouldn't. I didn't even worry when they called Carlitos, even though he's a convicted burglar. I believed you when you said he'd found God and we could trust him. And if I hadn't found the keys after one last look on the floor of the car, I would have let them do it.

"And as I was falling asleep that night I thought, 'That's what a good neighbor is. Someone you would trust to break into your house, knowing that they'd never do it without your permission.' It's even stronger than saying someone you'd give a key to, because they could rob you, but you wouldn't necessarily know it was them . . . it's an even higher degree of trust. Would you trust these companies to break into your house?"

"If they ever came and knocked, I would bar the door," she replied.

Julia's personal experience at her job heavily influenced her view of pharmaceutical good will toward the surrounding residents. And it is interesting to note that this same manager she disliked so much was the same one that Don Reynaldo had told me was always polite to him (if not very helpful). What both views of the manager suggest is that he did not seem to view Julia, an outsourced security guard, as a member of the community of stakeholders, in spite of her direct economic reliance on the factory for work. He could not deny Don Reynaldo's claim, but once the lawsuit was in place, the potential for legal liability likewise trumped community membership.

5

The Pharmaceutical Industry and the Problem of "Stakeholders"

In consequence, business social responsibility requires a change of
organizational culture from within the companies of the private
sector, which permits them to redefine their internal and external
relations.
        —Héctor Mayol and Bartolomé Gamundi (2004, 5;
translation mine)

There *is* a business case for CSR, but it is much less important or
influential than many proponents of civil regulation believe. CSR
is best understood as a niche rather than a generic strategy: it
makes business sense for some firms in some areas under some
circumstances.
        —David Vogel (2005, 3)

In the Puerto Rican context, corporate philanthropy, let alone Corporate
Social Responsibility (CSR), has emerged comparatively recently. In fact,
CSR in the United States really took off as corporate philanthropy was just
gaining traction on the island. While philanthropy can be a component of
social responsibility, the underlying social relationships that are affected by
philanthropy tend to be characterized by one-way obligations, and therefore inequality. The social relationships idealized in the CSR model are more
characterized as partnerships. This competing set of narratives created some
confusion even among those who wished to promote the significant social
responsibility in business practices. This chapter describes attributes of the
emerging CSR movement in Puerto Rico, and will consider where and with
what success the pharmaceutical companies fit into that movement.

    Some of the challenges in Puerto Rico to advancing what is often
referred to as "transformative" CSR are unique to the island. However, as
a society that in many ways represents a blend of U.S. and Latin American cultural qualities, the lessons to be learned there about the influence

and behavior of corporate entities can provide insight in many diverse locations. In particular I witnessed an ongoing debate within the rising CSR establishment as to whether an "American" version of CSR should dominate practice, as opposed to a more "Latin" version. In anthropological terms it was often competing ideas about meaning, culture, and community that were at play both in the corporate setting and in local communities.

Unsurprisingly, much of the current literature on CSR emerged out of existing debates about corporate governance and business ethics. It is replete with phrases that sound like slogans, graphs that look ready-made for powerpoint presentations, and generally reflects a discourse steeped in the language of business itself. However, there are some fundamental ideas that appear with regularity,[1] and advocates of the movement to enhance corporate social responsibility tend to see corporate policies and behavior in a developmental, perhaps evolutionary, framework. On the one hand, this perspective assumes that corporate entities can improve themselves, and all could be, in theory, on a trajectory to do so. In this sense the discourse of CSR can come across as unrelentingly optimistic. On the other hand, most independent CSR professionals start their developmental scale essentially at zero, where zero is "Compliant" with current legal standards across all regulated activities, and the highest level of achievement is considered "Transformative." This nirvana of corporate existence is characterized by behaviors that "change the game," create new markets through their sustainable contributions to economic development, engage in active, culturally relevant partnerships with local communities, and maintain a fully transparent system of governance and financial operations.[2] In other words, they imagine a world in which corporations function as they were originally intended, as "public institution[s] whose purpose was to serve national interests and advance the public good."[3]

This is the vision of several CSR professionals I worked with in the field, a group of dedicated people focused on launching what they viewed as a revolutionary social movement among corporate entities in Puerto Rico. When I asked the head of the CSR NGO spearheading this campaign about the state of pharmaceutical CSR programs, she shook her head.

If you're talking to the folks from the pharmaceuticals, in reality, as far as [transformative] CSR goes, they have zero concept, I mean *zero* concept of what we're talking about. Philanthropy, yes, but how to be a force for true development, no. And that's why we want the perspective of those working

in Latin America because we need the experience of *developing* countries
as much as we need the perspective from the States. We need to really get
to the bottom of the pyramid, you know?

This was a reference to C. K. Prahalad's treatise, much touted in CSR circles,
The Fortune at the Bottom of the Pyramid: Eradicating Poverty Through Profits
(2005). This approach has been criticized for overemphasizing the poor as
consumers, rather than as producers or innovation partners with businesses,[4]
a critique particularly relevant in the Puerto Rican context. In this case, there
tended to be a split in the CSR establishment between those who identified
most strongly with business, and emphasized markets, and those who identified more with people, and emphasized partnerships. Interestingly, I found
that Liria, the CSR advocate quoted above, typically sympathized with residential communities and small businesses. The reference to Prahalad's book
inadvertently represents the pervasive influence of the business perspective,
in which what might be called discursive "creep" occurs. In trying to pull
large businesses, particularly multinational corporations, into the CSR fold
in Puerto Rico, it was necessary to emphasize the business case, even when it
distracted from what many saw as the main focus of the movement.

For the majority of independent CSR professionals I encountered, their
mission was deeply tied into a broader vision of sustainable development,
an area in which Puerto Rico occupied an intermediary space. For example,
there were, and continue to be, serious doubts as to what degree capital-
intensive industries like the pharmaceuticals could contribute to an economically sustainable Puerto Rico. This was notable in the stated emphasis
on strengthening small businesses, which represented the majority of Puerto
Rican companies. However, in spite of their vision of Puerto Rico's future,
these dedicated proponents of CSR often found themselves in the position
of legitimating corporations that were, by their own standards, barely more
than "Compliant."

Corporate Philanthropy—Why "Doing Well
By Doing Good" Isn't Good Enough

Corporate Social Responsibility, with respect to the pharmaceutical industry, is often spoken of in terms of issues such as Access to Essential Medicines[5] or the ethics of drug trials and safety in both economically developing
and developed contexts.[6] In the first decade of the twenty-first century there
was increased attention in academic literature and the press to these topics,

and all the companies present in Nocorá were implicated to one degree or another in these analyses. However, my concern in this work is to focus on what might be called "community-based" CSR, as it is the most immediately relevant in the Puerto Rican context and the people of Nocorá. It is therefore important to understand how local CSR is related to corporate philanthropy, and where it diverges into an altogether different phenomenon—at least in theory.

The literature on corporate philanthropy makes frequent use of the notion of doing well by doing good, namely, improving corporate name recognition through good works, and thereby raising market appeal. Good works in this sense are generally donations of money, goods somehow related to the mission of the company,[7] or volunteer time of company employees. However, it was a notion of "doing good" in a much broader sense that was used to frame this ethnographic project from the beginning. My research suggests that considering the potential positive impact of a corporation in a local community *beyond philanthropy* opens up the possibility for corporations to behave more like the citizens they claim to be.

The philosophy of a corporation as a benevolent entity has been used as both a strategy for company policy, and the basis for academic critiques of corporate giving. Jerome Himmelstein notes that corporate philanthropy programs insert corporations into a web of relationships in which they are owed not tangible returns, but a diffuse regard and understanding, giving big business a subtle but distinct edge in political life and in the market.[8] Therefore, from a theoretical perspective, the pharmaceutical companies in Nocorá seemed likely to invest in local programs not for the benefit of the needy, but for broader maintenance of community relationships. I have suggested that the prime benefit to employee volunteerism in Nocorá, for example, is the fomenting of "feel good" *communitas* between workers and management, fulfilling the need to smooth over doubts or dissatisfaction workers may feel toward their employer. However, one of the most important desired outcomes of the systematic giving of time, as well as direct monetary donations, to various causes may well be securing of relationships specifically among the elite.[9] In Nocorá, however, social relationships at the level of the elite nevertheless have significant community-wide consequences.

In the new paradigm of corporate philanthropy that emerged in the 1990s, initiatives should serve both company and society; the company should use the tools of its trade for the solution of particularly relevant social problems.[10] Following Richard Wilk's schematization of time and self-interest (figure 5.2), the move of businesses toward a broader notion of

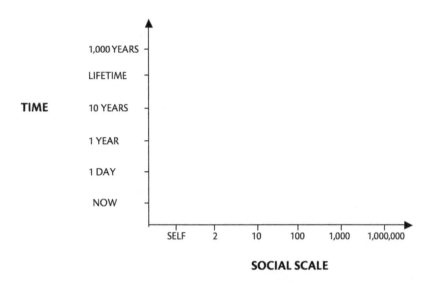

Figure 5.2. The social-temporal grid. This can be used to map different kinds of decision-making, showing that the conventional notions of selfishness and altruism form a continuum. [©Copyright 19960101 Wilk, Richard R. Reprinted by permission of Westview Press, a member of the Perseus Group.]

self-interest (the social) represents an evolutionary step, suggesting a continuing need to examine organizations as parts of broader social systems.[11] It also begs the question of whether certain businesses are moving beyond the traditional time perspective of quarterly bottom lines and engaging the tenets of sustainable development.[12] Significant positive movement along *both* of Wilk's axes (time and social scale) constitutes what is, in the twenty-first century, considered to be the ideal practice of corporate social responsibility.

As mentioned above, even corporate philanthropy as we know it in the United States was a relative newcomer to the socioeconomic scene in Puerto Rico, in part because it is associated with the giving of charity. As one local CSR expert put it, "In Puerto Rico we're very big on the *ay benditos*, oh, poor things. . . . But helping has always been something the church does, or that people do within their own families."

There have long been very distinct boundaries for cultural notions of social responsibility. While the church or the government (particularly since the 1940s) was perceived to have social and economic responsibilities to the populace at large, many people expressed to me a shared understanding that individuals, in general, do not particularly help strangers.

This cultural model of constraints on charity in general, as well as on the definition of to whom one is obligated, severely affected the growth of corporate philanthropic activities on the island. This was especially true with regard to multinational corporations. They might have practiced more substantial philanthropy or civic engagement in other contexts, but had been able to use "the local culture" as an excuse for minimizing their giving programs, or for not offering expensive benefits, like health care.[13] Likewise, as explored in chapter 3, how a corporation defines "community" is crucial to understanding the corporate perspective as to where its activities rate on the "social" axis.

To make a comparison between community-directed financial commitments in Puerto Rico, versus the mainland, I visited the offices of one of the pharmaceutical companies (which I here call MegaDrug) that happened to have facilities in both Nocorá and in the town in which I grew up. My hometown, Median (in the northeastern United States), boasted a population of about 148,000 people as of the 2000 Census, while its metropolitan area numbered about 730,000. The community activities/philanthropic support budget in 2003 was $250,000. In Puerto Rico, where the community affairs office of MegaDrug covers four facilities across the island, the total population for those four locations is approximately 224,000. The budget for the analogous purposes in Puerto Rico, as described to me by the community affairs director, was $30,000. Even assuming the community affairs budget for the U.S.-based factory was intended to reach the wider metropolitan area of Median, the Puerto Rican budget was still only 40 percent of the U.S. budget. The Median MegaDrug plant also utilized the "Neighbor of Choice" philosophy[14] in its corporate-community relations, including the production of a community relations newsletter and the ongoing presence of an active Community Advisory Panel. When asked about these kinds of programs in Puerto Rico, the MegaDrug representative responded that that type of program had never been necessary.

Still, the increasing flow of information along global communication networks had begun to increase the pressure on multinational corporations to improve their global standards for both responsible behavior and philanthropic giving. It was increasingly easy for information about how companies behave in local contexts to travel to previously underserved areas. Corporations sometimes claimed the need (or the desire) to conform to local cultural norms in Puerto Rico, because it could be considered culturally only a quasi-U.S. context, with traditionally low expectations for corporate-community involvement. However, some companies also recognized the opportunity to make a good show with their outreach and service programs on the island. Among the pharmaceutical companies I encountered in my research, the managers in charge of this area tended to present an interesting discursive juxtaposition: There was a good bit of ignorance expressed about the more substantial requirements dictated by the current state of CSR philosophy, and yet also a certain nonchalance that was summed up by one manager who stated that they were "already doing all those things." An industrial ecology researcher who worked with the pharmaceuticals in Nocorá summed up their perspective to me in the terse phrase, "We're doing what we can." When I asked what impact she thought her work on improving cooperation for conservation of resources had, she reluctantly admitted that she thought that overall it would have little or none.

Eager though they were to broadcast that they were already fulfilling CSR goals, with that title or not, the managers often seemed quite unaware of how their own corporate-cultural norms put severe constraints on their ability to be on the "cutting edge" of socially responsible behavior. In particular, the desire to limit legal liability, intrinsic to modern corporate entities, made it virtually impossible to substantively connect to, and to understand, community concerns. It could be said that in the terms of social theory, their actions demonstrated that it is not possible for corporate "persons" to empathize. This is because community concerns are, by their nature, *shared*, while fear of legal liability and its accompanying costs drove the drug companies in Nocorá to reflexively respond to many queries with, "That is not *our* problem."

This Land Is (Not) Our Land

Several poignant examples of this "not our problem" outlook by pharmaceutical companies and their partners in Nocorá help illustrate the limits to community participation, and therefore to the idealized version of Corporate Social Responsibility I have outlined. The first was raised as a part of my fieldwork in Tipan with the environmental activists of CDAN. The second was presented to me during an interview with the Community Affairs representative from SuperMed.

In chapter 1 I described in detail the concerns of Tipan with respect to the wastewater treatment plant, and discussed several issues related to corrosion in pipeworks leading from the factories to the plant. The buildup of hydrogen sulfide, as well as very extreme pH conditions, both issues raised in expert reports on the Nocorá treatment plant and its influent, had caused some of the influent pipes to be completely corroded through. Evidence suggested that the type of corrosion in the Nocorá pipeline would likely have allowed wastewater to leak into the surrounding environment.[15]

When I interviewed a member of the alcalde's staff who worked closely with the factories and on environmental and health issues in 2005, he recalled that about five years earlier a major renovation of the central industrial pipe to the treatment plant had been undertaken. The project had reportedly cost the pharmaceutical Consortium several million dollars. This informant recalled that other repairs had periodically been done to various portions of the pipe,[16] but that this installation of a high-tech "membrane" within the pipe[17] had been commissioned specifically to guard against leakages from internal damage to the pipe. As scholars of CSR have described,[18] this approach was fundamentally reactive to a well-established problem that could no longer be ignored, rather than the behavior of a highly responsive set of corporate citizens.

The activists of Tipan did not object to some kind of fix to the pipe, even a reactive one. But the unanswered question remained: if corrosion had been a problem since practically the beginning of the pipes' existence, what had leaked into the soil and the aquifers in the meantime?[19] This sentiment was echoed by a biologist I interviewed who had worked for the water company before becoming an environmental educator. Particularly concerned with the issue of accidental leaks, she said,

> Often when they discover that there was a certain kind of leak, it can mean that there were goodness knows how many leaks before. The problem is, it's very hard to say how much contamination has happened over a certain period—what they actually find, in all probability, is only scratching the surface.

Don Lirio of CDAN had once tried to draw for me a map of Tipan, identifying the current owners of the large, uninhabited portions of land once cultivated for sugarcane by the Commonwealth Land Authority. As he hunched over the paper his difficulty became clear: The Land Authority still owned much of the land, but leased or otherwise ceded it to the water and sewer company (PRASA), the Department of Natural Resources, the municipality, and who knew who else? It became even more confusing when trying to raise questions or complaints with any of the putative landholders because whenever a problem was raised they would tell the questioner, often with the utmost politeness, "You will have to contact the people at Organization X to ask about that. That area does not belong to us."

In a meeting I attended between representatives of the municipal leg-islature and managers of the Tipan wastewater treatment plant, a series of exchanges took place, demonstrating that this appeal to blame shifting could also serve to diffuse confrontations between relative equals. Driving toward the treatment plant with one of the Tipan legislative representatives, he explained to me that one of the issues he wanted to raise was the collapse and flooding of one of the sewer pipes due in part to excess debris and other maintenance failures. He and the other legislators were informed that even though the part of the pipe they were talking about was in Nocorá, the divi-sion of PRASA (the Commonwealth water company) in charge of maintain-ing that section of the pipe was the Bajas office,[20] in the neighboring munici-pality. When asked about the pipe collapse, the manager of the Tipan plant courteously suggested they call Bajas, and gave them the name of the person in charge and the phone number. As a generous afterthought, he also offered to call the Bajas office himself, to lend support to the Legislature's request for service.

I witnessed the second example of the "not our problem" perspective midway through a conversation that began with a joke about tearing up the roads. I arrived at SuperMed's metropolitan San Juan offices exactly on time for my meeting, no thanks to the spontaneous decision on the part of the Public Works department to begin tearing up the highway between San Juan and Nocorá during rush hour that morning. When I sat down at the confer-ence table, I broke the ice with the community affairs representative by men-tioning that I had been afraid of being late because "they were breaking up the road *por que le da la gana*" [because they felt like it]. The woman shared my smile and said, in the gently sarcastic way that Puerto Ricans repeat the well-worn tourism phrase in response to everyday problems, "Welcome to Puerto Rico."

As our conversation moved forward she described for me the company's notion of their local community—in this case the neighborhoods in their immediate vicinity. She then detailed the methods through which they had attempted to ascertain what the community's needs and wants might be, vis-à-vis the factory. One of the key findings of an initial survey, she explained, was that people's biggest concerns were about things that did not pertain to the factories. Recalling the start of our conversation she said, "They wanted us to fix the roads, for example." She shrugged as if to say, *You understand how it is.* Their budget for community activities was very limited, she said, and besides, that was the job of the government. Business, I was to hear over and over again, was not in business to do the government's job for it, no mat-ter how poorly the government operated.[21]

The example of road improvement and construction is a good one for see-ing how the power dynamics of Nocorá played out with regard to corpo-rate-community relations. During my time there, one of the biggest ongoing transportation projects was the widening of the road between the express-way and route 4 in the neighborhood of Salvador la Cruz, where the phar-maceuticals are located. This project demonstrated, like the channeling proj-ect of Río Bajas, how skilled the alcalde was at bringing together resources from diverse sources (mostly government and many federal grants) for a large infrastructure project. This particular road, previously just one lane in each direction, received a massive amount of traffic to the pharmaceu-tical factories (see map, figure 1.2). In fact, this exit, directing traffic from the expressway toward Salvador, was not originally designed as the exit for Nocorá when the highway was built. The original exit was located less than a mile to the east, at an intersection leading directly into the urban center of the pueblo to the north, and to route 4 to the south. However, the pharma-ceuticals had this second Nocorá exit built, and their influence was apparent in the exit sign which read:

SALIDA
La Cañita [the town to the south]
Farmaceuticas

The further widening of this road was clearly favorable to the factories, though the government was financing the project.[22] Hence, it was difficult to imagine, after wielding so much influence at apparently little expense, in the matter of certain roads, why a company would shy away from pressuring the local government to seek financing for other, smaller roads. One only needed to drive down any of the side streets connecting to route 4 one afternoon in the rain to know that smaller roads were only unimportant to those who never drove on them.

The Struggle for Self-Definition and Vision: TransformaRSE

It was precisely this abdication of responsibility that the Corporate Social Responsibility NGO *TransformaRSE* sought to eradicate through educa-tion and advisory support services to companies operating all over Puerto Rico. An outgrowth of an organization that was founded to encourage volun-teerism and community involvement by businesses (which I call *MeteMano*), TransformaRSE attempted to promote "the application of ethical values, *beyond* what the law requires, at all levels of an organization (manufacturing, hiring, marketing, products, everything)," as one member described it to me.

This goal, however, was not so easy to accomplish for many reasons. First, a consensus on a definition of CSR (and therefore the precise measurement of what constitutes "beyond") has yet to be reached internationally.[23] Additionally, TransformaRSE was in a position in which its directors felt the need to respond to both U.S. and Latin American cultural models of social responsibility,[24] which were not always in line with one another. The principal members of the organization generally agreed on their goal of promoting ethical behavior beyond what the law required, and promoting *alianzas* or partnerships that brought business into greater and more meaningful contact with their various "communities," or "stakeholders." However, many policy and operational details remained unclear as the organization strove to find its place on the political-economic landscape. During my fieldwork and several years after, the emphasis of TransformaRSE lay strongly in creating and raising the consciousness of businesses, government, and higher education about CSR. Unfortunately, my research suggests that this process was made extremely difficult for a number of reasons.

One issue that arose time and again in conversations with people working with or advising TransformaRSE was the pernicious tradition of paternalism in Puerto Rico. Paternalism, as one might describe the behaviors and attitudes of Nocorá's alcalde Martínez, can sometimes masquerade as social responsibility in the workplace, but reinforces relations of inequality. It is founded in expectations that flow from structural dependency. The need to break from local dependency models, which were embedded within Puerto Rico's larger political and economic dependency on the United States, was one area in which proponents of CSR were particularly emphatic about not overemphasizing corporate philanthropy. As one local businessman put it, "CSR requires a contract of social investment," a recognition that businesses exist as part of a broader, existing social contract. However, in my observation the fear of what has been called *cuponazgo*, or relationships based on welfare-type handouts, and thus further dependency on the part of those receiving aid,[25] proved to be a double-edged sword. In the practice of community-based giving and social responsibility, I often heard that "the pharmaceuticals do not want the commitment of established partnerships" (for example with individual local schools), for fear that they would be doing the government's job (or would be called on to do so in the future). A narrow focus on preventing dependency, through avoidance of "cuponazgo," also obfuscated the many ways in which the capital-intensive pharmaceutical industry had contributed to more broadly based dependency on the island. As such, CSR advocates often found themselves promoting economic sustainability as a goal, while being forced to appeal to industries that had long undermined that same goal.

Can CSR Be Transformative?

As it continued to find its feet as an organization, TransformaRSE ran directly into the problem that Ronen Shamir has identified as the "The De-Radicalization of Corporate Social Responsibility." In his critique Shamir particularly targets what he calls market NGOs for their business or corporate orientation. Their role, whether explicitly corporate-funded or not, is to "shape notions such as 'social responsibility' and 'social change' in ways that are amenable to business and employers' concerns."[26] During my fieldwork I participated on a consulting committee for TransformaRSE's Education and Research initiatives, and witnessed the internal struggles around how to avoid such cooptation without alienating local businesses (including outposts of multinationals). As a consequence, disagreements also emerged over what might be considered the "philosophical" aspects of CSR. For example, TransformaRSE members were troubled by the question of whether or not individual leaders of corporations needed to experience some kind of "spiritual" or personal revelation in order to run a transformative, ethical business.

David, a special advisor to the organization and a full-time CSR consultant, was a strong proponent of the spiritual conversion argument. He seemed to think that the personal connection to ethical principles would prevent "the use of subterfuge to hide maneuverings around the law, and thumbing their nose at ethical behavior." He was very preoccupied with the idea that TransformaRSE could unwittingly produce a "greenwashing" effect, through an unwillingness to criticize businesses expressing interest in CSR. In David's view, the commitment of TransformaRSE was not to back away from intense critical engagement, but to provide examples of how being a transformative business was really the best, most successful, and most profitable. It is worth noting that while David was perfectly willing to criticize business practices, he did not question, for example, the emphasis on profitability.

Other members expressed concern that TransformaRSE not take the role of policing businesses, or carrying out activities that are the bailiwick of enforcement agencies such as EPA and Hacienda (the local IRS). All members agreed that creating a self-evaluation for businesses (thereby providing them with an example of what true CSR is really about) was a good first step. There was, however, some concern that the evaluation should not be too onerous, else the companies, "who are already fed up with evaluations, questionnaires, and indicators," would decide that going beyond the requirements of the law was not really worth the effort. For these TransformaRSE members, the emphasis in their work was on making the "being responsible pays" argument as convincing as possible.

While the question of power dynamics and dependency was implicitly raised by TransformaRSE in discussions about the overall cultural paternalism on the island, when it came to considering actual corporate-community relationships there was little, if any, analysis of power differentials between companies and their resident neighbors, their so-called stakeholders. Even David, for all his talk of spirituality, perhaps because of his grounding in more traditional economics, did not seem overly concerned with power. "Of course you have power differences," he said once in an offhand tone. "You have them all throughout society, you have neighbors living next to people with more power, people who abuse the power they have, more wealthy and well-connected people. That's always an issue." This was a stark example of how easy it was for proponents of CSR to echo the views of business: recall the way, in chapter 2, one of the community affairs managers reflected this lack of understanding when he expressed his distaste for the influence of "outsiders."

Some of TranformaRSE's advisors were more cognizant of the problem of power. Eugenio, a business management consultant, stated his concerns like this:

> One thing that really bothers me in this process, is if the organizations [the businesses] see this as "I'm better than you" . . . the chemistry of the process won't work right. If it's "I'm this powerful thing, doing something for you" . . . if it goes that way . . . [*shakes his head*]. It's got to be, "I'm here, you're here, let's work together in ways that move us forward.

In practical terms, however, TransformaRSE's members struggled with maintaining their concerns for the local community, in the face of a business environment that was generally resistant to the type of paradigm shift being promoted by the CSR advocates. The problem, as David perceived it, was that too many people for too long had believed that in order to be successful at business you had to, in his words, "leave your soul at home." What was required, he suggested, was for mangers to be educated to see not only what was the morally correct choice (whether it be ecological, financial, etc.), but to understand that the same morally correct choice is also correct for business in the long run. In Wilk's framework (figure 5.2), David was arguing primarily for an expansion of notions of what constituted self-interest.

"You see it in everyday life, in families, in your friends," he lamented, picking up a copy of Jared Diamond's book *Collapse* from his desk as if using it to support his thesis. "People can't get it together to see the dangers ahead, and the result is people, societies, businesses, collapsing." Human beings were so tragically flawed, he surmised, that they could not seem to help themselves investing in the small-scale, in their own egos or short-term needs, that it is just a "train wreck. You see it in business all the time," he said. The role of CSR, according to David, was to try to present the broader facts to a business person making a decision, but then you step back and they make the decision—and sometimes all you can do is watch that "train wreck."

David's argument, following many critiques of capitalism run rampant,[27] was that engaging in business, and its axiomatic short-term outlook, was spiritually damaging for the businessperson as well as the worker, and the results were potentially disastrous for everyone. This is not a unique argument in the sustainable development arena, but the difference was that in David's view the core of the problem somehow rested in the nature of human beings, rather than the nature of capitalism. This idealized view of business, emphasizing the entrepreneurial spirit and the individual, and neglecting the more bureaucratic aspects of organization, offered both the solution and a new set of problems. It is in these sites of bureaucracy particularly in which I would argue much of what David describes as "soul loss" actually occurs. It is precisely in the gaps of formal organization (in which decisions can be blamed on unseen forces, the ubiquitous and vague "culture" or "company policy" of the organization, on those higher-ups in the decision-making structure) in which business is most often permitted, or even expected, to have no soul. For David the answer to achieving sustainable development was not to dismantle the global capitalist system,[28] or to reimagine it systemically as valuing natural resources,[29] but rather to change it through individual innovation. This perspective appeals to empowering models of individual agency and subjectivity,[30] but neglects the more pervasive, systemic rigidity exposed in the literature on critiques of capitalism, consumption, and the world system.[31] As such, and in spite of some internally acknowledged criticisms of corporate structural tendencies, TransformaRSE as a whole was never publicly critical of the larger limitations on the potential for the transformative CSR it sought.

It must be recognized here that the structure of corporations, created as legal entities for the express purpose of minimizing personal risk, can off-set the threat of being seen as a "bad guy," because accountability has a way of becoming structurally elusive.[32] The maintenance of the corporate image as a whole has become a delicate balance of being seen as doing enough of the right things at the right times, while maintaining profitability. The result is a type of "responsibility phobia" through which "a cynic might define power—always an elusive concept—as the right to be unaccountable."[33] Likewise, the discourses of responsibility, or failures of responsibility, *within* corporations tend to emphasize isolated circumstances ("bad apples" if you will)—individuals, or departments associated with a given problem, such as environmental contamination. Making systemic (and expensive) changes to improve accountability in a complex organization is typically resisted. In an atmosphere of pervasive responsibility phobia, those called to give an accounting can at least fall back on the usual protests of ignorance, "I didn't *know* that would happen. I didn't know that was our land/problem/fault/obligation." These protests of ignorance with respect to CSR indicators is legitimated by the fact that the indicators themselves, like other forms of measurement, are often a site of ideological and methodological contestation.[34]

Liria's goal for CSR in Puerto Rico reflected a deep understanding of some of the problems described in earlier chapters, the ways in which the development process had further stressed existing fissures in Puerto Rican society. She said,

> My vision really is to facilitate connections between all the diverse groups. Education, providing information is part of that, building relationships is part of that. Without the relationships, without *confianza*, people will not work together. And when each group feels the other is not listening, it breaks *confianza*, destroys it. We have to build *confianza*. You can't build social capital without it. And that won't happen without communication.

However, in spite of her history of working in communities, it was evident that her strategy, like that of GUIA, suffered from its roots in deeply captured assumptions about what it would take to bring corporations to sit "at the same table" as the community:

> In pulling together our initial activities we really tried to make it happen from the *point of view* of the businesses, not the communities. This is not

because my heart is not with the community—it is, and before this I've worked mostly with the community. But it's necessary to get the message out, to try to influence public policy.

Eugenio also acknowledged the need to recognize the business case for CSR, but he clearly held misgivings about the pervasiveness of what he called the "financial logic" argument:

If we hurt people's dignity in the process of economic development, we're in trouble. Everybody has the right to have dignity. There are people inside these companies, just like there are people inside the communities. We need to try to work with that.

A Brief Detour: The Practical Fallacy of the Fiduciary Responsibility Argument

As implied in the discussion of TransformaRSE above, Milton Friedman's oft-cited article "The Social Responsibility of Business Is to Increase Its Profits," raises an important contradiction still plaguing the CSR movement today, namely that "corporations are artificial people . . . 'business' as a whole cannot be said to have responsibilities."[35] Those who argue for social responsibility, and further, for social equity with corporate entities, might disagree with Friedman in principle. But his argument nevertheless exposes certain weaknesses from the activist view, as well as that of typical corporations, which must be addressed. Although my research took place prior to the *Citizens United v. Federal Election Commission* U.S. Supreme Court decision (in 2010), the specter of corporate personhood loomed large in the struggles I witnessed.

Friedman argues that the legal responsibility of a corporation is to make money for its shareholders,[36] legally known as the "fiduciary responsibility" of corporate enterprise.[37] This is not only a social burden, in that the corporation is made up of individual members with a financial stake in the company, but it is legally bound to behave so that those financial stakes are secure. As one small business owner said to me, echoing a widely held sentiment, "the purpose of a business is to make money—they are not non-profits."

The pharmaceutical industry is generally acknowledged to be pretty good at making money. In fact, the Kaiser Family Foundation and Sonderegger Research Center reported that

For every year from 1995 through 2002, the pharmaceutical industry was the most profitable industry in the U.S. Since 2002, however, its profitability has declined, with drug companies ranking as the third most profitable industry in 2004 (15.8%), with mining, crude-oil production the most profitable industry (22.1%). [Nevertheless] drug companies were three times more profitable than the median for all Fortune 500 companies in 2004 (15.8% compared to 5.2%).[38]

Before any reader begins to shake her head in dismay with the idea that new corporate social responsibility burdens emerging since 2001 have caused a drop in pharmaceutical profitability, it is instructive to take a look at another of Friedman's points: He argues that for a corporate executive to spend money on any program that goes *beyond* that which is required by law is *spending someone else's money* (emphasis mine). It seems fair to presume that poor management practices would likewise constitute spending someone else's (namely the stockholders') money.

In August 2005, *MSN Money*'s "Company Focus" column declared one of the Nocoreño multinationals' CEOs one of the "Most Outrageously Overpaid" in America, citing his collection of $41 million in compensation while "shareholders have seen the stock decline by 48% over the past four years."[39] The following year he joined two other CEOs of companies with outposts in Nocorá (for a total of three out of four) in being fired for severe mismanagement issues, among them legal troubles relating to marketing of drugs, obscuring of clinical trial risk data, and "shareholder disappointment."[40] A look at the five-year stock performance charts suggested that these companies were not showing particular concern for their fiduciary responsibilities to stockholders, in spite of continuing to make strong appearances in other indicators of the Fortune 500. Broader indicators also suggest that the pharmaceutical industry was not alone in the trend toward overcompensation for executives at the expense of regular investors.[41]

Bringing the attention back to on-the-ground social responsibility, two facts stand out to further argue against an overly simplistic notion of the social responsibility of corporations. For the first half of 2005, *Caribbean Business* (the weekly publication of record for Puerto Rico's business community) reported that overall sales for nine of the pharmaceutical companies operating in Puerto Rico had increased by 5.7 percent, though company earnings from that same period had remained flat.[42] In assessing the lackluster earnings it was pointed out that several of the blockbuster drugs that had previously increased profit margins, such as Vioxx and Paxil, had been removed from the market due to problems in manufacturing or to under-reported health risks. Sales of other drugs, such as Bextra and Celebrex, had also suffered from newly reported health side effects (Bextra was also temporarily removed from the market pending new warning labels). While other drugs faced increased competition from generic competitors, it is arguable that these setbacks could have been prevented had individual companies responded more proactively to clinic trial data on drug-related risks. Though not the primary focus of the present research, these examples suggest that (1) the pharmaceutical industry had some work to do in the arena of transparency[43] as regards safety issues, and (2) damage to profit margins has been more likely to come from internal sources than from any external demands on community activities or other philanthropic programs.

This second point is also echoed in the literature on corporate social responsibility: Singling out one of the pharmaceutical companies I studied (along with the Gap and Hewlett-Packard, among others) for "above-average" expenditures on CSR programs, political scientist David Vogel notes:

One reason CSR often appears to "pay" is not so much because its benefits are so substantial as because its costs have usually been modest. Most firms' CSR expenditures fall well within their limits of discretionary spending. . . . [and] are small in comparison with their earnings.[44]

His observation was evident in the limited resources available to CSR managers in Puerto Rico, as well as in the reluctance of the Pharmaceutical Consortium of Nocorá to spend money to address pollution problems.

Though Vogel argues that there are distinct limits on a "market for virtue," and CSR continues to have its detractors in the business world,[45] the consensus that business has more responsibility than it has traditionally acknowledged has surely grown. The far greater challenge is getting polluters to admit to being the source of past and present harms, even when they can claim to have been in compliance with what were later proven to be insufficient laws. Additionally, in the enforcement of environmental protection, or rather its absence, ignorance has long been a favorite excuse for how industry has managed to pollute as much as it has already. Even supposedly pro-environment engineers and other experts, while acknowledging the mistakes of the past, were apt to prefer to focus on how to prevent further contamination in the future. Through a variety of discursive practices, the pharmaceuticals used this refocusing on the present and the future to take the eye off the damage done, as well as to paint those, such as the Tipanecos, as backward thinking and even under-informed.

The Multinationals, in a Class by Themselves

The challenges to promoting transformative corporate social responsibility in this setting were legion. However, with respect to the fundamental problem for TransformaRSE, namely convincing upper-level management in a business in Puerto Rico to embrace CSR, one issue particularly emerged. On the one hand, Puerto Rican CSR promoters seemed to have a ready-made emotional appeal at their disposal, particularly suited to wooing Puerto Rican–owned and -operated businesses. If one of the basic issues facing the island was that development in Puerto Rico had emphasized industrial growth without sufficient attention to environmental or economic sustainability, then the challenge was to create long-term strategies to develop Puerto Rico sustainably.[46] All the key players in TransformaRSE were in agreement on this issue. As such, they were interested in bringing two groups on board both to promote CSR *and* to put it into practice: government, which they viewed in this sense as a business, and which many believed to be the most corrupt and environmentally unsound business on the island; and small- to-medium-sized local enterprises which, as David noted, often fall through the cracks in terms of watch-dogging, and yet can have a substantial impact on locally based issues of concern to CSR.

The local nature of their focus, then, was promoting a vision of a sustainably developed future Puerto Rico. It was a vision that fundamentally did not mesh with the traditional incentives that drew multinational industries like the various chemical manufacturers to the island in the first place. However, taking on the tax incentives, whether federal or local, would automatically draw TransformaRSE into the political status debate. This was an outcome they consciously sought to avoid, as party politics on the island were perpetually deadlocked. For these reasons, they seemed willing to let the pharmaceutical industry in Puerto Rico off the hook, in a sense. Most of the big pharmaceutical manufacturers were involved in TransformaRSE's activities, either as sponsors of certain programs, or participating in public relations events related to CSR. Two appeared prominently on their list of Corporate Friends. As far as key members of TransformaRSE were concerned, the pharmaceuticals were not even remotely on the cutting edge of social responsibility—they were still stuck somewhere in the shift from philanthropy to something deeper, and as a very conservative industry, not moving more quickly than they felt was absolutely necessary. In fact, many aspects of the business of ethical drugs belied the ability of drug manufacturers to be transformative: intra-industry competition has been a deal-breaker on several efforts at providing access to essential medicines, concerns about profitability have created massive anti-environment lobbying efforts, and the necessity of guarding "trade secrets" was often used as an excuse to hide other types of information, such as product safety.

But TransformaRSE was also willing to allow the pharmaceuticals to be associated with their mission, for two basic reasons. Most obviously, as with the case of environmental NGO GUIA, they helped provide funding and logistical support for projects. But perhaps more significantly, as the perceived backbone of the Puerto Rican economy (apart from tourism), the pharmaceuticals had a lot of prestige in the island's business world, and with regular people. The bottom line for a CSR NGO seemed to be: you will not get anywhere, even with the smaller businesses, if big businesses do not take you seriously. And while the long-range goal of the organization was to secure core funding from autonomous philanthropic sources to operate independently from corporate influences, these problems remained: (1) The associations TransformaRSE had with the pharmaceutical industry would be hard to erase in the mind of skeptics, even when financial ties were cut; and (2) Corporate Social Responsibility in Puerto Rico would always struggle with skepticism from those who promoted grassroots and community-based interests, because it was fundamentally pitched from a business perspective.

The multinational pharmaceutical companies were not part of the long-term strategic plan, per se, of TransformaRSE's promotion of CSR. But by a careful association with TransformaRSE, through their various philanthropic activities, and their perception as necessary in the broader public imaginary, the pharmaceuticals had been able to shore up their local reputations within the population at large. An island-wide survey in 2005 listed the pharmaceutical industry as second on a list of "trustworthy" institutions, behind only the church,[47] and tied with the National Guard. Seventy-eight percent of people surveyed mentioned the pharmaceutical industry specifically.[48] It is instructive to compare this to a poll cited in the New York Times that indicated that in 2004, only 9 percent of mainland Americans believed "drug companies are generally honest."[49]

Following the widely publicized "death" of Section 936, many Puerto Ricans seemed disposed to be grateful to the companies for every investment they made following the phasing out of the federal tax benefits that lured them in the first place. In an interview with a local school principal, in which we discussed their community involvement, she commented anxiously, "PharmaGigante is going to leave, I know it." Although she did not view their community-based activities as particularly impressive, she absolutely saw them as economically necessary. The longer the companies stayed, the more they gained a certain popular status for performed commitment to the island. However, it is worth noting that, among the general populace, they may have been getting more credit than they deserved: while 936 was gone, the pharmaceutical industry continued to benefit from similar tax benefits: In 2008, according to the Puerto Rico Industrial Development Company (PRIDCO) website,[50] companies incorporating as "Controlled Foreign Companies" (CFCs), including many based in the United States, continued to enjoy "no U.S. federal income tax," and "a local corporate income tax rate of 2%–7%." In 2012, they also continued to receive a wide range of other cost- and administrative-related benefits and incentives while making use of Puerto Rico's "highly skilled, bilingual and productive labor force," available at "manufacturing wages 65–80% lower than mainland U.S." As a front page article in *Caribbean Business* announced, "Puerto Rico's pharmaceutical industry remains strong despite end of 936/30A."[51] Indeed, at the time of this writing (2012), PRIDCO's website also stated, "With only one word, we can explain why we are a major manufacturing location in the world and why 13 out of the top 16 medical device companies have presence in Puerto Rico: *INCENTIVES*." With the continuing promotion of, and reliance on, financial incentives, it becomes more questionable as to whether the pharmaceutical industry could be considered a dedicated partner in Puerto Rico's sustainable development. Which in turn casts some doubt as to whether the industry could be legitimately viewed as a stakeholder in Puerto Rico's sustainable future.[52]

A Qualitative Look at Nocoreño Attitudes

It is evident from the data presented in chapter 3 that citizens of Nocorá were not completely taken in by industry's public face, even if they were not environmental activists. To further explore the complex outlook of Nocoreños, this section will examine some of the more qualitative responses to the survey described earlier. Here I place the commentary of several respondents in the context of their agree/disagree responses to the survey, as well as in the broader framework of the mandates of corporate social responsibility to treat the local community as valued stakeholders.

To review, there were three survey questions which related particularly to the perceived role of the pharmaceuticals in "the community": The first two were presented as statements, and respondents were asked to agree or disagree: (1) The pharmaceuticals are good neighbors, like part of our community. (2) The pharmaceuticals maintain a relationship of good faith and good communication with the community. And (3) Between the good things and the bad things that the pharmaceuticals bring to our community there are: (a) more of the bad, (b) of equal proportion, (c) more of the good.

In order to probe further into the feelings of Nocoreños about the interactions between factory and community, here are the nonstandardized commentaries of two respondents from the sample of elementary school teachers I took in the Nocorá school district. Local schools are a key place where the pharmaceutical companies like to concentrate their philanthropic and volunteer activities. So, I sampled teachers from five of the elementary schools in Nocorá, and interviewed administrators from all seven, to represent the views of people with firsthand experience of the companies.[53] On average, this sample rated the pharmaceuticals a little better than other folks on the "good faith and communication" question.

The first respondent, a lifelong resident of Nocorá, marked the questionnaire as follows: Good neighbor, more or less agree; Good faith, more or less disagree; Between good and bad, in equal proportion. On the reverse of the sheet she wrote: "A relationship of good faith, I don't believe. Seeing as they contribute to the pollution and use innumerable chemicals that can damage the community in the long-term. But, as they provide work . . ." (written as ellipsis). In spite of this acknowledgment of presumed long-term damage to the environment, and one could interpret to health, she marks "community activities" as the area she would like to see the pharmaceuticals most improve their services: "The community activities they offer are not community-oriented as such, rather only directed at the families of the people who work in the company. But offer an activity to the community close to them, never, and I have lived in this neighborhood 48 years, and I was born in the neighborhood in which I live." She made no mention of any positive participation by the companies in her school.

Another educator responded as follows: Good neighbor, more or less agree; Good faith, more or less agree; Between good and bad, more of the good. When ranking areas of needed improvement, she ranked Health and Community Activities 1 and 2 respectively, and Environment, 5 out of 5. But again, her written comments are instructive: "I would like if they helped to employ more people from the community where the industries are located, and give more help towards the necessities of the neighborhood, as a series of catastrophic illnesses have recently been noted in people close by."

The first respondent, like a number of people I spoke with, seemed to have accepted that a "good neighbor" provides economic benefits, but may not necessarily act in good faith with regard to the negative impacts they bring. Her answer also suggests that she did not believe there were great incentives for the industry to improve environmentally, or that the residential community had the ability to demand the improvement. This sentiment was echoed by many residents who said simply, "What can we do?" in response to my enquiries.

Community activities, constituting a wide range of activities such as health clinics, educational fairs for kids, street fairs, and concerts, presumably all fell into a range of things she believed the industry capable of, and potentially interested in, providing. The factories, for example, were well known for sponsoring science fairs (complete with attractive medals for the winners) and building covered basketball courts. As one informant described it, "We have more ball courts, and less physical activity than ever!" In chapter 6 I will return to the question of physical activity, and suggest ways in which it could be a vital area of positive community impact for the pharmaceutical companies. At the time of my research, however, most informants tended to view existing efforts as having limited impact.

The second respondent was interesting in that she placed both the economic *and* physical health of the community squarely in the category of responsibility of the pharmaceuticals. However, she made no explicit connection between the environment and physical health, whereas for others, particularly, though not exclusively, in Tipan, the connection was an intimate one. This may be, in part, because Tipanecos have experienced what they consider to be a more active, rather than passive, betrayal of good faith on the part of the factories. For the rest of Nocorá the pharmaceutical companies are polluters, but in a sense no one promised they would not be. Their job was generally perceived to be to make medicines, provide jobs, and act philanthropically, whereas in Tipan, there was a record of promises made and broken that went back to 1981. And, as similarly described in the principles of the Corporate Social Responsibility movement, for Tipanecos philanthropy and technical compliance were not enough, taken in account with the belief that the factories continued to cause them harm.

As can be seen in comparing these two sets of comments, and supported by the quantitative responses to the statement, "There is great concern over issues related to pollution from the pharmaceuticals," most people in Nocorá were keenly aware of the pollution from the pharmaceutical factories. At the same time people had all sorts of methods for prioritizing their concerns. For many Nocoreños environmental contamination, even if it caused distress, was more of a long-range concern. In contrast, having a peaceful life in a smaller, more traditional town was often valued highly. My neighbor

Héctor, a security guard contractor at a local factory, and a recent arrival to Nocorá from Bayamón, summed up this perspective:

> Bayamón is full of drugs. I was really young when I saw my first person with track marks on their arms. We moved here because life is tranquil— we're standing here [after dark, in front of his house] having a nice conversation, there aren't five guys down the street selling drugs, others threatening each other with guns. That's why we moved here, where there's a lot of contamination . . . but you can be safe, have a tranquil life. Life there is so stressful, so tense all the time.[54]

For Héctor and his family, environmental quality was not a factor in how peace was measured. Another neighbor, Sarita, had moved back to Nocorá after a divorce and living much of her life on the mainland. She told me that people she knew had decided not to move to our recently built neighborhood in Salvador la Cruz because of the pollution. On the other hand, she allowed, the neighborhood had been built for lower-income first-time home buyers. And many of our neighbors were not originally from Nocorá. "I'm not sure . . . if you were young, just starting out, you might not be able to move later." Sarita was not inclined to activism herself, and was not one to dwell on the broader sociopolitical implications of industrial pollution. However, she nevertheless clearly demonstrated the different levels of consciousness that were constantly at play for Nocoreños. "Nocorá does have its advantages," she acknowledged, admitting that she herself had always much preferred the life of a small town. "The trade-off is the pollution."

Positive Examples of Pharmaceutical Actions: A Case Study

The most extreme example I encountered of Nocoreños who emphasized other quality of life considerations over a clean environment was in the community organization of La Planchita, a neighborhood near the border of Bajas. A "Special Community"[55] designated by the commonwealth to receive community development support, the group in La Planchita was nevertheless very impressive in their level of organization and their accomplishments. I learned that the barrio had for many years had an organized core, led by Don Nelson, a member of a family that had long been prominent in neighborhood politics. Retired, Don Nelson was a former employee of SuperMed, whose factory was situated over the hill just behind La Planchita, and through his ongoing social ties with management he was able to promote some very effective community programming. His experience in negotiating with his former employers had also given him the *gravitas* to approach other companies directly with requests for donations to his organization.

Don Nelson's wife, Doña Alegra, was very much his partner in the organization, and contributed greatly to the administrative support of the group's activities. She explained to me that one of the reasons they were so successful was that they were well organized, and they were incorporated, an assessment echoed by the official Special Communities organizer assigned to several neighborhoods in the region. Incorporation, and the government financial oversight it required, gave potential donors confidence that the funds they gave would be used appropriately. The La Planchita community organization had, through the beneficence of at least two nearby companies, made the small building donated to them by the municipality a neat and functional space to host educational programming and planning for their future activities. I noted that the structure and their facilities (including expensive new audiovisual equipment) were superior to those used by the CDAN group in Tipan. This undoubtedly stemmed in part from the inability of CDAN to approach the companies with which they had a very confrontational relationship. However, my experience with CDAN also suggested that they lacked the more specialized type of organizational experience to seek external resources to bring their message to a broader community, or to see themselves as community leaders outside of a fairly narrow mission.[56] In contrast, Don Nelson and his group were not tied to one central theme (apart from location) and could serve as facilitators of corporate-community relationships, while at the same time advocating for local needs.

This is not to say that barrio La Planchita had been without its own environmental concerns. However, there were several issues that prevented direct confrontation with any one factory about pollution. Most obviously, Don Nelson's ties to nearby SuperMed were well known, and he both implicitly, and at times explicitly, served to reduce public criticism of the company. Not one to act in a dictatorial style, he countered questions about pollution by pointing out, accurately, that in La Planchita the pollution was much less of an issue than it used to be. Supporting his view Doña Alegra assured me that the air in the valley[57] used to be *"mortal,"* but that "now it's fine." They went on to explain how supportive the factories had been of their activities, particularly SuperMed. "We're up at the factory talking to them all the time," she told me.

One particularly interesting activity that took place in the SuperMed factory during my association with La Planchita exemplified the degree to which the factory-resident relationship represented almost an inversion of what was typical. Through his relationship with the Community Affairs office, Don Nelson and Doña Alegra arranged a workshop for factory workers, in which La Planchita members taught workers to make traditional Puerto Rican masks known as *vejigantes*. Unlike most activities coordinated between community and factory (including the one described below), the mask-making workshop created the illusion of the community bringing something of value (in this case cultural knowledge) to the corporation. It appeared to have been the ultimate feel-good activity, in which it was the community performing the act of *noblesse oblige*, for which the factory workers and management expressed gratitude. As such, it was a powerful example of the "anti-structural" reversal of roles,[58] a process through which the social order is maintained, but the lower status members feel as if higher status members have been brought down to their level.

My emphasis on the performative aspect of their relationship with SuperMed is not to say that the La Planchita community organization was not interested in the environment or in health. In fact, in the original Special Communities survey which served as a baseline for understanding the concerns and development needs of the neighborhood, 56.7 percent of residents reported that air pollution was one of their concerns related to infrastructure.[59] However, in their approach to the environment the community organization was primarily engaged in trying to get the whole barrio to recycle, a goal that matched nicely with efforts in the pharmaceutical industry to promote a narrow definiton of environmental awareness through personal responsibility. I attended an activity co-sponsored by SuperMed, the alcalde's office, and the La Planchita group, a Kite Festival, one spring afternoon. The purpose, as explained to me by the lieutenant alcalde, was to connect the goal of recycling with a family activity that also promoted outdoor exercise and good nutrition. "If your kite flies, we give you a prize. If not, we give you a prize. We're providing fruit and other healthy foods," he told me. The activity was part of a larger effort partnering with the Department of Health to try to bring the public health message of its "*Salud te recomienda*" campaign to improve eating habits and increase exercise. This program had been directed at stemming the rising tide of obesity and chronic disease, especially diabetes, on the island. The municipal administration of Nocorá had also made these health problems part of its argument for the renewal of public space in the town's urban center. However, the barriers to promoting a publicly supported exercise program were much more complex that simply a question of improving space.

To be successful, exercise promotion in neighborhoods like La Planchita and Tipan, which were not within easy walking distance of the ever-beautifying pueblo of Nocorá, needed to more directly address linger-ing local concerns about the environment. The following chapter considers the implications of high rates of diabetes in Nocorá in light of both con-ventional and more holistic approaches to environmental health. It reflects on both the negative impact and positive potential that the pharmaceutical industry has in health promotion.

Figure 6.1. An educational display presented by one of the pharmaceutical companies during the American Cancer Society's "Relay for Life" fund-raiser. The seats of the Ferris wheel are labeled with the individual responsibility strategies for addressing cancer: Nutrition, Exercise, Prevention (in this case through personal behavior modification, such as quitting smoking). Photo by the author.

"Salud te recomienda"

I met Benicia at her house and we walked to the park a few blocks away. "The program is sponsored by the Health Department," she told me, "they are providing logistical support to encourage people to walk for their health."

We climbed into the bleachers with the rest of the crowd, about 25 people, mostly women, to receive our orientation materials. Included were a t-shirt and an inexpensive pedometer, donated by a pharmaceutical company (though not one with a factory in Nocorá). After listening to a general outline of the program, we lined up to climb on a scale and receive a baseline indicator of our body fat percentage.

I was impressed with the planning that had obviously gone into the program, helping participants create realistic targets for weight loss or maintenance, and creating an environment of social support. While there might be some question as to whether an exercise program based exclusively on walking can produce significant weight loss, I got the impression that dietary advice and other types of exercise programming would be offered in tandem with the walking program. According to various sources, the Department of Health was hoping to frame these new programs for chronic problems, such as cardiovascular disease and diabetes, as a signature accomplishment of the Calderón administration. The clever title of the program, encompassing dietary and exercise recommendations to encourage behavioral change in an increasingly overweight population, blurred the lines between public health prescription and good health "common" sense.

Benicia and I walked in the afternoons for several weeks, and while there were never quite the numbers of people walking as attended on that first day, people seemed to be inspired by the program. So I was shocked when, about two weeks before the elections, I received a phone call from the regional health office, informing me that the program was being suspended until after the elections. "Please continue to exercise on your own," the voice on the other end exhorted me before hanging up.

I found out later that this turn of events, while unfortunate, was not unusual. Many programs begun by one gubernatorial administration were likely to be cancelled by the succeeding administration, including public health campaigns. Benicia and I continued to walk, but as the holidays approached, participation dwindled. Nevertheless, shortly after the new year we received notice that the sports and recreation division of the municipality would be taking up the program, and indeed they did. Though I found much to criticize about the local government, this was a definitive example of public health action, funded in part, albeit indirectly, by pharmaceutical corporate taxes. The only problem was, the program was targeted at the *pueblo urbano*, where infrastructure was receiving the most attention, and Norocá was most walkable. Additionally, air quality (due to relative distance from both the factories and the wastewater treatment plant) was reasonably good. What about the other barrios?

6

Radical Redistributions of Knowledge

A Holistic View of Environmental Health

Another assumption behind most education interventions is that knowledge flows from the top to the bottom of social hierarchies, and from experts to lay people. According to this position, if people act in ways that professionals deem unhealthy, they must do so from ignorance.

—James Trostle (2005, 126)

Asked what should be done to help the poor, otherwise articulate middle-class professionals suddenly grope for words. They profess ignorance. This, they say, enters the realm of politics and economics, neither of which is possible for ordinary people to understand. Probably it will take experts to figure it out.

—Robert Wuthnow (1996, 289)

In the evolving social relationships between corporate entities and local actors, complex forms of moral commitment and priorities continue to take shape.[1] For outside observers, these commitments frame what can look like contradictory policy decisions and alliances. In the case of Nocorá, government and corporate actors often dedicated resources to projects that were legitimately for the public good, while avoiding the deeper roots of health problems and economic stagnation. This chapter looks at some of the broader health and economic implications of the industry moving forward, and I analyze a number of examples in which the structural context makes it difficult for Nocoreños to make "good health choices." In this context, I explore strategies though which activists and educators can promote a more equitable redistribution of knowledge for the benefit of residents and employees exposed to both ambient pollution and unhealthy pharmaceutical work environments. I also suggest some philanthropic and programming opportunities for the drug companies to support these efforts, as well as a broader notion of environmental health, in the event that they are legitimately interested in changing the long-term patterns in their community relationships.

Education, Jobs, and Health

Toward the end of my fieldwork the pharmaceutical industry was taking steps to help Nocoreños attain access to the better employment that had so long eluded them. In partnership with the municipal administration, they contributed substantively to the creation of a new technical studies campus of one of the private university systems on the island. The center, which opened in 2008, was dedicated to training students in the skills needed to compete for work in the biotechnology sector. Pharmaceutical employees and high school graduates were able to pursue training in areas such as quality control, which would help them become or remain competitive for jobs in the industry. My neighbor Héctor whom, as I mentioned, was a contracted security guard at one of the local factories, had heard of the new training site:

> The new university is a great thing, because it will also help the pharmas keep employees . . . because the less well trained, they can't keep up, and eventually have to get laid off, because they haven't been well educated enough to keep increasing their training . . . and if they know that their time is short, they also are more likely to steal.

The promise of the new university was a significant source of pride among municipal leaders. One afternoon I had the opportunity to walk around Tipan with some members of the legislature, and we stopped at the site of some broken down ruins of an old coastal hotel. Expressing dismay at a location he referred to as an "ecological disaster" (figure 3.1), one of the alcalde's key allies told me that such things could hold Nocorá back. "We're going to have a University here," he said, shaking his head. The plans for the school fit Nocorá's new image, and stood in stark contrast to the ruins. The university was to be housed at the site of a renovated and remediated factory near the pharmaceutical corridor, one that was once a federal Superfund site. As such the university represented not only a future of improved economic prospects, but one in which notoriously contaminated areas could be rehabilitated for the public good.

There continued to be a few issues that threw a wrench into this very respectable endeavor to improve the competitiveness of Nocoreños in the local job market. One of the main contributions to the university by the drug industry was to make the facility as like a factory as possible, thereby making the training as hands-on as possible. However, it remained unclear whether the type of training offered (emphasizing primarily vocational skills and associate's degrees, as opposed to more advanced degrees in the chemical sciences) would open as many doors as hoped. In an interview with *Caribbean Business* in 2002, a local manager boasted that about 76 percent of the workforce in the Nocorá plant had degrees in science and engineering, allowing that the rest had vocational and technical degrees. As a percentage of an already small workforce, those high school graduates pursuing technical training with the goal of working in the pharmaceutical industry, or even in the burgeoning biotechnology sector, might be at risk of simply creating and facing stiffer competition for available work. While estimates from the 2010 Census and American Community Survey indicated that the population of Nocorá was beginning to grow, data from these same sources, as well as the Bureau of Labor Statistics, revealed that the unemployment rate in the same time period was fairly stable. These estimates also showed that only 18.3 percent of the civilian workforce was employed in manufacturing.

Additionally, there have long been educational problems that a technical university could not address as a stand-alone solution. Although all the pharmaceutical companies had education programs aimed at improving science and math achievement in local K–12 schools, there appeared to be substantial room for improvement. A series of interviews with school administrators, as well as qualitative comments submitted through the survey of elementary school teachers, suggested that there were powerful constraints on the quality and duration of pharmaceutical investment in Nocorá public schools. While the key industry players often touted their donations of lab equipment, prizes for science fairs, and the time scientists devoted to the training of science teachers, several I spoke to admitted, "We could do much more."[2] Furthermore, there remained the broader problem that significant numbers of students were failing to complete high school. This suggests that the students in need of the most help were not benefiting from existing programs. And without a high school diploma, or equivalency, they would not even qualify for enrollment in the new technical programs.

Finally there remained the crucial question of what would happen to technical workers when they finally attained their pharmaceutical jobs. It is true that the wages and benefits for those who worked full-time (as opposed to the increasing numbers of temporary workers and contract workers) were among the highest on the island. But many of these workers worked in rotating shifts, working sequentially in different eight-hour time slots. A neighbor of mine explained the rigors of working "*turnos*" in a pharmaceutical factory one evening, concluding that she had finally quit when the factory, after promising all the women on her shift a permanent work slot, shifted the worst complainers to the infamous fourth shift (working all the hours that other workers get off). Félix, who lived next door, had what was considered a highly enviable position as the leader of a team that washed tanks for PharmaGigante. While he and Julia in many ways had a stable economic life, it was evident that his rotating shift schedule took its toll in other ways, both social and physical.

The potential health consequences of shift work have been well described in the literature, the most commonly reported risk factors being related to heart disease. A significant association has been found between rotating shift work and ischemic heart disease.[3] Shift work can also be a significant predictor for abdominal obesity in workers 50 years of age or younger, and numerous studies have found higher serum triglyceride levels (and therefore increased risk of coronary heart disease) for shift workers of all ages.[4] In the year and a half I knew Félix, a strikingly handsome man in his twenties, his waistline expanded noticeably.

The health of workers in the pharmaceutical industry presents an ongoing practical challenge,[5] in spite of longstanding efforts in occupational health and safety. This stems in large part from the undeniable fact that the chemicals going into and coming out of the productive process have serious effects on human health. I heard several anecdotes from employees and residents about the consequences and concerns of working in, or even in the immediate vicinity of, the factories. A security guard explained:

> We had a training at the plant when I started working there, you know, a safety training. What to do if there is a chemical leak or something. And they told us that whatever chemical it was, you had to spray water on it, and then it would come out of the air, and could be washed away. But I kept thinking to myself, "What if it gets outside the factory? They've had explosions,[6] you know. What if it gets into the air outside, and then it rains?" But they just gave us the training like, "Here's what you do, no big deal."

Although residents and employees alike expressed great concern, the training by the pharmaceutical companies in environmental health and safety was also, ironically, received with some skepticism by their non-management employees. It may be in part because the industry had a well-known, or at least widely perceived, history of low-level concern about chemical safety. One informant, who worked for another plant in accounting, asked me if I knew that there was a man who lived down the block from his mother who used to work in one of the factories, and who had no hair left on his entire body.

Well, the dust, you know, the chemical dust, before they had those suits they wear now—well even if you wore a mask, the dust could just get into every pore. And after a while, all his hair just fell out. Like he'd had chemotherapy for cancer.

Everyone in Nocorá knew stories like these. Another woman told me that after seeing so many of her co-workers become ill, her mother eventually requested to be moved off the line and into office work for PharmaGigante.

She's worked for them for, I don't know, 25 years? And finally, she took a look around and said, "I need to get off the line." She told me she and some of her coworkers were talking about it and they realized that a lot of the women they started out working with aren't around anymore. She had one friend who got a really rare kidney disease—something that doesn't just *happen*, you know? And this woman, well, she didn't really like to follow the safety procedures. She seemed to think nothing bad was going to happen to her—she was strong, she didn't need to do that stuff. But eventually this kidney thing happened. And Mom says that it surely must be related.

Resistance to factory-based discipline techniques can be construed as "weapons of the weak"[7] and surely fits into the Puerto Rican cultural idiom of *bregar*. Workers may feel temporary victory over their bosses or the company by not following safety protocols, but in the long run their triumph is hollow. Such actions often have primarily short-term benefits for workers, and are unlikely to serve to create a substantial basis for class-based struggle.[8] In this setting *la brega* became an endless war of position, or minor victories, forever failing to culminate in paradigm-changing wars of maneuver (as Antonio Gramsci[9] would distinguish them). Negrón-Muntaner has offered a powerful argument that the techniques of la brega (such as jaibería) may have contributed to the success of social movements, such as ousting the navy from Vieques.[10] However, resistance to capitalist discipline in the form of ignoring rules on the pharmaceutical factory floor has little potential to disrupt production at a cost to the corporation. From a public health perspective, the celebration of "agency," or the making of choices within the narrow boundaries available to workers and residents explored in the present research, opened a space in which there were few options for gaining ground in comparison to the personal damage it could create. In an extreme example such as the woman described above, some workers chose to put themselves, and even others, at risk by refusing to comply with safety regulations in a factory setting. I spoke with other residents who reported that they would not accept a job on the factory line because the safety regulations were too burdensome, and the remuneration for the temporary position was not worth it.[11] These acts can be construed as ways to maintain one's sense of self in such a corporate-dominated environment, both inside and outside factory fences. I would argue that this is the result when institutions like corporations and government exploit the language, and even at times the form, of family and community while simultaneously sending the message in published materials and other modes of communication—"everyone for herself."

In public health, these kinds of observations are not necessarily new, and the discourse about occupational safety parallels the highly problematic traditional clinical and public health framing of "compliance" and "difficult" patients. We still have few practical tools being mobilized to deal with, on a *structural level*, those broader components of negative health outcomes, which are only becoming more entrenched through public policy.[12] As anthropologists, we should be able to contribute meaningfully to the policy conversation by documenting the specific, grounded connections between these structural discourses, and health behaviors or other health outcomes.[13] Furthermore, in a cultural atmosphere that emphasizes the individual responsibility for causes of disease, we need to better understand the well-worn question of social and cultural "variables" in disease causation, the shared burden, and the broadly defined environmental cause, of community-based illnesses. These co-occurring problems are best understood as "syndemics," or health outcomes with intersecting contributing causes, and which mutually exacerbate disease and mortality.[14]

Health Promotion and "Responsibility" in
the Production of Knowledge

The official epidemiology of Tipan, in terms of what was prioritized by the municipal administration, did not contain evidence of unique health problems. What local data they had came from the municipal clinic,[15] but as the health care resources of Nocorá were limited, and there were many hospitals in Bajas at which people might seek care instead, there were limits to these data. Additional data by municipality were available from the Department of Health, but these were for the entire population of Nocorá. Based on the commonwealth data for Nocorá and its neighboring municipalities, in terms of both reported morbidity and mortality, Nocorá was an outlier in what might have been a surprising disease category: diabetes.[16]

Given the available data, it is not surprising that during my interview with the lieutenant alcalde (who was in charge of health policy for the municipality), he emphasized public health programming directed at diet and exercise. When asked about health concerns in the municipality, he acknowledged that the director of the municipal clinic had reported that Nocorá had somewhat higher rates of cancer, though he did not know the numbers specifically. "Not like Vieques,"[17] he assured me. In jumping right to a concern about cancer he inadvertently disclosed two underlying assumptions: (1) that carcinogens were perceived as being a concern, and that therefore, (2) cancer was presumed to be the most significant risk from a polluted environment. These biases, while very common, can have profound policy implications. By referring to the perceived cancer-environment connection, and then minimizing the cancer concern, he downplayed environmental health as a whole.

In a further effort to shift the focus away from the environment, he stated that lifestyles were more his concern than pollution-related disease, particularly diets high in fat and alcohol. Stressing his belief that education was important, he praised Dr. Johnny Rullán (the secretary of health at the time, and member of his own PPD party), saying that the "*Salud te recomienda*" campaign was going in the right direction. It was extremely unfortunate, he said with passion, that people did not understand that nutrition and exercise were the keys to public health. Citing in support of his statement that the health secretary was an epidemiologist, the lieutenant alcalde reasoned, "he would know the causes of disease." Absent from the conversation about obesity and its role as a risk factor for heart disease and diabetes were questions about the role of both environmental and occupational health considerations for all three. As evidenced in the design of the kite-making workshop described in chapter 5, this public official embodied the belief that if people could just be brought out into the open air for a fun activity, and be offered free fruit, they would begin to exercise and eat more healthily. From this perspective government, perhaps in conjunction with partners in private industry, was primarily responsible for identifying problems, and providing information. There was an assumed relationship between the possession of knowledge, combined with the right attitude (or belief), to predict health practices, known as KAP in public health.[18] The notion of KAP assumes that the individual is responsible for acquiring and maintaining the "right attitude" toward his or her personal health, and consequently, that if the individual has the knowledge and fails to behave in a healthy manner, then the individual is at fault. Though research has identified the existence of a KAP-gap,[19] or patterns of behavior in which knowledge does not accurately predict practice, there remains a persistent belief present in health discourse around chronic disease that the individual ultimately bears responsibility for the gap. In the present example, if exercise is one of the primary cures for obesity, and therefore a weapon against heart disease and diabetes, we must reframe the approach to the solution. We must ask: What are the factors that limit people's abilities to make "healthy choices" about not only diet, but exercise? How can we expect people to "get outside" when they perceive the air outside to be harmful to them?

In his classic collection *Health, Culture and Community*, Benjamin Paul wrote that the success of public health programs requires starting "with people as they are and the community as it is," and further stipulating that "a willingness to meet them must be matched by a knowledge of the meeting place."[20] James Trostle invoked Paul's words in his work *Epidemiology and Culture*, reminding readers that the anthropological perspective that helps reveal local rationalities and ways of seeing can help inform epidemiological practice, which is both methodologically robust and community-relevant.[21] My research supports these theoretical and practical orientations, arguing that environmental as well as epidemiological investigative activities in communities should not be mysterious to the participants (i.e., to the members of the communities requesting the study). It is too easy to treat the scientific investigation of disease and/or environment as an expert-policed black box, with seemingly unrelated, or worse, misleading, survey questions or research methods as the first line of defense.

As previously described, one of the proposed epidemiological surveys for Tipan emphasized personal behaviors that could lead to respiratory problems, such as diet, exercise, and smoking habits. While a public health practitioner might see these questions as necessary control variables, community leaders and their professional activist advisors saw them as designed to "blame the victim" in a survey that, to their knowledge, did not account for environmental variables. In the absence of a measurement of ambient air quality, or the content of air exhaled from the lungs of residents, the health survey was virtually guaranteed to find a relationship between any number of control variables and participants' reported health problems. And in the case of Tipan specifically, there is evidence that the intent, as it was understood among public health workers, was not value-free. Indeed, while all previous efforts to address health concerns in Tipan avoided the methodology of testing air quality, the settlement of the lawsuit in 2008 eventually required that precisely that action be taken. The community's concerns were clearly justified.

Professionals working in specialized fields notoriously find it irksome to work with "the community"; I have even heard this aversion expressed, in its most extreme, as "a horror," both in Puerto Rico and on the mainland. In my own field experience I encountered this attitude on a number of occasions, as I was sometimes identified by people of authority (such as a field investigator from the Environmental Quality Board) as something of an "expert" myself, if only because I had substantially higher academic credentials than many of my Tipan informants.[22]

Epidemiological methods do not necessarily have to be sacrificed when working with communities unfamiliar with those methods. However, public health professionals must be more broadly aware of the contexts of their work, and be able to anticipate, for example in an investigation of air pollution, concerns the community might have about the role of certain questions in a survey. Field workers conducting the surveys must build rapport, at a minimum, with designated community leaders who were likely involved in bringing the study to the location in the first place. Working together to use the research methods as a way of sharing information with the people themselves should be a priority as much as collecting rigorous data. Indeed, having to engage with non-experts in this manner may well be one way to guard against, as Marilyn Nations put it, the dangers of intellectual rigor mortis in pursuing quantitative rigor.[23] Additionally, the use of new technologies, such as GIS mapping and sophisticated air or water testing equipment, is an example of how expertise can, even inadvertently, obfuscate the knowledge-gathering process for community nonexperts. Orientation to the uses of technology, and ideally, development of programs to train local groups to monitor their own air and water quality, should not serve to simply dazzle. Speaking from the experience of working in Tipan on such a project, I know it can be frustrating and time-consuming to bridge technical and local understandings. But that does not absolve those of us who have the status of "experts," ostensibly working for the public good, from treating knowledge itself *as* a public good. For example, when testing the pH of a local water source, the reading itself is unlikely to be meaningful to a person without a high school level background in science. However, to be able to say that a measurement of three is "roughly the same as vinegar" can give a concrete sense to an otherwise context-free number. Explaining concepts like "within the range of normal" can also make unfamiliar measurements less intimidating. Likewise, technical experts can learn a great deal from local residents about the history and social context in which they are taking measurements and gathering other data.

Janice Harper, writing about minority communities and air pollution in Houston, observes:

> If anything, community-based public health efforts regarding asthma have been focused on changing the perceptions of asthmatics and their families, making them more cognizant of their own role in degrading their environments by not cleaning up the mold, by not washing their sheets well enough, by not eradicating cockroaches. Although cockroaches and dust mites do, indeed, contribute to asthma, such educational programs remain top-down. They draw out people's perceptions of their health and environment in order to reshape them.[24]

In situations like those of Tipan's residents, there are additional constraints on the practical study of environment-related health problems. The necessity (acknowledged by people on several sides of the problem) of a lawsuit to bring the plant into good operational status created a situation in which a health needs assessment could not be carried out without prejudicing the legal outcome. The specifics of the Tipan case have also exacerbated the process of "delegitimation" of personal experience of illness through expert knowledge.[25] Absent standard measures of disease, it is easy for health officials to claim that no problem is present.

This rendering of chronic suffering as socially invisible is frequently reported by sufferers of chronic pain in a variety of examples.[26] Research in ethnomedicine and so-called alternative healing systems suggests that, grounded in Turner's formulation of communitas,[27] the positive-belief-trust complex engendered by the sharing of difficult experiences and consequent emergence into a more complete, socially whole person, serves to support the healing process. If so, then the isolation and delegitimation[28] faced by Tipan residents in the social and political processes through which their physical suffering was denied was contrary to communitas, and disrupted their abilities to heal.

In Puerto Rico, and particularly in Nocorá, the process of changing perceptions has been further manipulated by the sponsorship of culture, and the insinuation and cementing of the corporate presence into the local community through ritual and celebrated association with local government. Thus, the government and its corporate partners have been able to play both sides of the equation to their own advantage: they have gained communal goodwill by performing a brand of social responsibility, while encouraging individual responsibility for health outcomes. And yet, as we have seen in the example of the respiratory problems in Tipan, there was a significant household and community burden of caregiving produced by chronic ailments. Further research as to how it has affected day-to-day household economics and other dynamics would be necessary to evaluate this burden, but there is no doubt about its existence. Finally, the importance of trust for perceptions of risk[29] cannot be underestimated in Tipan. Given the potential for a patient's negative experiences and expectations to influence health outcomes and affective state (as in a *placebo* or *nocebo* effect),[30] low levels of *confianza* appear to compound a variety of chronic problems for the seaside residents.

And so, with reference to a place that is axiomatically clichéd as a "paradox," I would like to suggest yet another theoretical paradox with potential for policy relevance: On the one hand there is no doubt that individual behavior, embedded in an environment compromised by corporate behavior, continues to have a measureable impact on health in Puerto Rico. On the other hand, overemphasizing the agency, or "resilience" of Tipanecos or other Puerto Ricans for the sake of not "speaking for the subaltern" or supporting their human dignity, relieves the pharmaceuticals and the various government agencies and actors discussed of their collective responsibility.

Consciousness and Communitas: El Pais
Posible [The Possible Country]

I have expropriated the tagline "El Pais Posible" from the Special Communities (SC) propaganda as the subheading of this section because I believe that one of the underlying messages of the SC initiative was that corporate sponsorship was and will be part of the solution to Puerto Rico's socioeconomic woes. If not through sponsorship outright, this will occur through corporate-community partnerships, with the benevolent facilitation of government, as exemplified by the activities and relationships of barrio La Planchita (chapter 5). In some cases SC leaders have called into question the benevolence of the municipal governments, because, as Don Nelson put it, many of them "*no quieren bregar con las comunidades*" [they don't want to work/struggle with/ alongside the community]. Many SC leaders believed, and my observations suggest correctly in some cases, that the alcaldes have found too much community empowerment threatening. In such cases, leaders who did not have combative relationships with local industry could find it tempting to align themselves with businesses, who in turn seemed to appreciate their new-found capacity and, from a certain perspective, enlightened self-interest.

The traditional environmental rhetoric in Puerto Rico is closely allied with that of political independence, because it is based in a critique of a colonized mentality.[31] In this frame it is easy to diagnose certain kinds of anti-environment behavior as being the product of a dependence mentality: throwing the trash over the fence, or leaving garbage on the beach becomes an exercise in independence simply because it is the least responsible way of dealing with it (bearing a resemblance to the factory worker not following safety regulations). A useful critique of dependence, however, as explored in earlier chapters, goes much deeper than advocacy for political independence. In order to be successful, those with environmental concerns need to forge understandings of local connectedness and commitment, rather than political independence.[32]

This connectedness might sound suspiciously like the idealistic demand of the Corporate Social Responsibility movement to promote and engage in so-called stakeholder dialogue. However, dialoguing with stakeholders has proven to be a much easier mandate to fulfill if corporations are able to effectively choose who gets to be a stakeholder, and who does not. In some cases representation of "the community" emerged in an arguably more organic fashion.[33] However, cementing these positive, noncombative relationships with select segments, combined with structural limits on participation in public forums, allowed for the isolation and diminution of adversaries like those in Tipan.[34] Likewise, the limited resources of public health, however well-meaning, were ultimately marshaled in support of these exclusionary narratives of progress, either through the failure to prioritize the needs of a small group of people, or more insidiously, by filtering out important data through study design.

The group CDAN of Tipan was unique because they worried about the future in a way that was *specific to the environment*, as opposed to politics or economy or symbolic culture. They had become environmental subjects, a process often achieved through the perception of a very direct threat to one's ecology[35] (and often health). Returning once again to Wilk's framework (figure 5.2), the more people are able to embody concerns that reach out from the immediate present and the immediate self, the more quickly they have consciousness of the connection between themselves and their environment, or, "environmentality."[36] In Nocorá, as in many places, concerns over economics combined with social rituals of dependence served to muddle the connections between ecology and survival. If representatives of the pharmaceutical industry had wished to act on legitimate concerns for the long-term health of Nocorá and Nocoreños, those decision-makers would have invested in programs and people that fomented the sense of connectedness people felt between their environment and their immediate and long-term health. However, the industry, like at times the professional sciences represented in medicine, public health, and environmental administration, has had too much invested in the persistent disconnect from local community to accomplish meaningful change.

The contrast between La Planchita and Tipan is useful in illustrating the consequences of two different tactical approaches within the industry: Tipan had, to a certain degree, achieved its "environmentality" because it had never really been the subject of corporate philanthropy or goodwill. Geographically separate from the industrial parks of Salvador, waste arriving in Tipan was already de-identified with any one particular factory, eliminating the theoretical incentive for any one corporation, except the water company (PRASA), to perform as a good neighbor. The lawsuit by CDAN on behalf of the Tipanecos, even if it failed to establish a legal liability, was the only means by which this isolated group of residents could create a binding *social* liability to improve the plant. In La Planchita, while a general legal liability for improving air quality had been enforced by federal regulation on individual factories, there also existed an undeniable social relationship to local residents, in which the companies needed to work to some degree (however limited) to socially acknowledge and engage with those who lived nearby.

The greatest barrier to these steps for social (and thereby health and environmental) progress is that in general corporations have little or no incentive to alter their established patterns of behavior. In early 2012, the *New York Times* reported on an explosion in a factory in China that supplied components for Apple's best-selling iPad, a deadly accident that brought the issue of CSR front and center in the global news cycle. Among other points made in the story,[37] Apple's contradictory attitude toward health and safety along its supply chain exemplifies the primacy of the corporate desire to reduce costs. While sources from within the company asserted that there was a commitment to maintaining Apple's code of conduct for suppliers, they nevertheless admitted that, like for the pharmaceutical industry, such a high premium was placed on competition and secrecy that accountability ultimately suffered. In conclusion, the authors noted that without intense outside pressure, primarily from consumers, companies like Apple will focus on their bottom line. As one Apple executive was quoted as saying, "right now, customers care more about a new iPhone than working conditions in China."[38] In the case of pharmaceuticals, customers are likewise reluctant to demand any changes that could cause already high drug prices to go up, though they do express concerns about the safety of the products themselves. Still, average consumers have little awareness of the conditions of drug production, let alone any downstream environmental impact.

Modeling the Redistribution of Knowledge

In order to accomplish change what is necessary is a radical redistribution of knowledge. One example of how corporate philanthropy by the pharmaceutical companies could contribute to transformative social responsibility would be through the funding of competitive, no-strings, grants for groups of a certain (small) size to create locally based education and information sharing. Several pharmaceutical companies tout their "no-strings" grants for high-tech basic science research. These grants are good investments in the system which produces the lifeblood of the industry, and also produces goodwill between individual "star" scientists and industry. Nevertheless, they are investments in an abstract future benefit, one aspect of the perspective necessary for the grants I am recommending, and which I do not think is the biggest leap for corporate perspectives. Providing opportunities for communities to choose their own environmental priorities, however, also opens the possibility that the companies themselves might come under scrutiny, which makes the plan unlikely. However, examples of this kind of activity do exist, some of which were presented in a 2005 CSR conference in San Juan.

If funding incorporated groups is generally considered necessary to ensure non-profit status and financial reporting, then one of the areas targeted for funding should be to provide the necessary resources for grassroots groups to engage in the process of incorporation. Further funds should be made available for the purchase of equipment and the hiring of experts *of an organized community's own choosing*, to create community-based knowledge-sharing programs between public health and environmental protection representatives and residents and workers concerned about their health and the environment. As concerns about conflict of interest would inevitably arise as soon as environmental groups began receiving funds from pharmaceutical companies, I suggest that the funds be deposited in a mixed account, to be administered by a consortium constituted primarily of representatives of resident-based organizations. The governing board could have one or two industry representatives, as well as representatives from organizations such as TransformaRSE, to monitor transparency in the grant-giving process. Members of the board would be prohibited from receiving any additional payments or consulting fees of any kind from industry organizations. The desired effect on the relationship between individual monies and individual industry interest would be similar to that between individual wastes and individual industries: pooling the funds together would disperse the social obligations felt by any individual community group to any one company. Additionally, companies would need to make long-term commitments to the funding pool, reducing the concern that any actions critical of the industry would result in immediate reduced funding.[39]

An example of the kind of knowledge-exchange relationship I am promoting was demonstrated by several environmental activists who provided support to CDAN over many years. An environmental economics professor who grew up in Nocorá expressed her approach to building community knowledge and capacity bases like this: "When I come here, I don't come here as a professor. I come here as Paula." She acknowledged that they treated her with the respect accorded a highly educated person in Puerto Rico, but she was always mindful that their knowledge, and their priorities, while at times different than those she might choose, were important. She tried to share with them knowledge to which she had access, such as the equipment and technical ability necessary to measure certain water quality indicators. And while it was sometimes an uphill battle, in part because many of the older members of CDAN were so impressed by the technology, she warned that technology is not sufficient. "There are people who mean well, who sweep in and give impressive presentations, using GIS mapping and PowerPoint—and then they sweep out again." When technology takes the place of communication, at the end of the day the community is not really left in a different knowledge state than they were before.

The approach of redistributing knowledge was also echoed by another environmental advisory group in a series of educational activities they sponsored called "Measuring Our Beach." In the face of overbuilding on the coasts, including the receipt of permits to build in zones which were at regular risks for flooding due to tidal flows, the workshops brought groups of residents in beach neighborhoods to physically measure the maritime zones. The workshop created a physical (or embodied) experience, as well as an intellectual understanding of the meanings of the laws that were meant to protect the publicly owned, severely ecologically burdened shorelines. As such, the activities contributed to a sense of shared ownership of the coastal resources, which the organizers hoped would improve accountability in the regulation of construction and tourism.

Conclusion

In a 1999 article on the risks of groundwater contamination in Puerto Rico, Constantina Skanavis argued that a combination of targeted educational programs (sponsored by EPA) and engagement with religious leaders to raise environmental consciousness would be the ingredients to a successful public health campaign on that issue. Relying on a study of political attitudes from the late 1960s, Skanavis proposed to make use of the tendencies toward what I have described as the island's personalistic political relationships in order to spread environmental awareness about both institutional and personal risk behaviors. She particularly suggested that traditional Church hierarchies would be useful, because "The traditional Puerto Rican understanding of a leader involves someone who defines the goals of the group, makes decisions for it, and sees to it that they are carried out."[40] While this may be an understandable means-to-an-end formula for raising environmental awareness, I believe it is ultimately counterproductive, because it completely overlooks the need for ownership of and connectedness to knowledge and place.

In contrast, Arturo Escobar's recent framing of a political ecology is attentive not only to inequality, but to difference across a broad range of areas related to the environment and to culture.[41] He argues for recognition of the inextricable relationship between the degradation of the environment and the degradation of local cultures. Conflicts over ecological distribution, such as the changes wrought on the landscape, air, and waters of Nocorá by the presence and pollution of the pharmaceutical industry, have modified the ways in which people relate to their environment. Thus, broadening the narrow cultural ecology equation between physical work and culture,[42] the fact that the waters in which children used to swim are now visibly contaminated, for example, resonates throughout the local culture. The local knowledge base has been forever altered, although the conflict of expertise I have described created an ongoing contest of local versus scientific knowledge. In this contest decisions made about protecting community health are often compromised.

Finally, in the context of Puerto Rico there are many challenges, economic, cultural, and political, facing communities in their transition along the axes of Wilk's decision-making framework, described in earlier chapters. As Jorge Duany has described it, Puerto Rico is ever-increasingly a "nation on the move," at once transnational and fiercely nationalistic; mobile, and yet emotionally tied to the island.[43] These qualities create a society, both on and off the island, rich in contradictions, ambivalent about political status, and economically and politically dependent in ways that can likewise contradict a sustained commitment to environmental protection and alternatives to high-intensity industrialization. These same qualities do have the potential to become technologies of mobilization, under some circumstances, as exemplified by the success of the protests against the navy in Vieques.[44] However, workers and residents alike must be attentive to the ways in which refusing certain types of corporate or government order can be detrimental to their health. Rejection of occupational health protections or refusing to participate in public health programs can be counterproductive in the long run.

A radical redistribution of knowledge, as well as a greater valuation placed on local residential knowledge of the environment, is essential to ensure the sustained local connectedness that is required for long-term ecological accountability of corporate entities, government agencies, and local residents. Only through an unrelenting commitment to this broad understanding of community health and well-being will Nocorá, and indeed all of Puerto Rico, achieve some degree of ecological balance, and sustainability.

Figure E.1. The author with members of CDAN, surveying the land and water of Tipan.

In the time following my fieldwork several important events changed, and may yet change, the everyday lives of Nocoreños. The Tipan court case was declared a class action and was settled for several million dollars, including substantial investments in infrastructure for the wastewater treatment plant, and the hiring of a professional monitor. In the context of such settlements the dollar amount was not actually that significant, and at most families in Tipan received a few thousand dollars. The majority of residents nevertheless accepted the settlement in the spirit of hoping that it would create long-term accountability for management of the plant. In conversations with residents in 2011, however, they still expressed concerns. Don Eduardo, whose efforts with CDAN had become reinvigorated since the settlement, expressed the ongoing potential for pollution as "still worrying." In addition to sporadic problems with odors, residents remained extremely concerned about the potential for water pollution from runoff from the fields where the sludge from the plant was spread for recycling. In 2012, after years of being told how harmless the process was, the sludge program was finally brought to an end.

In the summer of 2012, working in conjunction with both of the Tipan community groups, we inaugurated a water monitoring program through the World Water Monitoring Challenge (www.worldwatermonitoringday. org). While sophisticated equipment for such a program would be expensive, through programs like WWMC, communities can gain access to tools to measure basic water quality. The posting of the data in a global internet database would be one step toward creating both awareness and accountability for local environments.

In a more surprising turn of events, the alcalde, whom I have called Estrello Martínez, was arrested and confined without bail, on charges of accepting bribes from contractors in exchange for privileged access to certain potential construction sites. The story, as it trickled out into the media, gave cause for some vindication of local community and environmental activists and critics who had long expressed concern over his style of governance. As one media commentator put it with a shrug, "absolute power corrupts absolutely." Officials chose to keep him locked up during the arraignment and trial because he was judged, based on threats he made at various times, to be a danger to himself and others. These threats gave further credence to reports that in dealing with Tipanecos in particular, he had used tactics of intimidation. He pleaded guilty to several charges, and it appears likely that he will spend several years in prison. His former planner, who had bragged to me about being in charge of deciding which properties to expropriate, was likewise charged, and cooperated with authorities in the investigation.

The arrest was the final straw in a year that had seen Martínez come under increasing scrutiny from agencies and concerned advocates outside of Nocorá. In particular, it was found by a government investigation that he had broken the law in the process of expropriating several properties in Tipan, unlawfully taking both homes and businesses from longtime residents. This action gave rise to a new social movement in the neighborhood of Barco de Caña at the far eastern border of Tipan, where a new generation of activists created new and intriguing strategies to contest the development plans of the alcalde. In particular, the group organized around a group of interrelated concerns, the environment, cultural patrimony, and community, linking their own personal histories and property rights with protection of the environment and the broader history of Nocorá and beyond. They offer small workshops in local crafts, hold informational meetings in the community, and also coordinated the legal actions against the alcalde for illegal expropriations.

In Puerto Rico more broadly I noted that the CSR movement had weakened substantially, in part due to the heavy weight of the late-2000s economic crisis. In speaking to members of TranformaRSE I received the impression that what limited impulse toward partnerships had existed before had diminished under the perceived limitation on financial resources combined with increasing global hostility toward corporations. As I have described the internal culture of the organization, they found their hands tied in an economy where companies were tending to retreat into severe cost-cutting and fear of creative engagement. I noted this retreat symbolically in Nocorá, where the site of the much-hyped "symbolic planting" (figure 5.1) had been leveled in favor of building a new drugstore in a nearby lot.

The emergence of powerful anti-corporate movements in 2011, exemplified by the Occupy Wall Street protests, resonated with Nocoreños I spoke with. However, these social movements had not yet caused most to rethink their community's ongoing ties to the pharmaceuticals in a substantial way. And in spite of the apparent success of the new training schools, according to the most recent data from the USDA's Economic Research Service, Nocorá's unemployment rate was 2.4 percent higher than the island-wide average, and remained much closer to rural municipalities than urban metropolitan areas. In the wake of the alcalde's resignation it was reported that the town had a significant budget deficit, which would severely limit planned development projects. In response to this reality, the new activists in Tipan were proposing a new approach to local development, in which small businesses like those providing services for visitors to the local beaches would take a lead. This new movement, while still quite small, suggested that a cultural shift in Nocorá had begun, in which the potential for local connectedness I have described had the possibility to take root.

A. Demographic information (please circle the option that represents you).

1. Gender: M / F

2. Age: 18–24   25–29   30–34   35–39   40–44   45–49   50–54   55–59
60–64   65–69   70–74   75–79   80 or more

3. Municipality of Residence: Nocorá/other Northern Region/other non-Northern Region (if not Nocorá, skip to #5)

4. Sector of Municipality: Tipan / Bo. Pueblo / Salvador la Cruz / Delfín / Cañita Afuera

5. How long have you lived in the Northern Region? (if you are not from the North, skip to #6)
___ Years ___ Months

6. Do you or a family member work for, or have you or a family member ever worked for, a pharmaceutical?
Mark all those that apply: You / Family Member / None

B. Questions about the relationship between the pharmaceutical industry and the community. Please circle the option that *best* represents your opinion:

1. Our quality of life would be worse if the pharmaceutical industry leaves Puerto Rico.
Totally agree / More or less agree / More or less disagree / Totally disagree

2. There is great concern over issues related to pollution from the pharmaceuticals.
Totally agree / More or less agree / More or less disagree / Totally disagree

3. The pharaceuticals maintain a relationship of good faith and good communication with the community.
Totally agree / More or less agree / More or less disagree / Totally disagree

4. The pharmaceuticals are good neighbors, like part of our community.
Totally agree / More or less agree / More or less disagree / Totally disagree

5. Between the good and the bad things that the pharmaceuticals bring to our community:
There are more of the bad / There are equal amounts / There are more of the good

6. The pharmaceuticals offer the best community services in (mark in order, best to worst, 1–5):
____ education   ____ sports   ____ health
____ environment/nature   ____ community activities

7. The pharmaceuticals should do more in the area of (mark 1 as the most important, 5 as the least important):
____ education   ____ sports   ____ health
____ environment/nature   ___ community activities

If you have any additional comments, you may write them on the other side of this sheet.

INTRODUCTION

1. Angell 2004; Newman 2009.
2. USAToday 2009.
3. All told my time spent in Puerto Rico has totaled over 18 months, including exploratory research and language study in the summer of 2001, as well as several shorter return trips in 2008 and 2011.
4. See Michaels 1988.
5. Bakan 2004.
6. 477 F. Supp. 2nd 413; U.S. Dist. LEXIS 12067. The general aim of the Clean Water Act (CWA) is to prevent the discharge of pollutants into navigable waters of the United States, including its states, territories, possessions, and authorized tribal lands. The CWA also seeks to protect wildlife and provide for the recreational uses of water. It is worth noting that in recent years there has been some debate in the courts over what exactly constitutes "navigable waters," and there has been some attempt to weaken the jurisdiction of the CWA by disputing that some creeks and smaller bodies are not "navigable." This perspective makes it clear that even in a pro-environment law such as the CWA, there is a strong economic undercurrent of value on water itself, as the classifying of water as "navigable" assumes the possibility of commercial use (33 U.S.C.S. § 1251).
7. Of course, as do many Puerto Ricans in the early twenty-first century.
8. See particularly Whyte et al. 2002; van der Geest and Whyte 1991.
9. See Nichter 1996; Petryna et al. 2006.
10. Webster's Dictionary (online) 2006.
11. See Benson and Kirsch 2010; Welker et al. 2011 for a review.
12. See e.g. Grimes 1984; Hunter and Arbona 1995; Kennicutt et al. 1984; Skanavis 1999.
13. Pharmaceutical Research and Manufacturers of America 2007.
14. The move toward CSR, an outgrowth of earlier practices of corporate philanthropy, makes this research even more important, as our knowledge of these areas of society has typically been collected under the auspices of the quantitatively driven disciplines at home in schools of business (e.g., Vogel 2005). These studies, while very useful in understanding the field as a whole, are often carried out by researchers with an interest in "best practices" rather than critique, have said little about the qualitative impact of business on an ethnographic scale (see Auyero and Swistun 2009; Partridge et al. 2011; Welker 2009 for exceptions).
15. In smaller scale societies, sociopolitical organization may rely more heavily on kinship networks. Arguably, even in more complex societies with larger-scale institutions, who

190 190 << NOTES TO INTRODUCTION

you know, or who you are, can still matter a great deal. All of these relationships are ultimately constructed and given meaning through culture.

16. Turner 1969.
17. Davila 1997, xv.
18. Paul 1955.
19. Checker 2007; Satterfield 1997.
20. See e.g. Bakan 2004; Kairys 2010; Korton 2001, for discussion of the theoretical and
    applied legal question of how corporations came to be considered *persons* under U.S. law.
    The legitimacy of the claims of corporate personhood is an ongoing debate of significant
    social and political importance.
21. See e.g. Briggs 2002.
22. An early critical medical anthropology study of the effects of industrialization on a
    Puerto Rican community suggested that anthropologists needed to pay as much attention
    to unemployment, politics, and corporate policies as to "folk" aspects of local culture
    (Susser 1985). Emerging scholars of CMA have taken up crucial questions of the health
    consequences of militarization (Torres-Velez 2010), HIV/AIDS policy (Garriga-Lopez
    2010), and managed care practices (Mulligan 2010), all of which are of vital importance
    in twenty-first-century Puerto Rican life. My research is in dialog with this work, and has
    been vitally informed by it.
23. This refers to risk assessed by strictly statistical methods, such as by epidemiologists and
    insurance actuaries (see Krieger 1994; Marchant 2003; Susser 1994). As Checker (2005,
    2007) and others have noted, political pressure (see also Freudenburg 2005; Griffith 1999;
    Satterfield 1997, 2002), economic rewards, and even methodological limitations (see
    Susser and Susser 1996a, 1996b) can influence the outcomes of the most rigorous-appear-
    ing risk assessment, particularly when the variables in question are environmental.
24. See e.g. Beck 1992; Boholm 2003; Douglas and Wildavsky 1982.
25. Boholm 2003.
26. Slovic 1999.
27. Susser and Susser 1996b.
28. In research exemplified by anthropologist Merrill Singer (see 1989, 1995, 1998; Singer and
    Baer 1995) two main theoretical foci are interrelated: (1) to make central to the under-
    standing of health and illness political and economic forces that create class inequalities
    (often compounded and confounded by racial and ethnic discrimination), and therefore
    unequal access to basic nutritional sources and health services, and unequal exposure to
    harm; and (2) to critique applied anthropological work that has, unwittingly or not, been
    "handmaiden" of hegemonic health institutions, while suggesting concrete, politically
    informed examples of applied health work (see Singer 1995).
29. McElroy and Townsend 2008; Johnston 2011.
30. Baer and Singer 2008.
31. Singer 2009.
32. See Farmer 1996.
33. Scheper-Hughes and Lock 1987.
34. See Watts and Bohle 1993.
35. Leatherman 2005.
36. Ethnographic literature on the environment, development, and globalization has exploded
    in recent years (e.g. Agrawal 2005; Tsing 2004). These studies engage theoretically along
    the axes of culture and power, addressing the question of what happens when traditionally

isolated communities meet the world economic system, global and local bureaucracies, becoming what Agrawal has termed "environmental subjects." Likewise, the work of Arturo Escobar (e.g. 2006) in the field of political ecology is concerned with locally situated economies, ecologies, and their cultural qualities. Escobar's research emphasizes the importance of localized access to, and ownership of knowledge for, those traditionally disempowered. This emphasis on the value and control of knowledge is central to my own research. However, following the admonition not to lose sight of the ecology in political ecology (Vayda and Walters 1999), I have also attempted to ground my analyses in historical and ecological data, so as to examine the interaction between social dynamics and the environment itself over time.

37. Auyero and Swistun 2009.
38. Hawken 1993.
39. Padilla Seda 1966 [1956]; Seda Bonilla 1964.
40. See appendix.
41. See also Nash and Kirsch 1988.
42. That is to say, a statistical analysis of a potential exposure-disease relationship.

CHAPTER 1

This chapter is based on my essay *Corrosion in the System*, which received the Virchow Award from the Critical Anthropology of Health Caucus, and material from it has been published in a different format (Dietrich 2008). Used by permission of The Rowman & Littlefield Publishing Group.

1. George 2008.
2. This is not only the case for wastewater. There has been increased concern over the need to manage solid waste, and corresponding debates over the building of incinerators versus other options.
3. Padilla Seda 1966 [1956]; Seda Bonilla 1964.
4. The term *urbanización* is used to describe a defined area of residential development, while *parcelas* are individual allotments within that defined area. The name of an urbanization is often used as part of the postal address.
5. Singer 1998: 107.
6. See e.g. Brown 1992.
7. National Center for Environmental Health 2005. In chapter 2 I will return to the theme of Environmental Impact Assessment (EIA). It is worth noting, perhaps with a touch of irony, that in spite of a highly contentious debate in the literature regarding environmental causes of cancer and the ability to statistically detect them (see, e.g., Ames and Gold 1998; Epstein et al. 2002), cancer has long been essentially the *only* disease risk evaluated in the EIA process.
8. Windsor 2006.
9. See Hunter and Arbona 1995; Office of Drinking Water 1979.
10. García-Martínez 1982; Neumann 1981.
11. Agencia EFE 1998.
12. Kennicutt et al. 1984.
13. Neumann 1981.
14. Office of Drinking Water 1979.
15. Hunter and Arbona 1995.
16. García-Martínez 1977; Goitía n.d.

17. García-Martinez 1975.
18. Neumann 1981.
19. Goitía n.d.
20. López Acevedo 1976; Partido Socialista Puertorriqueño 1977.
21. Goitía n.d.; Kennicutt et al. 1984.
22. The original dumpsite for untreated wastes was approximately 45 miles offshore, with an estimated depth of 3.5 miles. See Kennicutt et al. 1984.
23. A more recent project to build a deep-water ocean outfall pipe for the Ponce Regional Wastewater Treatment Plant on Puerto Rico's southern coast underwent an extensive design and revision process, due to the complexities of placing such a pipe in high-force ocean waters. The ultimate distance for the outfall of that pipe was over three miles.
24. Goitía n.d.; Kennicutt et al. 1984.
25. Lorenzo and Serrano 2002.
26. Grimes et al. 1984; Grimes and Colwell 1989.
27. Grimes 1985.
28. Kennicutt et al. 1984, 548.
29. Campos Bistani 1983.
30. Witherspoon et al. 2004.
31. See Estado Libre Asociado de Puerto Rico 2004.
32. Campos Bistani 1983.
33. Ibid.
34. Schafer 1983.
35. Campos Bistani 1983.
36. Campos Bistani 1983.
37. US-EPA Office of Water 2003.
38. Federal Register 1998.
39. Notice and Comment rulemaking, such as happens with agencies like EPA, is time-consuming, requires significant external input, and the agency has to respond to all comments. It can easily take five to ten years.
40. Interestingly, environmental regulations tend to anticipate and dismiss this type of argument. In describing mixing zone regulations, the EQB has stated, "Authorizations for mixing zone shall not be transferable and do not imply a property right of any kind or exclusive privilege, nor do they authorize any harm to persons or property or the invasion of the private rights of others, or the infringement of any laws or federal or state regulations" (Environmental Quality Board 2010).
41. See e.g. Bakan 2004; Hartmann 2002 for a discussion of corporations and the law.
42. See e.g. Friere 2000; Patterson 1985.
43. See e.g. Bourgois and Schonberg's (2009) discussion of the *lumpen* characteristic of homeless people. This perspective is also uncomfortably reminiscent of long-held, though disproven, ideas within medical science that lower classes (or people of color, or animals, or even infants) do not experience pain.
44. Campos Bistani 1983.
45. Odors have long been considered in public health to be a warning sign of potential danger, but not a danger in and of themselves. However, there is now a consensus that in an increasing number of cases the odors themselves can have cumulative health effects (Schiffman et al. 2005).

46. Don Reynaldo and his wife Beatríz retired to Tipan in 1995, having lived in New York City for most of their lives. They chose Tipan because Don Reynaldo's brother (a drug factory supervisor) lived there, and they wanted to be near the water and near family. He arrived at a time when the environmental movement still existed, but many of its original members were weary. Don Reynaldo had only a third-grade formal education, but his years as a foreman in a factory in New York gave him a voice of authority. He was a person whose integrity and dedication gained the admiration of friends and foes alike.

47. It would be possible, in theory, to create a less expensive, comparative study design between Tipan and an otherwise similar community to demonstrate that location was a factor in reported illness. However, there was no indication that this was the approach to be taken with the survey discussed here. If that type of survey had been the intention of the study design, then the obligation of those sponsoring and conducting the survey to explain the full implication of the design was not met. This type of conflict between expert knowledge and the health needs of communities has been described by Checker (2007), Harper (2004), and others on the U.S. mainland, and will be discussed further in Chapters 5 and 6.

48. Brown 1992.

49. Montealegre et al. 2004.

50. Pérez-Perdomo et al. 2003.

51. I will return to these new development plans in the Epilogue, based on recent return trips to Nocorá. However, I will note here that the animosity between Alcalde Martínez and Tipan did not abate, and his willingness to disregard the views of the resident community took a more material turn. He greatly expanded his use of the municipality's powers of expropriation, and repossessed the land originally used for CDAN's headquarters. It was, ironically, turned into a PRASA pumping station.

52. See Estado Libre Asociado de Puerto Rico 2004; Huertas 2004.

53. Jimenez Barber 1994.

54. This principle of the mixing zone (Alaska Division of Water Quality Standards 2005) is typically used as an economical way of achieving water quality for treated wastewaters that do not meet drinking water quality, being emitted into natural bodies of water.

55. Jimenez Barber 1994.

56. Lorenzo and Serrano 2002.

57. Jimenez Barber 1994.

58. Roberts 1995.

59. Southern Technology Council/Southern Growth Policies Board 2000.

60. Estado Libre Asociado de Puerto Rico 2004.

61. Many residents in Tipan were in fact *not* connected to the sewer system. These neighborhoods lie very close to the water table, and the design of the sewer underwent many revisions to accommodate this technical issue. Questions remained as to whether the eventual design (as well as the engineering oversight of PRASA) would cause sewer backups and other problems once it was built.

62. The role of the alcalde in the life and culture of Nocorá will be explored in greater detail in chapter 3.

63. See especially Freeze 2000.

64. Public Citizen 2002.

CHAPTER 2

1. See e.g. Collins et al. 2006; Dietz 2003; Sotomayor 1998, 2004.
2. It has also been the subject of (or subject to) a great deal of social science research generally, so much so that there is an ongoing counter-discourse on the topic (see Freidenberg 2001; Lapp 1995; Pantojas-García 2000).
3. Pantojas-García 1990.
4. Dietz 2003, 21.
5. Ibid., 22.
6. Collins et al. 2006; Lopez 1994.
7. Dietz 2003, 169.
8. See also Lopez 1994.
9. See Dietz and Pantojas-García 1993; Rivera-Batíz and Santiago 1996.
10. Rivera-Batíz and Santiago 1996.
11. See Richards 2006.
12. See Grusky 1996.
13. Hunter and Arbona 1995.
14. Molina-Rivera 1996.
15. Molina-Rivera 2005.
16. Some examples of the chemicals used in drug production, and which have subsequently been found in the environment of Nocorá, are dichloromethane and carbon tetrachloride, among many solvents that are regulated as toxic by the U.S. government.
17. See e.g. López Acevedo 1976.
18. In my survey of 213 residents of the region in 2005, 62 percent agreed with the statement that their quality of life would be worse if the pharmaceutical industry left Puerto Rico. When the sample was limited to only residents of Nocorá, a majority (58%) still agreed with this statement. The survey methodology and more detailed findings are presented in chapter 3.
19. See Etheridge 1992; Ettling 1981.
20. Briggs 2002, 101.
21. An important aspect of Briggs' (2002) work is the demonstration that a wide spectrum of social development ideas, including those resulting in improved health and living conditions, nevertheless drew on some of the basic assumption of "eugenics" during this crucial period of emergent modernization.
22. This practice otherwise went against the general Rockefeller policy of funding projects not people.
23. Briggs 2002, 101.
24. Seda Bonilla 1964, 12.
25. See e.g. Dávila 1997.
26. Romberg 2003, 152.
27. Dávila 1997.
28. See also Duany 2002; Rivera 2007.
29. Sánchez-Cardona et al. 1975.
30. Bosworth and Collins 2006, 39.
31. Oficina de Gerencia y Presupuesto Estado Libre Asociado de Puerto Rico 2005.
32. Concepción 1990, 224.
33. The overall cultural dominance of this organizational pattern, known as "regulatory capture," will be discussed in greater detail in chapter 4.

34. Concepción 1990, 37.
35. Alvarez de Choudens 1973.
36. Harmony is a recurring theme in debates about economic development and the environment, and will be explored more thoroughly in chapter 4.
37. Concepción 1990; see also Steinemann 2000: 631 for further distinctions.
38. Concepción 1990: 226. As Steinemann (2000) notes, the federal requirement for an EIS occurs, "if the potential impacts are deemed significant." Concepción's argument, a point of view confirmed by my own interviews with EPA officials, is that Puerto Rico's original version of the federal law was in fact *stronger*, and was subsequently weakened. This process of weakening had the further effect of weakening the position of the EQB as an enforcement agency more generally.
39. See Dávila 2009.
40. Steinemann 2000.
41. See also Checker 2007.
42. See Susser 1998.
43. Steinemann 2000, 634.
44. Boholm 2003.
45. Steinemann 2000, 635.
46. Bakan 2004.
47. The practice of injecting processed waste into shallow fields is sometimes called "recycling" because the nutrients in the waste are used as fertilizer, even as the exposure to air and plant life assists the breakdown of various bacteria (see Overcash et al. 2005). As noted in the previous chapter, all activities related to the plant have long been mismanaged, resulting in suspicion as to whether these materials were being handled according to regulations. I recorded a number of incidents in which runoff from the sludge fields appeared to pollute local canals and streams.
48. Again, by culture they basically meant the intertwining elements of economy, social relationships, and abstract systems of belief. Though definitions of culture are as numerous as anthropologists themselves, this general model remains a useful way to think about it.
49. Padilla Seda 1966 [1956], 265.
50. Ibid., 279.
51. Seda Bonilla 1964.
52. Ibid.
53. Ibid., 278.
54. Ibid.
55. See Córdova 1980. Not to be confused with the Puerto Rican Socialist Party (PSP) founded in 1971 (see Torres and Velázquez 1998 for further reading on Puerto Rican revolutionary politics and links between the island and the mainland).
56. The ideological heirs of the Coalition of Republicans and Socialists in Nocorá tend to support statehood and the PNP. Those who maintain a more traditional Socialist perspective are more likely to support independence and the PIP, although support for this party is waning even among *independentistas*.
57. Padilla Seda 1966 [1956], 271.
58. Seda Bonilla 1964, 17; all translations mine.
59. Ibid.
60. See Ayala 1996.

61. Seda Bonilla 1964.
62. Maldonado 1979.
63. Seda Bonilla 1964, 20.
64. Ibid., 28.
65. See also Bossen 1984.
66. In the late 1950s, in the midst of extreme economic uncertainty, increased government aid was beginning to make the lives of Puerto Ricans a bit less fragile. The first signs of what would become an extreme example of consumerism (Hernández 1991) were beginning to appear. Repatriation payments from migrant farmworkers in the States also contributed substantially to local incomes at this time. It should be noted that as the migration for farmwork was also orchestrated by the government, it still fits into the model of expectations being described here.
67. Seda Bonilla 1964, 128.
68. Ibid., 123.
69. Ibid.; see also Foster 1976.
70. Lewis-Fernández and Kleinman 1994.
71. Ríos 1993, 95.
72. Briggs 2002; Ramírez de Arellano and Seipp 1983.
73. García 1982.
74. Ramírez de Arellano and Seipp 1983, 127.
75. Briggs (2002) has convincingly argued against the presence of an island-wide mass sterilization campaign. However, Ramírez de Arellano and Seipp's classic study (1983) supports the notion that Nocorá was one of the few municipalities in which the traditional provision of "social and charity medical assistance to their residents" by the local administration extended to readily available sterilizations.
76. García 1982.
77. Ayala 1996.
78. The Land Authority had invested substantially in pineapple cultivation, seeking a substitute for the declining sugar industry. However, after an early peak in production and profit, by 1960 costs had quickly outstripped gains. The Land Authority opened its first cannery in Nocorá in 1957, although canning operations had been uniformly unprofitable, and the factory, too, operated at a loss. In an attempt to stanch the flow of money in 1961, the factory was leased to a private company in a profit-loss sharing arrangement (Rosenn 1963).
79. Calero 2005b.
80. Turner 1969, 96.
81. Seda Bonilla 1964.
82. See Herzog 1987.
83. This pattern was still evident in the 2004 elections I witnessed.

CHAPTER 3
1. Briggs 2002, 145; emphasis mine.
2. Such as Victor Turner's work on the ritual process (1969).
3. Díaz Quiñones 2000.
4. Negrón-Muntaner and Grosfoguel 1997.
5. Negrón-Muntaner 2009.
6. Schwartzman 1989.

7. During the time of my fieldwork, expropriations in poor communities were becoming an increasing concern among advocates for social and environmental justice. In the time since, several conflicts over expropriation erupted in the Tipan neighborhood of Barco de Caña.

8. It is interesting to note that political leaders in Nocorá have been drawn almost exclusively from the ranks of former teachers and educational administrators. Teachers were held in extremely high regard, perhaps because education was seen as necessary for economic success. The irony, considering the failure of Nocoreños to break into the limited local high-tech labor market, is profound.

9. Seda Bonilla 1964.

10. The alteration of a natural stream by excavation, realignment, lining or other means to accelerate the flow of water.

11. While the dam and related infrastructure work has prevented the annual flooding of downtown Nocorá, areas lying outside the wall, such as Tipan and Salvador, are still subject to frequent floods, particularly during hurricane season. There is also concern that protecting the town center, the core of Martínez's urban revitalization initiatives, has resulted in worsening flood conditions in both Nocorá and Bajas, as the rivers all over the island swell with silt and other by-products of construction.

12. Turner 1969.

13. Dávila 1997.

14. Though it can be argued that through the *patentes* (local taxes) the pharmaceuticals indirectly sponsored at least half, on average, of any municipal function.

15. Activities of any size also require security and emergency-response units. The municipality had a substantial staff for these events, easily identified by their uniforms and new vehicles. According to a 2004 article in *Caribbean Business* (Ramos 2004), annual expenditures for total municipal police forces on the island are estimated at $114 million, part of an increasing trend toward non-state protection services. Nocorá's own municipal police force was in the process of being created during 2004, as part of the effort to increase security and foment urban renewal.

16. It is not unusual for island-wide, and even internationally recognized, Spanish-language artists to perform.

17. In 2011, I was informed that laptops were now the item being given away selectively by the most affluent municipalities, including Nocorá.

18. Martínez had been alcalde since 1986—it was not inconceivable that he could have given a new bicycle, or the equivalent, to every child in town.

19. Seda Bonilla used Tönnies' term *Gemeinschaft* which I am using interchangeably with Turner's *communitas* (Tönnies 1957; Turner 1969).

20. De Vries 2002; see also Heine 1993.

21. Dávila 1997.

22. A *velorio cantado* is a tradition of singing (often the Catholic rosary) in honor of a saint. In this case the event is traditional Puerto Rican Christmas music in honor of the coming of the Three Kings (Epiphany).

23. Don Teodoro, in his 80s at the time of my fieldwork, was, like the alcalde, a former teacher, and very well-respected in Nocorá. He managed to be involved with the environmental movement CDAN and yet still have cordial relations with both the pharmaceutical companies and the alcalde due to his standing as president of the Centro. His commitment to the Centro was so strong that it always publically superseded his other potential conflicts.

24. This NGO, Grupo Uniendo Iniciativa Ambiental (GUIA), will be discussed in later chapters.

25. At that time I had not yet succeeded in establishing contact with that company, which I later did.

26. In Wade's (2006) terms, transparency runs on a scale from "trust me," to "tell me," to "show me" (the most transparent state).

27. Wade 2006, 135.

28. The term "stakeholder" is problematic, and some of the issues related to its usage are a subject of current debate in the literature. Here I do not mean to take the term at face value, and the intent of my survey was to challenge the typical concept of stakeholder as it is deployed in Nocorá. This and other discourses of Corporate Social Responsibility will be addressed further in chapter 5.

29. Wilk 1999.

30. The proportion of women to men in the sample is most likely explained by the fact that women are overrepresented in the labor force of the sample locations listed, as teachers, nurses, and secretaries.

31. The only options would be for the benefit of the few very high-ranking managers who might not speak Spanish, or for any English-speaking tourists who may have strayed down to the local beach. Though sometimes popular with surfers, in general Nocorá beaches merit a "pass" from most guidebooks.

32. Vogel 2005.

33. They can have the positive side effect of creating a context for outdoor exercise (see Killingsworth et al. 2004: 11), increasingly rare in Puerto Rico. The issue of public health promotion of exercise will be discussed in chapter 6. I am indebted to Lesley Sharp for first suggesting to me a critical perspective on the social phenomenon of health-related walk-a-thons and similar fundraisers.

34. Turner 1969: 202.

35. At best companies will match, or partially match, pledges made to participants. They also sponsor refreshments for their company "teams," provide the ubiquitous t-shirts, and sometimes provide transportation to the site of the event.

36. See Epstein 2000.

37. The debate over the vaccine for Human papillomavirus (HPV), Gardasil, illustrates many of the complexities of this specific question, particularly as it relates to the ethics of developing preventative drugs that may compete with or distract from the less invasive, and often more sustainably effective, methods of promoting positive health behaviors (see Jain 2011; Wailoo et al. 2010). There is also some evidence that efforts on the part of pharmaceutical companies to work for prevention are focused on getting doctors to prescribe existing curative medications (such as statins) to otherwise healthy patients (Wilson 2010; see also Oldani 2004 for examples of the pushing of "off label" prescriptions by drug salespeople).

38. All the questions in the survey (apart from the demographic items) were developed based on participant observation and qualitative interviews during the first nine months of fieldwork. The survey was designed to be short and accessible across a wide range of people, and it was pilot tested with people of different ages, genders, and educational attainment.

39. Kleinbaum and Klein 2002.

40. Dávila 1997.

41. It has also made a wealth of goods and services available to the populace that were previously lacking, though many have purchased such goods on the also-recently-available

credit. Oscar Lewis's (1966) famed "La Esmeralda" neighborhood in San Juan is still considered poor and dangerous—but digital satellite dishes adorn many of its rooftops. For further analysis of this complex set of socioeconomic relationships, see Ortiz-Negrón (2009).

42. Sabater 2005.

43. So far I have seen little evidence that pharmaceutical shareholders represent an outspoken group of environmental activists capable of altering the behaviors of the companies in locations like Nocorá. This is likely in part due to the strong tendency of annual reports to paint the brightest environmental picture possible. There is some evidence that in other industries, activist shareholders may have the power to create greater accountability (see Welker and Wood 2011).

44. In a strict Marxist analysis of wage-labor, where skill levels (and therefore training) are minimal, and therefore workers are easily replaced, treating workers well does not pay. In the present pharmaceutical labor market of Puerto Rico there tend to be two classes of workers: those who are "part of the family," the higher skilled, well-compensated; and those whose work is less skilled and increasingly farmed out to contractors/temporary services, such as security guards and those working in packaging. When a high-profile robbery of a drug shipment occurred from a Nocorá factory and it became clear that it was an "inside job," several security guards I knew commented that it was no surprise: as contractors they had no special loyalty to the company, and were not treated especially well, in spite of needing to speak English.

45. Peterson 2004.

46. Díaz Quiñones 2000: 20. On a number of occasions I have discovered that my use of this verb in conversation is often taken as definitive evidence, despite my explanations to the contrary, that I myself am Puerto Rican.

47. Diaz Quiñones 2000: 22.

48. See e.g. Berman Santana 1996.

49. Here I am using power in the Foucauldian sense, as present, and persistent, throughout social relations (see e.g. Foucault 1990).

50. Negrón-Muntaner 2007; see also McCaffrey and Baver 2006.

51. See Duchesne Winter 2007; Torres-Velez 2010.

52. Though not immediately germane to this discussion, it is important to mention that Diaz Quiñones also notes yet another connotation for *bregar*, which one also sometimes hears in connection particularly with the expression *bregar bien*, a double entendre that might be considered to underlie the reference to politicians. An older usage of *bregar* translates loosely as "to fornicate" and was used to describe people having extramarital affairs, for example. In this case a politician might be viewed positively for his masculine strength used on behalf of his people (a paternalistic connotation), or in a neutral/negative sense this could connote that while the politician works for the people, he is simultaneously lining his own pockets. Many Puerto Ricans I knew seemed to accept this "win-win" self-benefit for politicians, though there is also an acknowledgment that working both sides of the equation can easily cross the line until one is simply "screwing" the public good.

CHAPTER 4

This chapter is an updated and revised version of an earlier article (Dietrich 2011), and is used by permission.

1. Mercer 2002.

2. See e.g. Horowitz 2009; Welker 2009.

3. Pharmaceutical Research and Manufacturers of America, www.phrma.org; accessed March 1, 2007.

4. Auyero and Swistun 2009; Berglund 2001; Zonabend 1993.

5. See Carroll 1999; Welker 2009.

6. Nader 2002: 118.

7. Here I am distinguishing between groups focused on justice, rather than strictly on protection of the environment through other means—these other groups (of which there are several active on the island) do not emphasize the damages done to people in conjunction with environmental damage.

8. Nader 2002: 120.

9. Dietz et al. 1989.

10. Other than these two groups, the remaining positions are largely with regulatory agencies, a scenario that enhances the "capturing" of the profession in general.

11. Martin 1999.

12. Singer and Baer 2008: 26.

13. Hanson and Yosifon 2003.

14. Stigler 1971. See also Hanson and Yosifon 2003.

15. Frank 2009. Frank further elaborates his point: "The George W. Bush Administration . . . gave us a Food and Drug Administration that sometimes looked as though it was taking orders from Big Pharma . . . and a Consumer Products Safety Commission that moved like a rusty wind-up toy. . . . Misgovernment of this kind is not a partisan phenomenon, of course. . . . [T]oday we talk about this problem, with its nose-on-your-face obviousness, as though it didn't exist."

16. In this case the public good is presumed to be the desired outcome of the sum of the majority of individuals.

17. Hanson and Yosifon 2003.

18. Freudenburg 2005: 3.

19. See e.g. Doll 1976.

20. See Hardell et al. 2007.

21. Scott 1998.

22. Kairys 2010; see also Kairys 1998.

23. Legal scholar David Kairys notes (2010) that corporations are not in fact able to vote as citizens, although the recent Supreme Court decision in *Citizens United v. Federal Communications Commission* has now radically changed the landscape of their influence in U.S. federal elections.

24. Nader 2001; 1990.

25. See Pantojas-Garcia 1990.

26. López 1994.

27. Transfer payments significantly include those earned as veterans' benefits and social security, as well as nutritional and housing support.

28. "Puerto Rico is the perfect place for Biotechnology." http://biosciencepr.org/, accessed February 2, 2010.

29. Benson and Kirsch 2010.

30. Valdés Pizzini 2001.

31. A sample examination of the IRS form 990 of one of the parent company foundations of one of the local factories for fiscal year 2003 reports that the foundation gave $10,000 to GUIA; in 2005, another company was gratefully thanked during GUIA's anniversary

celebration for another donation of $10,000, in which Velázquez noted, "We have survived thanks to the economic help of the [local] industries."

32. Zonabend 1993: 125; emphasis in original.

33. Ashton 2008.

34. Prahalad and Ramaswamy 2004. In a market in which drugs increasingly support the quality of life, rather than provide obviously life-saving or life-extending remedies. It should be noted that their concern over reputation has had less impact on their behavior in Puerto Rico itself, (1) because the island does not represent a substantial portion of their market, and (2) until very recently word of their local pollution problems had not traveled much beyond Puerto Rico's borders.

35. See Auyero and Swistun 2009; Horowitz 2011; Welker 2009.

36. Hanson and Yosifon 2003.

37. Auyero and Swistun 2009; Nazarea 1999; Tsing et al. 2005.

38. See Haraway 1991.

39. Tsing et al. 2005: 2.

40. For the sake of the example we will leave aside the question of whether this connection negatively impacts the overloaded system as a whole. *Not* having a sewer connection is not a viable alternative.

41. See e.g. Checker 2005.

42. In contrast, the Puerto Rico Aqueduct and Sewer Authority (PRASA, or AAA by its Spanish title), the official managers of the NWTP, could be considered the government utility that everyone loves to hate.

43. Lyon and Maxwell 2004.

44. Hanson and Yosifon 2003: 217.

45. See also Checker 2005.

46. Morgan 1993.

47. Yalamanchili and Smith 2008; see also Schiffman and Williams 2005.

48. See Berglund 2001.

49. See Morris 1995. Much work in anthropology using the concept of performativity focuses on gender performance (see also Butler 1988); however, the notion clearly resonates in other contexts, with other social identities (such as "expert").

50. Nader and Ou 1998: 2.

51. Concepción 1990.

52. Gramsci 1971: 481.

53. Ismail 2007. The Center for Public Integrity (www.iwatchnews.org) has routinely reported on the pharmaceutical lobby in Washington, noting that between 1998 and 2006, drug manufacturers and their interest groups spent upwards of $733 million on lobbying activities.

54. In fact, I had acquired the document the week before through my own research on the Internet, and had asked CDAN about it. Shortly thereafter I was contacted by their lawyer asking, "Where did you get this?" Although it was indeed publicly available, it had been extremely time-consuming to uncover, and the lawyers for CDAN had limited research and support staff.

55. Auyero and Swistun 2009.

56. Jain's (2011) analysis demonstrates, for example, the fluidity with which pharmaceutical companies have managed to convince seemingly every category of cancer "stakeholder" (patients, families, doctors, epidemiologists, to name a few) that survival for five years after diagnosis is success, regardless of the age and desired life expectancy of the patient.

57. At the time of this writing, criticisms of "corporate personhood" have gained a great deal of traction, and the issue of corporations as immortal was brought into stinging relief by a quip appearing on a campaign-style button: "I'll believe corporations are people when Texas executes one."

58. Hanson and Yosifon 2003.

59. Scott 1998.

60. Berglund 2001; Haenn and Casagrande 2007; Hale 2006.

CHAPTER 5

1. Googins and Rochlin 2006.

2. Ibid., 114.

3. Bakan 2004, 153.

4. See Karnani 2007; Simanis et al. 2008.

5. See van der Geest 2006.

6. Consumers International 2005.

7. They may also be goods, such as water, to which a company has access by virtue of their production processes. An example of this is a beer company using its machinery to bottle potable water.

8. Himmelstein 1997, 146; see also Neiheisel 1994.

9. Rose-Ackerman 1996. A good example of mutual benefit to elites is the large donation by one of the Nocorá companies to rebuild the local library. The library, including its bank of computers, undoubtedly provides a valuable public service to Nocoreños. However, its holdings are not as impressive as one might expect from a sponsored library, and it seems likely that the main donation was for the structure, rather than the bibliographic resources themselves.

10. Smith 1996.

11. Stern and Barley 1996.

12. Diaz 2005.

13. This is not an unusual argument in the context of the developing world, and I heard it repeated by corporate managers across the region. It is an interesting parallel to the argument that drug treatments will not work (and therefore donation programs are scrapped) because of cultural or infrastructural limitations.

14. Burke 1999.

15. Román Seda 1996; US-EPA Office of Water 2003.

16. Pérez 1993.

17. The membrane was inevitably referred to by members of CDAN, though with some embarrassment in front of this female ethnographer, as "the condom."

18. Googins and Rochlin 2006.

19. Velez Arcelay 1984.

20. As I understood it, the Bajas office managed this section of pipe because it was connected to the waste pipe coming into the treatment plant from Bajas.

21. This comment raises an important set of questions beyond the purview of this ethnography, but nevertheless important to consider. In a context in which there is increasing pressure for the work of government agencies to be handled through private sector contracts, or through sale of public services to private companies, to what degree are private companies providing public services beholden to the wishes of the public itself?

22. Government financing, as Fischel points out in a discussion of Michigan's Poletown project, is hardly a limiting force on projects benefiting private enterprise (2004). The U.S. Supreme Court decision in *Kelo v. New London* also further enhanced the ability of local governments to expropriate (and therefore, in a sense, to financially facilitate private business through public means).

23. Crook 2005; Sharp 2006.

24. See e.g. Kliksberg and Tomassini 2000.

25. Mayol and Gamundi 2004: 6. In the time of Seda Bonilla's (1964) study this sentiment was described as *"mamalonería,"* or, metaphorically, the reliance on breastfeeding for sustenance. The word *cupón* is the translation of food stamps, the growth of which as a means of supporting Puerto Rican families, along with other types of payments, is discussed in earlier chapters (see also Dietz 2003). The neologism *cuponazgo* is a play on the term *compadrazgo*, or ritual co-parenthood, typical of Puerto Rican society prior to heavy industrialization. In this earlier context, the social ties of compadrazgo were "utilized daily in getting help, borrowing money, dividing up available work opportunities, and so forth" (Mintz and Wolf 1950: 360).

26. Shamir 2004, 669.

27. See Bakan 2004; Kovel 2002; Korten 2001.

28. Kovel 2002.

29. Hawken et al. 2010.

30. Such as those promoted in feminist and postmodern critical theory (see Ahearn 2001).

31. See e.g. Frank 1979; Ong 1987; Wallerstein 1991.

32. Unspoken here was the debate that came to a head in U.S. politics in 2011, as to whether or not corporations were persons in any real sense. From an anthropological perspective, elaborating on Bakan's analysis (2004), current theories now suggest that avoidance of accountability to a community would not have made for a strong survival strategy in human society. Cooperation is now believed to be a key component of a robust model for human evolutionary success (Fuentes 2004), suggesting that, by analogy, purely profit-driven "individual" corporations do not behave as humans typically do.

33. Herzfeld 1992, 122.

34. Merry 2011.

35. Friedman 1970. See also Gibson (1995) for additional counter-arguments. Gibson points out that traditional views of stakeholders distinguish between "primary" and "secondary" groups, where primary are those to whom the corporation is contractually accountable. In my work I found that the generic term stakeholder was often used to blur the boundary between these two types of stakeholders for public relations purposes, while they remained distinct in practice.

36. It is important to note that shareholders also have the potential to inspire accountability beyond financial transparency and profit margins. However, that type of change requires significant effort and awareness on the part of "activist shareholders," usually those who themselves own significant amounts of stock (see Welker and Wood 2011).

37. A key set of criticisms of corporate influence (see e.g. Korten 2001) particularly distinguish between capitalist economies and market economies. At the core of this argument is a belief that the corporate structure and its dominance, not market dynamics per se, are contrary to the public good.

38. Kaiser Family Foundation and Sonderegger Research Center 2004, 1.

39. Brush 2005.

40. Saul 2006.
41. Morgenson 2006.
42. Martínez 2005a.
43. Transparency in governance is a key aspect of corporate social responsibility, which has been strongly resisted by the pharmaceutical industry in the name of intellectual property and proprietary knowledge concerns.
44. Vogel 2005, 164–65.
45. See Crook 2005.
46. It is important to note that of the majority of people across the wide spectrum of perspectives with which I conducted research, very few advocated a retreat from an industrialized economy. The overall impression I received was that Puerto Ricans would like for industry, like government, to "do better"—in other words, to better meet the tenets of what has been defined here as socially responsible business.
47. This category presumably encompasses not just the Catholic Church, but religious institutions in general.
48. Gómez 2005.
49. Berenson 2005.
50. www.pridco.com.
51. Martínez 2005b.
52. Rhys Jenkins has noted that in general "the centrality of stakeholders within CSR also limits its usefulness in approaching poverty" (2005: 540). In the case of Puerto Rico at least, this is less accurate in the sense that Puerto Rico is so small, that an industry as a whole can have a significant impact on the whole island, both economically and environmentally. In this sense, the entire island is a stakeholder in the actions of the pharmaceuticals because a growing consensus that the island is generally polluted could be extremely detrimental to its other major industry, tourism.
53. The reason I was only able to get survey results from five of the seven schools was that two of the schools had interim principals. These interim principals, who were seemingly overwhelmed by organizational difficulties, were unable (or ultimately unwilling) to collect the distributed surveys (the collection method necessitated by strict limits on school access and teacher time).
54. I did not probe Héctor and his wife Daniela too much about the pollution because in the time I lived near them they had a baby, and the baby was quickly found to have asthma. However, while Daniela complained of the smell coming from the factories, and about the dust that caused us all to sweep out our rooms virtually every day, I never heard them connect the asthma to the air quality. I do know that no one in their house was a smoker.
55. The Comunidades Especiales initiative was the pet project of former governor Sila M. Calderón (Asamblea Legislativa de Puerto Rico 2001), designed to provide basic infrastructure and training to create more sustainable communities in traditionally poor neighborhoods. The results of the project have been very mixed, in part because, as one community support worker told me, if the communities were already organized they can make use of the resources. However, many were not well-organized, and there was also an element of political favoritism in the selection of the sites.
56. This is slowly changing, as CDAN has managed to attract some new blood to their leadership, including a new president in his late twenties. On a follow-up visit to Tipan in 2006, I witnessed the new president of CDAN presenting some of his ideas to become more of a resource for the community, which was received very positively. However, these are not

the kinds of activities, such as outreach and non-hierarchical community education, with which members have had much experience.

57. The valley of the neighborhood Salvador was for many years, I was told, especially prone to thermal inversions, trapping the high levels of industrial air pollution, as well as car exhaust from the well-traveled route 4, relatively near the ground. In neighborhoods like La Planchita, which wind up the karstic limestone hillsides, the air in earlier years would indeed have been deadly.

58. Turner 1969.

59. Among their other concerns were: lack of sewers (rainwater: 92%; sewage: 91%); roads in poor condition: 74%; housing (need: 69%; need repairs: 59%); area prone to flooding: 49%.

CHAPTER 6

1. Welker 2009.

2. This perspective, from those who knew the programs the most intimately, stands in stark contrast to the more managerial attitude, "We're doing what we can."

3. Fujino et al. 2006.

4. Karlsson et al. 2003.

5. Heron and Pickering 2003.

6. There was, in fact, an explosion caused by a short circuit in the factory closest to us around the time of Tropical Storm Jeanne. It was reportedly caused by an electrical "short circuit," but the local newspaper reported that there was some contact with a gas. None of us living near the factory ever knew what really happened, but the burning smell lingered for more than 24 hours.

7. Scott 1985.

8. Ong 1987.

9. Gramsci 1971.

10. Negrón-Muntaner 2007.

11. In an example that was expressed to me in a tone of adding insult to injury, one woman complained that for a temporary job in pharmaceutical packaging, she had to wear a special uniform provided by the company right down to the underwear, but that the cost of the uniform was deducted from her pay. In this case it seemed as if the uniform was designed as much to prevent theft as to ensure safety.

12. Mark Nichter, a highly respected medical anthropologist, asserted in a presentation to the 2006 joint meetings of the Society for Applied Anthropology and the Society for Medical Anthropology that medical anthropologists needed to "create a niche for themselves" in occupational health investigations of phenomena such as shift work.

13. Rylko-Bauer et al. 2006.

14. Singer and Clair 2003; Singer 2009.

15. Interestingly, interviews with health care workers and administrators at the clinic revealed that there were concerns based on anecdotal experience with air quality in Salvador la Cruz, near the factories, and in Tipan, near the treatment plant.

16. Calero 2005b; Ramos Valencia 2001.

17. See Wilcox 2001; Torres 2005. Though the rates of cancer in Vieques have been the subject of much debate, in part because of changing policies in cancer surveillance during the critical period of Navy bombing of the island, cancer and Vieques were undeniably linked in the public imaginary at this time.

18. Surveys to assess KAP are typically used in reproductive health and sexual behavior research, and increasingly gaining attention in environmental health. A number of researchers have noted what is called the KAP-gap, the fact that people seemingly in possession of both the right knowledge and attitude may nevertheless not practice the desired health behavior.

19. See Helitzer-Allen and Kendall 1992.

20. Paul 1955, 476–77.

21. Trostle 2005.

22. I am quite certain that while anthropologists often perform the role of expert outside of the field, it is rarer to be considered an expert in a traditional field setting. In the classic scenario the anthropologist is supposed to "learn like a child" from the communities in which we work (see e.g. Bowen 1964), and sometimes even maintain fictive kin relationships of lower status.

23. Nations 1986.

24. Harper 2004, 319.

25. Ware 1992.

26. See Del Vecchio-Good et al. 1994; Moloney et al. 2006.

27. Turner 1969.

28. This argument also appeals to the longstanding theoretical assertions of post-colonial, feminist, and queer theories that there is a subtle violence of its own to the process of being socially erased. As Paul Farmer has noted, "[e]rasing history is perhaps the most common explanatory sleight-of-hand relied upon by the architects of structural violence" (2004, 308).

29. Slovic 1999.

30. Colloca and Miller 2011; Hahn 1997.

31. See also Fanon 1991; Memmi 1991.

32. In the time since my fieldwork other social activists have come to this same conclusion, and new political parties have been formed in response. Some examples are *Partido Puertorriqueños por Puerto Rico*, PPR, which was ratified at the Commonwealth level, but lost its recognition when its candidate for governor failed to garner 3 percent of the vote. It is still an active organization, advocating for sustainable development, and taking no stance on Puerto Rico's political status. Parties are also formed on the municipal level, as was the case in Nocorá in 2011, when a local activist announced her candidacy for alcalde under the banner of the Partido Eco del Pueblo.

33. I would argue this was the case with groups like GUIA and the community board of La Planchita.

34. See also Concepción 2000.

35. Agrawal 2005.

36. Ibid.

37. Duhigg and Barboza 2012.

38. Ibid.

39. It is easy to retain skepticism as to whether such an endeavor would ever be sufficiently separated from the interests of the industry. However, my thinking here is inspired by such organizations as the Ford Foundation, which has long been an entirely independent organization from the Ford Motor Company, and whose actions appear to have no impact on public perception of that corporation.

40. Skanavis 1999, 35. She contrasts this with the idea that Anglo-American leaders are perceived as having been delegated to carry out the priorities that the majority has already agreed upon.
41. Escobar 2006.
42. In the case of Nocorá, the cultural ecology framework applies most directly to fishers (whose economic base has radically declined; see Griffith and Valdez-Pizzini 2002) and those who work in the factories.
43. Duany 2002. See also Aranda 2006.
44. See Negrón-Muntaner 2007; Sandoval 2000. I am also indebted to Jorge Duany for discussing with me some of the implications of his ideas for environmental activism.

Agencia EFE. 1998. "A pagar por la limpieza." In *El Nuevo Día*, el 18 de abril, p. 38. San Juan.

Agrawal, Arun. 2005. *Environmentality: Technologies of Government and the Making of Subjects.* Durham, NC: Duke University Press.

Ahearn, Laura M. 2001. "Language and Agency." *Annual Review of Anthropology* 30: 109–37.

Alaska Division of Water Quality Standards. 2005. 2003–2005 Triennial Review: Mixing Zones Fact Sheet (available at http://www.state.ak.us/dec/water/wqsar/trireview/trireview.htm; accessed 16 March 2006).

Alvarez de Choudens, José. 1973. "Resolución, Junta de Calidad Ambiental de Puerto Rico" [Resolution on Environmental Autonomy]. *Concepción 1990*, Appendix 3.

Ames, Bruce and Lois Gold. 1998. "The Causes and Prevention of Cancer: The Role of Environment." *Biotherapy* 11(2–3): 205–20.

Angell, Marcia. 2004. "Excess in the Pharmaceutical Industry." *Canadian Medical Association Journal* 171(12): 1451–53.

Aranda, Elizabeth M. 2006. *Emotional Bridges to Puerto Rico: Migration, Return Migration, and the Struggles of Incorporation.* Lanham, MD: Rowman & Littlefield.

Asamblea Legislativa de Puerto Rico. 2001. "Ley para el Desarrollo Integral de las Comunidades Especiales de Puerto Rico." 14ta Asamblea Legislativa, 1ra Sesión Ordinaria. Aprobado el 1 de marzo de 2001 (http://www.comunidadesespeciales.gobierno.pr/db/ley1.pdf).

Ashton, Weslynne. 2008. "Sustaining Industry on Small Islands by Harnessing Opportunities for Collaborative Resource Management." *Business, Finance & Economics in Emerging Economies* 3(1): 37–59.

Auyero, Javier, and Débora Alejandra Swistun. 2009. *Flammable: Environmental Suffering in an Argentine Shantytown.* New York: Oxford University Press.

Ayala, César J. 1996. "The Decline of the Plantation Economy and the Puerto Rican Migration of the 1950s." *Latino Studies Journal* 7(1).

Baer, Hans and Merrill Singer. 2008. *Global Warming and the Political Ecology of Health: Emerging Crises and Systemic Solutions.* Walnut Creek, CA: Left Coast Press.

Bakan, Joel. 2004. *The Corporation: The Pathological Pursuit of Profit and Power.* New York: Free Press.

Beck, Ulrich. 1992. *Risk Society: Towards a New Modernity.* London: Sage Publications.

Bellman, Beryl L. 1984. *The Language of Secrecy: Symbols & Metaphors in Poro Ritual.* New Brunswick, NJ: Rutgers University Press.

Benson, Peter and Stuart Kirsch. 2010. "Capitalism and the Politics of Resignation." *Current Anthropology* 51(4): 459–86.

Berenson, Alex. 2005. "Big Drug Makers See Sales Decline with Their Image." *New York Times*, November 14 (www.nytimes.com).

Berglund, Eeva. 2001. "Self-defeating Environmentalism?: Models and Questions from an Ethnography of Toxic Waste Protest." *Critique of Anthropology* 21(3): 317.

Berman Santana, Déborah. 1996. *Kicking Off the Bootstraps: Environment, Development, and Community Power in Puerto Rico*. Tucson: University of Arizona Press.

Boholm, Åsa. 2003. "The Cultural Nature of Risk: Can There Be an Anthropology of Uncertainty?" *Ethnos* 68(2): 159–78.

Bossen, Laurel H. 1984. *The Redivision of Labor: Women and Economic Choice in Four Guatemalan Communities*. Albany: State University of New York Press.

Bosworth, Barry P. and Susan M. Collins. 2006. "Economic Growth." In *The Economy of Puerto Rico: Restoring Growth*, S. M. Collins, B. P. Bosworth, and M. A. Soto-Class, eds. New York: Brookings Institution Press.

Bourgois, Philippe and Jeff Schonberg. 2009. *Righteous Dopefiend*. Berkeley: University of California Press.

Bowen, Elenore Smith. 1964. *Return to Laughter*. Published in cooperation with the American Museum of Natural History New York: Anchor Books.

Briggs, Laura. 2002. *Reproducing Empire: Race, Sex, Science, and U.S. Imperialism in Puerto Rico*. Berkeley: University of California Press.

Brown, Phil. 1992. "Popular Epidemiology and Toxic Waste Contamination: Lay and Professional Ways of Knowing." *Journal of Health and Social Behavior* 33(3): 267–81.

Brush, Michael. 2005. Company Focus: The 5 most outrageously overpaid CEOs (posted: 8/25/2005): moneycentral.msn.com (accessed January 2007).

Burke, Edmund M. 1999. *Corporate Community Relations: The Principle of the Neighbor of Choice*. Westport, CT: Praeger.

Butler, Judith. 1988. "Performative Acts and Gender Constitution: An Essay in Phenomenology and Feminist Theory." *Theatre Journal* 40(4): 519–31.

Calero, Heidie. 2005a. Encuesta de Hogares en Municipio de Barceloneta.

———. 2005b. Perfil Socioeconómico del Municipio de Barceloneta.

Campos Bistani, Luis F. 1983. Memo Re: Barceloneta Wastewater Treatment Plant, To: Files (EPA Caribbean Field Office).

Carroll, A. B. 1999. "Corporate Social Responsibility: Evolution of a Definitional Construct." *Business & Society* 38(3): 268.

Checker, Melissa. 2005. *Polluted Promises: Environmental Racism and the Search for Justice in a Southern Town*. New York: NYU Press.

———. 2007. "'But I Know It's True': Environmental Risk Assessment, Justice, and Anthropology." *Human Organization* 66(2): 112–24.

Collins, Susan M., Barry P. Bosworth, and Miguel A. Soto-Class, eds. 2006. *The Economy of Puerto Rico: Restoring Growth*. New York: Brookings Institution Press.

Colloca, Luana and Franklin G. Miller. 2011. "The Nocebo Effect and Its Relevance for Clinical Practice." *Psychosomatic Medicine* 73, no. 7 (September): 598–603. doi:10.1097/PSY.0b013e3182294a50.

Concepción, Carmen M. 1990. "Environmental Policy and Industrialization: The Politics of Regulation in Puerto Rico." PhD diss., University of California, Berkeley.

———. 2000. "Justicia ambiental, luchas comunitarias y política pública." *Revista de Administración Pública* 31–32 (1998-1999/1999-2000): 89–113.

Consumers International. 2005. *Branding the Cure: A Consumer Perspective on Corporate Social Responsibility, Drug Promotion and the Pharmaceutical Industry*. London: Consumers International.

Córdova, Gonzalo F. 1980. *Santiago Iglesias: Creador del Movimiento Obrero de Puerto Rico*. Barcelona: Editorial Universitaria.

Crook, Clive. 2005. "The Good Company: The Movement for Corporate Social Responsibility Has Won the Battle of Ideas." *The Economist* 374: 3–4.

Dávila, Arlene. 1997. *Sponsored Identities: Cultural Politics in Puerto Rico*. Philadelphia: Temple University Press.

———. 2009. *Latin Spin: Public Image and the Whitewashing of Race*. New York: NYU Press.

Del Vecchio-Good, Mary-Jo, Paul E. Brodwin, and Byron J. Good. 1994. *Pain as Human Experience: An Anthropological Perspective*. Berkeley: University of California Press.

De Vries, P. 2002. "Vanishing Mediators: Enjoyment as a Political Factor in Western Mexico." *American Ethnologist* 29(4): 901–27.

Diaz, Alexander F. 2005. "Position Paper on Corporate Social Responsibility." *RumboNovo* (San Juan, Puerto Rico).

Díaz, José O. 1995. "Puerto Rico, the United States, and the 1993 Referendum on Political Status." *Latin American Research Review* 30(1): 203–11.

Díaz Quiñones, Arcadio. 2000. *El arte de bregar*. San Juan: Ediciones Callejón.

Dietrich, Alexa S. 2008. "Corrosion in the System: The Community Health By-products of Pharmaceutical Production in Northern Puerto Rico." In *Killer Commodities: Public Health and the Corporate Production of Harm*, M. Singer and H. Baer, eds. Lanham, MD, Alta Mira Press.

———. 2011. "Coercive Harmony, Deep Capture and Environmental Justice in Puerto Rico." *Development and Change* 42(6): 1441–63. doi:10.1111/j.1467–7660.2011.01738.x.

Dietz, James L. 2003. *Puerto Rico: Negotiating Development and Change*. Boulder, CO: Lynne Rienner.

Dietz, James and Emilio Pantojas-Garcia. 1993. "Puerto Rico's New Role in the Caribbean: The High-finance/Maquiladora Strategy." In *Colonial Dilemma: Critical Perspectives on Contemporary Puerto Rico*, E. Meléndez and E. Meléndez, eds. Cambridge, MA: South End Press.

Dietz, Thomas, Paul C. Stern, and Robert W. Rycroft. 1989. "Definitions of Conflict and the Legitimation of Resources: The Case of Environmental Risk." *Sociological Forum* 4(1): 47–70. doi:10.1007/BF01112616.

Doll, Richard. 1976. "The Contribution of Epidemiology to Knowledge of Cancer." *Rev. Epidém. et Santé Publ.* 24: 107–21.

Douglas, M. and A. Wildavsky. 1982. *Risk and Culture*. Berkeley: University of California Press.

Duany, Jorge. 2002. *The Puerto Rican Nation on the Move: Identities on the Island and in the United States*. Chapel Hill: University of North Carolina Press.

Duchesne Winter, Juan. 2007. "Vieques: Protest as a Consensual Spectacle." In *None of the Above: Puerto Ricans in the Global Era*, F. Negrón-Muntaner, ed. New York: Palgrave Macmillan.

Duhigg, Charles and David Barboza. 2012. "Apple's iPad and the Human Costs for Workers in China." *New York Times*, January 25, Business Day section. http://www.nytimes.

com/2012/01/26/business/ieconomy-apples-ipad-and-the-human-costs-for-workers-in-china.html.

Environmental Quality Board of Puerto Rico. 2010. "Puerto Rico Water Quality Standards Regulation." http://water.epa.gov/scitech/swguidance/standards/wqslibrary/upload/prwqs.pdf.

Epstein, M. J. and K. O. Hanson, eds. 2006. *The Accountable Corporation*. Santa Barbara, CA: Praeger Publishers.

Epstein, Samuel S. 2000. "Legislative Proposals for Reversing the Cancer Epidemic and Controlling Run-Away Industrial Technologies." *International Journal of Health Services* 30(2): 353–71.

Epstein, Samuel S., et al. 2002. "The Crisis in U.S. and International Cancer Policy." *International Journal of Health Services* 32(4): 669–707.

Escobar, Arturo. 2006. "Difference and Conflict in the Struggle over Natural Resources: A Political Ecology Framework." *Development* 49(3): 6–13.

Escobar, Arturo, Dianne Rocheleau, and Smitu Kothari. 2002. "Environmental Social Movements and the Politics of Place." *Development* 45(1): 28–36.

Estado Libre Asociado de Puerto Rico. 2004. Informe de Auditoria CP-05-13 (Autoridad de Acueductos y Alcantarillados de Puerto Rico (PRASA)): Oficina del Controlar.

Etheridge, Elizabeth. 1992. *Sentinel for Health: A History of the Centers for Disease Control*. Berkeley: University of California Press.

Ettling, John. 1981. *The Germ of Laziness: Rockefeller Philanthropy and Public Health in the New South*. Cambridge, MA: Harvard University Press.

Fanon, Frantz. 1991. *Black Skin, White Masks*. New York: Grove Press.

Farmer, Paul. 1996. "On Suffering and Structural Violence: A View from Below." *Daedalus* 125(1): 261–84.

———. 2004. "An Anthropology of Structural Violence." *Current Anthropology* 45(3): 305–19.

Federal Register. 1998. "Pharmaceutical Manufacturing Category Effluent Limitations Guidelines, Pretreatment Standards, and New Source Performance Standards; Final Rule," 63, no. 182, 40 CFR Parts 136 and 439.

Fischel, William A. 2004. "The Political Economy of Public Use in Poletown: How Federal Grants Encourage Excessive Use of Eminent Domain." *Michigan State Law Review* (4): 929–56.

Foster, George M. 1976. "Disease Etiologies in Non-Western Medical Systems." *American Anthropologist* 78(4): 773–82.

Foucault, M. 1990. *The History of Sexuality, Volume 1: An Introduction*. Trans. Robert Hurley. New York: Vintage.

Frank, Andre Gunder. 1979. *Dependent Accumulation and Underdevelopment*. New York: Monthly Review Press.

Frank, T. 2009. "Obama and 'Regulatory Capture.'" *Wall Street Journal*, online edition (http://online.wsj.com/article/SB124580461065744913.html; retrieved 29 June 2009).

Freeze, R. Allan. 2000. *The Environmental Pendulum: A Quest for the Truth about Toxic Chemicals, Human Health, and Environmental Protection*. Berkeley: University of California Press.

Freidenberg, Judith. 2001. "Applied Anthropology/antropología de la gestión: Debating the Uses of Anthropology in the United States and Latin America." *Journal of Latin American Anthropology* 6(2): 4–19.

Freudenburg, William R. 2005. "Seeding Science, Courting Conclusions: Reexamining the Intersection of Science, Corporate Cash, and the Law." *Sociological Forum* 20: 3–33.

Friedman, Milton. 1970. "The Social Responsibility of Business Is to Increase Its Profits." *New York Times Magazine*, September 13.

Friere, Paulo. 2000. *Pedagogy of the Oppressed* (30th anniversary edition). New York: Continuum.

Fuentes, Agustin. 2004. "It's Not All Sex and Violence: Integrated Anthropology and the Role of Cooperation and Social Complexity in Human Evolution." *American Anthropologist* 106(4): 710–18. doi:10.1525/aa.2004.106.4.710.

Fujino, Yoshihisa, et al. 2006. "A Prospective Cohort Study of Shift Work and Risk of Ischemic Heart Disease in Japanese Male Workers." *American Journal of Epidemiology* 164(2): 128–35.

García-Martinez, Neftalí. 1975. Informe Sobre Industria Quimico-Farmaceutica y Plantas de Tratamiento: Archives SCTInc. Folder 1975: #7.

——. 1977. "Ni Una Quimica Ni Una Farmaceutica Mas Para el Area de Manatí-Barceloneta." Misión Industrial y Servicios Legales.

——. 1982. Acerca de la Contaminación de los Pozos de Agua Potable en Arecibo y Barceloneta. con Tetraclouro de Carbono: Archives of SCTInc. Folder: 1982, #5.

García-Passalacqua, Juan M. 1994. "The Grand Dilemma: Viability and Sovereignty for Puerto Rico." *Annals of the American Academy of Political and Social Science* 533(1): 151–64.

Garcia, Ana Maria. 1982. *La Operación* (documentary film). New York: Cinema Guild.

Garriga-Lopez, Adriana. 2010. "A Puerto Rican Privilege: Health Care as Human Right and the HIV/AIDS Service Industry." Paper delivered at the American Anthropological Association Annual Meeting. New Orleans, LA.

George, Rose. 2008. *The Big Necessity: The Unmentionable World of Human Waste and Why It Matters*. New York: Macmillan.

Gibson, Kevin. 1995. "Fictitious Persons, Real Responsibilities." *Journal of Business Ethics* 13(9): 761–67.

Goitía, José R. n.d. Barceloneta's Regional Wastewater Treatment Plant: Puerto Rico Aqueduct and Sewer Authority.

Gómez, Antonio R. 2005. "Desconfían de legisladores y de los partidos: Crítico retrato del país." In *Primera Hora*, 4 de marzo (www.primerahora.com). San Juan.

Googins, Bradley and Steven Rochlin. 2006. "Corporate Citizenship Top to Bottom: Vision, Strategy, and Execution." In *The Accountable Corporation Vol. 3: Corporate Social Responsibility*, M. Epstein and K. O. Hanson, eds. Santa Barbara, CA: Praeger.

Gramsci, Antonio. 1971. *Selections from the Prison Notebooks*. Trans. and ed. by Quintin Hoare and Geoffrey Nowell Smith. New York: International Publishers.

Griffith, D. 1999. "Exaggerating Environmental Health Risk: The Case of the Toxic Dinoflagellate *Pfiesteria*." *Human Organization* 58(2): 119–27.

Griffith, David and Manuel Valdés-Pizzini. 2005. *Fishers at Work, Workers at Sea*. Philadelphia: Temple University Press.

Grimes, D. J. 1985. "Microbiological Studies of Municipal Waste Release to Aquatic Environments." In *Ecological Considerations in Wetlands Treatment of Municipal Wastewaters*, P. J. Godfrey, E. R. Kaynor, and S. Pelczarski, eds. New York: Van Nostrand Reinhold.

Grimes, D. J. and R. R. Colwell. 1989. "Ocean Discharge of Industrial and Domestic Waste-water at Barceloneta, Puerto Rico: Bacteriological Considerations." *Oceanic Processes in Marine Pollution* 4: 139–48.

Grimes, D. J., et al. 1984. "Microbiological Effects of Wastewater Effluent Discharge into Coastal Waters of Puerto Rico." *Water Research* 18(5): 613–19.

Grusky, Sara L. 1996. "Political Power in Puerto Rico: Bankers, Pharmaceuticals and the State." *Studies in Comparative International Development* (SCID) 31(1): 48–64.

Haenn, N. and D. G. Casagrande. 2007. "Citizens, Experts, and Anthropologists: Finding Paths in Environmental Policy." *Human Organization* 66(2): 99–102.

Hahn, Robert A. 1997. "The Nocebo Phenomenon: Concept, Evidence, and Implications for Public Health." *Preventive Medicine* 26, no. 5 (September): 607–11. doi:10.1006/pmed.1996.0124.

Hale, C. R. 2006. "Activist Research v. Cultural Critique: Indigenous Land Rights and the Contradictions of Politically Engaged Anthropology." *Cultural Anthropology* 21(1): 96–120.

Hanson, J. and D. Yosifon. 2003. "The Situation: An Introduction to the Situational Character, Critical Realism, Power Economics, and Deep Capture." *University of Pennsylvania Law Review* 152: 129–2001.

Haraway, Donna. 1991. *Simians, Cyborgs and Women*. New York: Routledge.

Hardell, Lennart, Martin J. Walker, Bo Walhjalt, Lee S. Friedman, and Elihu D. Richter. 2007. "Secret Ties to Industry and Conflicting Interests in Cancer Research." *American Journal of Industrial Medicine* 50(3): 227–33. doi:10.1002/ajim.20357.

Harper, Janice. 2004. "Breathless in Houston: A Political Ecology of Health Approach to Understanding Environmental Health Concerns." *Medical Anthropology* 23: 295–326.

Hartmann, Thom. 2002. *Unequal Protection: The Rise of Corporate Dominance and the Theft of Human Rights*. Emmaus, PA: Rodale Books.

Hawken, Paul. 1993. *The Ecology of Commerce: A Declaration of Sustainability*. New York: HarperCollins.

Hawken, Paul, Amory B. Lovins, and L. Hunter Lovins. 2010. *Natural Capitalism*. Earthscan.

Heine, J. 1993. *The Last Cacique: Leadership and Politics in a Puerto Rican City*. Pittsburgh, PA: University of Pittsburgh Press.

Helitzer-Allen, Deborah L. and Carl Kendall. 1992. "Explaining Differences Between Qualitative and Quantitative Data: A Study of Chemoprophylaxis During Pregnancy." *Health Education & Behavior* 19(1) (April 1): 41–54. doi:10.1177/109019819201900104.

Hernández, Luis Alberto. 1991. "The Origins of the Consumer Culture in Puerto Rico: The Pre-Television Years (1898–1954)." *CENTRO Journal* 3(1): 39–54.

Heron, R.J.L. and F. C. Pickering. 2003. "Health Effects of Exposure to Active Pharmaceutical Ingredients (APIs)." *Occupational Medicine* 53(6): 357–62.

Herzfeld, Michael. 1992. *The Social Production of Indifference: Exploring the Symbolic Roots of Western Bureaucracy*. Chicago: University of Chicago Press.

Herzog, Hanna. 1987. "The Election Campaign as a Liminal Stage—Negotiations over Meanings." *Sociological Review* 35(3): 559–74.

Himmelstein, Jerome L. 1997. *Looking Good and Doing Good: Corporate Philanthropy and Corporate Power*. Bloomington: Indiana University Press.

Horowitz, Leah S. 2009. "Environmental Violence and Crises of Legitimacy in New Caledonia." *Political Geography* 28(4): 248–58.

———. 2011. "Interpreting Industry's Impacts: Micropolitical Ecologies of Divergent Community Responses." *Development and Change* 42, no. 6 (November 1): 1379–91. doi:10.1111/j.1467-7660.2011.01740.x.

Huertas, Evelyn. 2004. "Impact and Environmental Risk of Discharges from Wastewater Treatment Plants of the Puerto Rico Aqueduct and Sewer Authority." Master's thesis, Metropolitan University, Environmental Affairs Graduate School.

Hunter, John M. and Sonia I. Arbona. 1995. "Paradise Lost: An Introduction to the Geography of Water Pollution in Puerto Rico." *Social Science and Medicine* 40(10): 1331–55.

Ismail, M. Asif. 2007. "Spending on Lobbying Thrives." iWatch News by The Center for Public Integrity. http://www.iwatchnews.org/2007/04/01/5780/spending-lobbying-thrives.

Jain, S. Lochlann. 2011. "Survival Odds: Mortality in Corporate Time." *Current Anthropology* 52 (Supplement 3): S45–S56.

Jameson, Frederick. 1984. "Postmodernism, or The Cultural Logic of Late Capitalism." *New Left Review* 146: 53–92.

Jenkins, Rhys. 2005. "Globalization, Corporate Social Responsibility and Poverty." *International Affairs* 81, no. 3 (May 1): 525–40. doi:10.1111/j.1468-2346.2005.00467.x.

Jimenez Barber, Carlos. 1994. Status Memo: Water Quality Certificate for the BWTP. To: PRASA and Advisory Council Members, Meeting, dated December 7, 1994.

Johnston, Barbara Rose, ed. 2011. *Life and Death Matters: Human Rights, Environment, and Social Justice.* 2d ed. Walnut Creek, CA: Left Coast Press.

Kairys, David. 1998. *Freedom of Speech II. The Politics of Law,* 3rd ed. New York: Basic Books.

———. 2010. "Money Isn't Speech and Corporations Aren't People: The Misguided Theories behind the Supreme Court's Ruling on Campaign Finance Reform." http://www.slate.com/id/2242210/.

Kaiser Family Foundation and Sonderegger Research Center. 2004. "Exhibit 1.21: Profitability Among Pharmaceutical Manufacturers Compared to Other Industries, 1995–2004" (http://www.kff.org/insurance/7031/ti2004-1-21.cfm). In *Trends and Indicators in the Changing Health Care Marketplace* (accessed January 2007).

Karlsson, Berndt H., Anders K. Knutsson, Bernt O. Lindahl, and Lars S. Alfredsson. 2003. "Metabolic Disturbances in Male Workers with Rotating Three-Shift Work: Results of the WOLF Study." *International Archives of Occupational and Environmental Health* 76(6): 424–30.

Karnani, Aneel. 2007. "The Mirage of Marketing to the Bottom of the Pyramid: How the Private Sector Can Help Alleviate Poverty." *California Management Review* 49(4): 90–111.

Kennicutt, Mahlon C., James M. Brooks, and Thomas J. McDonald. 1984. "Volatile Organic Inputs from an Ocean Outfall Near Barceloneta, Puerto Rico." *Chemosphere* 13(4): 535–48.

Killingsworth, Richard E., Audrey de Nazelle, and Richard H. Bell. 2004. "A New Role for Public Health in Transportation Creating and Supporting Community Models for Active Transportation." Chapel Hill, NC: Active Living by Design National Program Office, UNC School of Public Health.

Kleinbaum, David and Mitchell Klein. 2002. *Logistic Regression—A Self-Learning Text,* 2d ed. New York: Springer-Verlag.

Kliksberg, Bernardo and Luciano Tomassini, eds. 2000. *Capital Social y Cultura: Claves Estratégicas Para El Desarrollo*. Buenos Aires: Banco Interamericano de Desarrollo y Fondo de Cultura Económica.

Korten, David C. 2001. *When Corporations Rule the World*, 2d ed. Bloomfield, CT: Kumarian Press.

Kovel, Joel. 2002. *The Enemy of Nature*. London: Zed Press.

Krieger, Nancy. 1994. "Epidemiology and the Web of Causation: Has Anyone Seen the Spider?" *Social Science & Medicine* 39(7): 887–903.

Lapp, Michael. 1995. "The Rise and Fall of Puerto Rico as a Social Laboratory, 1945–1965." *Social Science History* 19(2): 169–99.

Leatherman, Thomas. 2005. "A Space of Vulnerability in Poverty and Health: Political-Ecology and Biocultural Analysis." *Ethos* 33(1): 46–70. doi:10.1525/eth.2005.33.1.046.

Levins-Morales, Aurora. 1998. *Medicine Stories: History, Culture and the Politics of Integrity*. Cambridge, MA: South End Press.

Lewis, Oscar. 1966. *La Vida: A Puerto Rican Family in the Culture of Poverty—San Juan and New York*. New York: Wiley.

Lewis-Fernández, Roberto and Arthur Kleinman. 1994. "Culture, Personality, and Psychopathology." *Journal of Abnormal Psychology* 103 (1). *Personality and Psychopathology* (February): 67–71. doi:10.1037/0021-843X.103.1.67.

López Acevedo, Bernardo. 1976. "Desperdicios venenosos para la costa norte." In *Claridad*, 15 de mayo. Pp. 3. San Juan, PR.

Lopez, M. M. 1994. "Post-Work Selves and Entitlement 'Attitudes' in Peripheral Postindustrial Puerto Rico." *Social Text* 38: 111–33.

Lorenzo, Pedro, and Orisson Serrano. 2002. Comments on the Proposed 301(h) Secondary Treatment Waiver for the PRASA Bayamon/Puerto Nuevo Discharges (submitted by Puerto Rico Water Environment Association, American Water Works Association— Puerto Rico Section).

Lyon, Thomas P. and John W. Maxwell. 2004. "Astroturf: Interest Group Lobbying and Corporate Strategy." *Journal of Economics & Management Strategy* 13(4): 561–97.

Maldonado, Edwin. 1979. "Contract Labor and the Origins of Puerto Rican Communities in the United States." *International Migration Review* 13(1): 103–21.

Marchant, G. E. 2003. "From General Policy to Legal Rule: Aspirations and Limitations of the Precautionary Principle." *Environmental Health Perspectives* 111(14): 1799.

Martin, B. 1999. "Suppression of Dissent in Science." *Research in Social Problems and Public Policy* 7: 105–35.

Martinez, Marialba. 2005a. "Global Pharmaceutical-Drug Sales in 2005 for Nine Local Companies Up 5.7% to $102.5 Billion: Local Manufacturers' Sales Represent $42.1 Billion or 41.1% of Total Sales, 2.3% Less Than 2004." *Caribbean Business* 33(32): 30.

———. 2005b. "Puerto Rico's Pharmaceutical Industry Remains Strong Despite End of 936 / 30A: The Island Faces the Challenge of Remaining Competitive as Other Jurisdictions Court the Industry." *Caribbean Business* 33(46): 1, 16.

Mayol, Héctor and Bartolomé Gamundi. 2004. "Responsabilidad Social Empresarial: el desafío de la colaboración." Cámara de Comercio de Puerto Rico.

McCaffrey, Katherine T. and Sherrie L. Baver. 2006. "'Ni Una Bomba Mas': Reframing the Vieques Struggle." In *Beyond Sun and Sand*, S. L. Baver and B. D. Lynch, eds. New Brunswick, NJ: Rutgers University Press.

McElroy, Ann,and Patricia K. Townsend. 2008. *Medical Anthropology in Ecological Perspective*, 5th ed. New York: Westview Press.

Memmi, Albert. 1991. *The Colonizer and the Colonized*. Boston, MA: Beacon Press.

Mercer, Claire. 2002. "NGOs, Civil Society and Democratization: A Critical Review of the Literature." *Progress in Development Studies* 2(1) (January 1): 5–22. doi:10.1191/1464993402ps027ra.

Merry, Sally Engle. 2011. "Measuring the World: Indicators, Human Rights, and Global Governance: With CA Comment by John M. Conley." *Current Anthropology* 52(S3) (April 1): S83–S95.

Michaels, D. 1988. "Waiting for the Body Count: Corporate Decision Making and Bladder Cancer in the US Dye Industry." *Medical Anthropology Quarterly* 2(3): 215–32.

Mintz, Sidney W. 1966 [1956]. "Cañamelar: The Subculture of a Rural Sugar Plantation Proletariat." In *The People of Puerto Rico: A Study in Social Anthropology*. J. H. Steward et al., eds. Urbana: University of Illinois Press.

Mintz, Sidney W. and Eric R. Wolf. 1950. "An Analysis of Ritual Co-Parenthood (Compadrazgo)." *Southwestern Journal of Anthropology* 6(4): 341–68.

Molina-Rivera, Wanda. 1996. "Ground-Water Use from the Principal Aquifers in Puerto Rico During Calendar Year 1990." U.S. Geological Survey Fact Sheet FS-188-96.

———. 2005. "Estimated Water Use in Puerto Rico, 2000." U.S. Geological Survey Open-File Report 2005-1201.

Moloney, Margaret F., et al. 2006. "The Experiences of Midlife Women with Migraines." *Journal of Nursing Scholarship* 38(3): 278–85.

Montealegre, Federico, et al. 2004. "Exposure Levels of Asthmatic Children to Allergens, Endotoxins, and Serine Proteases in a Tropical Environment." *Journal of Asthma* 41(4): 485–96.

Morgan, L. M. 1993. *Community Participation in Health: The Politics of Primary Care in Costa Rica*. New York: Cambridge University Press.

Morgenson, Gretchen. 2006. "Peer Pressure: Inflating Executive Pay." *New York Times*, November 26. www.nytimes.com/2006/11/26/business/yourmoney/26peer.html (accessed December 9, 2012).

Morris, Rosalind. 1995. "All Made Up: Performance Theory and the New Anthropology of Sex and Gender." *Annual Review of Anthropology* 24(1): 567–92.

Mulligan, Jessica. 2010. "Reforming Risk: Markets and Managed Care in Puerto Rico." Paper delivered at the American Anthropological Association Annual Meeting. New Orleans, LA.

Nader, Laura. 1990. *Harmony Ideology: Justice and Control in a Mountain Zapotec Village*. Stanford, CA: Stanford University Press.

———. 2001. "Anthropology! Distinguished Lecture—2000." *American Anthropologist* 103(3): 609–20.

———. 2002. *The Life of the Law: Anthropological Projects*. Berkeley: University of California Press.

Nader, L. and J. Ou. 1998. "Idealization and Power: Legality and Tradition in Native American Law." *Oklahoma City University Law Review* 23: 13.

Nash, June and Max Kirsch. 1988. "The Discourse of Medical Science in the Construction of Consensus between Corporation and Community." *Medical Anthropology Quarterly* 2(2): 158–71.

National Center for Environmental Health. 2005. "About Cancer Clusters." http://www.cdc.gov/NCEH/clusters/about_clusters.htm (accessed June 18, 2006).

Nations, Marilyn K. 1986. "Epidemiological Research on Infectious Disease: Quantitative Rigor or Rigor Mortis?" In *Anthropology and Epidemiology*, Craig R. Janes, R. Stall, and S. M. Gifford, eds. Boston: D. Reidal.

Nazarea, V. D. 1999. "Introduction. A View from a Point: Ethnoecology as Situated Knowledge." *Ethnoecology: Situated Knowledge/Located Lives*. Tucson: University of Arizona Press.

Negrón-Muntaner, Frances, ed. 2007. *None of the Above: Puerto Ricans in the Global Era*. New York: Palgrave Macmillan.

Negrón-Muntaner, Frances, ed. 2009. *Sovereign Acts*. Cambridge, MA: South End Press.

Negrón-Muntaner, Frances and Ramón Grosfoguel. 1997. *Puerto Rican Jam: Rethinking Colonialism and Nationalism*. Minneapolis: University of Minnesota Press.

Neiheisel, Steven R. 1994. *Corporate Strategy and the Politics of Goodwill: A Political Analysis of Corporate Philanthropy in America*. New York: Peter Lang.

Netting, Robert M. 1986. *Cultural Ecology*, 2d ed. Prospect Heights, IL: Waveland Press.

Neumann, A. Lin. 1981. "U.S. Pharmaceutical Giants Move to Puerto Rico for Tax Breaks." *Multinational Monitor* 2(10) (multinationalmonitor.org).

Newman, Rick. 2009. "How Big Pharma Wins From Healthcare Reform." http://money.usnews.com/money/blogs/flowchart/2009/09/25/how-big-pharma-wins-from-health-care-reform (accessed November 26, 2012).

Nichter, Mark. 1996. "Pharmaceuticals, the Commodification of Health, and the Health Care–Medicine Use Transition." In *Anthropology and International Health: Asian Case Studies*, 2d ed. M. Nichter and M. Nichter, eds. Amsterdam: Gordon and Breach.

Office of Drinking Water. 1979. "Statement of Basis and Purpose: Underground Injection Control Regulations" (National UIC Program Docket Control Number D01062). Environmental Protection Agency.

Oficina de Gerencia y Presupuesto Estado Libre Asociado de Puerto Rico. 2005. "Historia de la JCA" (http://www.gobierno.pr/JCA/QueEsLaJCA/historia/) (accessed January 2007).

Oldani, Michael J. 2004. "Thick Prescriptions: Toward an Interpretation of Pharmaceutical Sales Practices." *Medical Anthropology Quarterly* 18(3) (September 1): 325–56. doi:10.1525/maq.2004.18.3.325.

Ong, Aihwa. 1987. *Spirits of Resistance and Capitalist Discipline: Factory Women in Malaysia*. Albany: SUNY Press.

Ortiz-Negron, Laura. 2007. "Space Out of Place: Consumer Culture in Puerto Rico." In *None of the Above: Puerto Ricans in the Global Era*, Frances Negron-Muntaner, ed. New York: Palgrave Macmillan.

Overcash, Michael, et al. 2005. "Beneficial Reuse and Sustainability: The Fate of Organic Compounds in Land-Applied Waste." *Journal of Environmental Quality* 31(1): 29–41.

Padilla Seda, Elena. 1966 [1956]. "Nocorá: The Subculture of Workers on a Government-Owned Sugar Plantation." In *The People of Puerto Rico: A Study in Social Anthropology*, J. Steward et al., eds. Urbana: University of Illinois Press.

Pantojas-García, Emilio. 1990. *Development Strategies as Ideology: Puerto Rico's Export-Led Industrialization Experience*. Boulder, CO and London: Lynne Rienner.

———. 2000. "End-of-the-Century Studies of Puerto Rico's Economy, Politics, and Culture: What Lies Ahead?" *Latin American Research Review* 35(3): 227–40.

Partido Socialista Puertorriqueño. 1977. Boletin Especial: "Unete al Piquete del Partido Socialista Puertorriqueña - ¡Salvemos Nuestras Playas y Nuestra Pesca! - ¡Alto a la Contaminación!"

Partridge, Damani J., Marina Welker, and Rebecca Hardin, eds. 2011. "Corporate Lives: New Perspectives on the Social Life of the Corporate Form." *Current Anthropology* 52 (Supplement 3).

Pastor, Robert A. 1992. *Whirlpool: U.S. Foreign Policy toward Latin America and the Caribbean*. Princeton, NJ: Princeton University Press.

Patterson, Orlando. 1985. *Slavery and Social Death: A Comparative Study*. Cambridge, MA: Harvard University Press.

Paul, Benjamin D., ed. 1955. *Health, Culture and Community*. New York: Russell Sage.

Pérez, José. 1993. "Pestilencias tóxicas arropan el área de Barceloneta (photo)." In *Todo Norte*, 15 de julio.

Pérez-Perdomo, Rosa, et al. 2003. "Prevalence and Correlates of Asthma in the Puerto Rican Population: Behavioral Risk Factor Surveillance System, 2000." *Journal of Asthma* 40(5): 465–74.

Peterson, Dane K. 2004. "Benefits of Participation in Corporate Volunteer Programs: Employees' Perceptions." *Personnel Review* 33(5/6): 615–27.

Petryna, Adriana, Andrew Lakoff, and Arthur Kleinman, eds. 2006. *Global Pharmaceuticals: Ethics, Markets, Practices*. Durham, NC: Duke University Press.

Pharmaceutical Research and Manufacturers of America (PhRMA). 2007. Home page of the Pharmaceutical Research and Manufacturers of America (www.phrma.org) (accessed February 23, 2007).

Prahalad, C. K. 2005. *The Fortune at the Bottom of the Pyramid: Eradicating Poverty Through Profits*. Upper Saddle River, NJ: FT Press.

Prahalad, C. K. and V. Ramaswamy. 2004. "Co-creating Unique Value with Customers." *Strategy & Leadership* 32(3): 4–9.

Public Citizen. 2002. "Pharmaceuticals Rank as Most Profitable Industry, Again: 'Druggernaut' Tops All Three Measures of Profits In New *Fortune 500* Report." http://www.citizen.org/documents/fortune500_2002erport.PDF.

Ramírez de Arellano, Annette B., and Conrad Seipp. 1983. *Colonialism, Catholicism, and Contraception: A History of Birth Control in Puerto Rico*. Chapel Hill: University of North Carolina Press.

Ramos, Luis A. 2004. "Puerto Rico's Security Army." *Caribbean Business* 32: 1, 18.

Ramos Valencia, Gilberto. 2001. "Datos Preliminares del Estudio Continuo de Salud para los Municipios de Puerto Rico." Río Piedras, PR: Universidad de Puerto Rico, Recinto de Ciencias Médicas, Escuela Graduada de Salud Pública, Departamento de Bioestadística y Epidemiología.

Richards, Kevin C. 2006. "Puerto Rico's Pharmaceutical Industry: 40 Years Young!" (originally published in Pharmaceutical Online - accessed at www.interphexpuertorico.com).

Ríos, Palmira N. 1993. "Export-Oriented Industrialization and the Demand for Female Labor: Puerto Rican Women in the Manufacturing Sector, 1952–1980." In *Colonial Dilemma: Critical Perspectives on Contemporary Puerto Rico*, E. Meléndez and E. Meléndez, eds. Cambridge, MA: South End Press.

Rivera, Raquel Z. 2007. "Will the 'Real' Puerto Rican Culture Please Stand Up?: Thoughts On Cultural Nationalism." In *None of the Above: Puerto Ricans in the Global Era*, F. Negrón-Muntaner, ed. New York: Palgrave Macmillan.

Rivera-Batiz, Francisco L. and Carlos E. Santiago. 1996. *Island Paradox. Puerto Rico in the 1990s*. New York: Russell Sage.

Roberts, Blanca O. 1995. Memo To: Alcalde de Barceloneta. Subject: Women's Executive Leadership Program—30-day Developmental Assignment: Summary of Activities while at the Barceloneta City Hall—Environmental Directorate. March 8, 1995.

Román Seda, Roque. 1996. Informe Pericial: Evaluación del problema de olores ofensivos producidos por la planta de tratamiento de aguas negras de Barceloneta y su impacto en la comunidad [Tipan]. Mayagüez, PR.

Romberg, Raquel. 2003. "From Charlatans to Saviors: Espiritistas, Curanderos, and Brujos Inscribed in Discourses of Progress and Heritage." *CENTRO Journal* 15(2): 146–73.

Rose-Ackerman, Susan. 1996. "Altruism, Nonprofits, and Economic Theory." *Journal of Economic Literature* 34(2): 701–28.

Rosenn, Keith S. 1963. "Puerto Rican Land Reform: The History of an Instructive Experiment." *Yale Law Journal* 73(2): 334–56.

Rylko-Bauer, Barbara, Merrill Singer, and John Van Willigen. 2006. "Reclaiming Applied Anthropology: Its Past, Present, and Future." *American Anthropologist* 108(1) (March 1): 178–90. doi:10.1525/aa.2006.108.1.178.

Sabater, Cristina. 2005. "Construir la *Confianza*." In *El Nuevo Día—Negocios del Domingo*, vol. el 14 de agosto, pp. 8. San Juan, PR.

Sánchez-Cardona, Víctor, Tomás Morales-Cardona, and Pier Luigi Caldari. 1975. "The Struggle for Puerto Rico: How to Undevelop an Island." *Environment* 17(4): 34–40.

Sandoval, Chela. 2000. *Methodology of the Oppressed*. Minneapolis: University of Minnesota Press.

Satterfield, T. 1997. "'Voodoo Science' and Common Sense: Ways of Knowing Old-Growth Forests." *Journal of Anthropological Research* 53(4): 443–59.

———. 2002. *Anatomy of a Conflict: Identity, Knowledge, and Emotion in Old-growth Forests*. Vancouver, BC: University of British Columbia Press.

Saul, Stephanie. 2006. "Drug Maker Fires Chief of 5 Years." *New York Times*, September 13 (www.nytimes.com/2006/09/13/business/13bristols.html).

Schafer, Jacqueline E. 1983. Letter to [CDAN] from EPA Regional Administrator. n.d. (received October 17, 1983).

Scheper-Hughes, Nancy, and Margaret Lock. 1987. "The Mindful Body: A Prolegomenon to Future Work in Medical Anthropology." *Medical Anthropology Quarterly* 1 (n.s.) (1): 6–41.

Schiffman, Susan S., and C. M. Williams. 2005. "Science of Odor as a Potential Health Issue." *Journal of Environmental Quality* 34(1) (February): 129–38.

Schwartzman, Helen B. 1989. *The Meeting: Gatherings in Organizations and Communities*. New York and London: Plenum Press.

Scott, James C. 1985. *Weapons of the Weak: Everyday Forms of Peasant Resistance*. New Haven, CT: Yale University Press.

———. 1998. *Seeing Like a State: How Certain Schemes to Improve the Human Condition Have Failed*. New Haven, CT: Yale University Press.

Seda Bonilla, E. 1964. *Interacción social y personalidad en una comunidad de Puerto Rico*. San Juan, PR: Ediciones Juan Ponce de León.

Shamir, Ronen. 2004. "De-Radicalization of Corporate Social Responsibility." *Critical Sociology* 30(3): 669–89.

Sharp, John. 2006. "Corporate Social Responsibility and Development: An Anthropological Perspective." *Development Southern Africa* 23(2): 213–22. doi:10.1080/03768350600707892.

Simanis, Erik, Stuart Hart, and Duncan Duke. 2008. "The Base of the Pyramid Protocol: Beyond 'Basic Needs' Business Strategies." *Innovations: Technology, Governance, Globalization* 3(1): 57–84. doi:10.1162/itgg.2008.3.1.57.

Singer, Merrill. 1989. "The Limitations of Medical Ecology: The Concept of Adaptation in the Context of Social Stratification and Social Transformation." *Medical Anthropology* 10: 223–34.

———. 1995. "Beyond the Ivory Tower: Critical Praxis in Medical Anthropology." *Medical Anthropology Quarterly* 9(1): 80–106.

———. 1998. "The Development of Critical Medical Anthropology: Implications for Biological Anthropology." In *Building a New Biocultural Synthesis: Political-Economic Perspectives on Human Biology*, A. H. Goodman and T. L. Leatherman, eds. Ann Arbor: University of Michigan Press.

———. 2009. *Introduction to Syndemics: a Critical Systems Approach to Public and Community Health*. New York: Wiley.

Singer, Merrill, and Hans Baer. 1995. *Critical Medical Anthropology*. Amityville, NY: Baywood Publishing.

———. 2008. "Introduction: Hidden Harm, the Complex World of Killer Commodities." In *Killer Commodities: Public Health and the Corporate Production of Harm*. Lanham, MD, Alta Mira Press.

Singer, Merill and Scott Clair. 2003. "Syndemics and Public Health: Reconceptualizing Disease in Bio-Social Context." *Medical Anthropology Quarterly* 17(4) (December 1): 423–41. doi:10.1525/maq.2003.17.4.423.

Skanavis, Constantina. 1999. "Groundwater Disaster in Puerto Rico: The Need for Environmental Education." *Journal of Environmental Health* 62(2): 29–35.

Slovic, Paul. 1999. "Trust, Emotion, Sex, Politics, and Science: Surveying the Risk-Assessment Battlefield." *Risk Analysis* 19 (4): 689–701. doi:10.1023/A:1007041821623.

Smith, Craig N. 1996. "Desperately Seeking Data: Why Research Is Crucial to the New Corporate Philanthropy." In *Corporate Philanthropy at the Crossroads*, D. Burlingame and D. R. Young, eds. Bloomington: Indiana University Press.

Sotomayor, Orlando. 1998. *Poverty and Income Inequality in Puerto Rico, 1970–1990*. Río Piedras, PR: Centro de Investigaciones Sociales.

———. 2004. "Development and Income Distribution: The Case of Puerto Rico." *World Development* 32(8): 1395–1406.

Southern Technology Council/Southern Growth Policies Board. 2000. "Invented Here: Toward an Innovation Driven Economy." www.southern.org/pubs/ih2000/pr.pdf.

Steinemann, A. 2000. "Rethinking Human Health Impact Assessment." *Environmental Impact Assessment Review* 20: 627–45.

Stern, Robert N. and Stephen R. Barley. 1996. "Organizations and Social Systems: Organization Theory's Neglected Mandate." *Administrative Science Quarterly* 41(1): 146–62.

Stigler, George J. 1971. "The Theory of Economic Regulation." *Bell Journal of Economics and Management Science* 2(1): 3–21.

Susser, I. 1985. "Union Carbide and the Community Surrounding It: The Case of a Community in Puerto Rico." *International Journal of Health Services: Planning, Administration, Evaluation* 15(4): 561–83.

Susser, Mervyn. 1994. "The Logic in Ecological: I. The Logic of Analysis." *American Journal of Public Health* 84(5): 825.

Susser, Mervyn and Ezra Susser. 1996a. "Choosing a Future for Epidemiology: I. Eras and Paradigms." *American Journal of Public Health* 86(5): 668–673.

———. 1996b. "Choosing a Future for Epidemiology: II. From Black Box to Chinese Boxes and Eco-epidemiology." *American Journal of Public Health* 86(5): 674–677.

Taussig, M. 1999. *Defacement: Public Secrecy and the Labor of the Negative.* Palo Alto, CA: Stanford University Press.

Tönnies, Ferdinand. 1957. *Community and Society: Gemeinschaft und Gesellschaft,* trans. and ed. by Charles P. Loomis. East Lansing: Michigan State University Press.

Torres, Andrés and José E. Velázquez, eds. 1998. *The Puerto Rican Movement: Voices from the Diaspora.* Philadelphia: Temple University Press.

Torres, Maria Idalí. 2005. "Organizing, Educating, and Advocating for Health and Human Rights in Vieques, Puerto Rico." *American Journal of Public Health* 95(1): 9–12.

Torres-Velez, Victor. 2010. "At the Margins of the Bio-Island: Environment, Health and Subjectivity in Vieques' Social Movements." Paper delivered at the American Anthropological Association Annual Meeting, New Orleans, LA.

Trostle, James A. 2005. *Epidemiology and Culture.* Cambridge and New York: Cambridge University Press.

Tsing, Anna Lowenhaupt. 2004. *Friction: An Ethnography of Global Connection.* Princeton, NJ: Princeton University Press.

Tsing, Anna. L., J. Peter Brosius, and Charles Zerner. 2005. "Raising Questions about Communities and Conservation." In *Communities and Conservation: Histories and Politics of Community Based Natural Resource Management,* J. P. Brosius, A. L. Tsing, and C. Zerner, eds. Walnut Creek, CA: Alta Mira Press.

Turner, Victor. 1969. *The Ritual Process: Structure and Anti-Structure.* Ithaca, NY: Cornell University Press.

USA Today 2009. "The Smokestack Effect: Toxic Air and America's Schools." http://content. usatoday.com/news/nation/environment/smokestack/index. Accessed February 9, 2012.

U.S. Census Bureau (2000). Summary File 1 (SF 1) and Summary File 3 (SF 3).

U.S.–EPA Office of Water. 2003. "EPA's National Pretreatment Program, 1973–2003: Thirty Years of Protecting the Environment." (EPA 833–F–03–001).

Valdés-Pizzini, Manuel. 2001. "Historical Contentions and Future Trends in the Coastal Zone: The Environmental Movement In Puerto Rico." Mayagüez: University of Puerto Rico Sea Grant College Program, Publication number UPRSGGCP-R-80.

Van der Geest, Sjaak. 2006. "Anthropology and the Pharmaceutical Nexis." *Anthropological Quarterly* 79(2): 303–14.

Van der Geest, Sjaak and Susan Reynolds Whyte, eds. 1991. *The Context of Medicines in Developing Countries: Studies in Pharmaceutical Anthropology.* Amsterdam: Het Spinhuis Publishers.

Vayda, A. P. and B. B. Walters. 1999. "Against Political Ecology." *Human Ecology* 27(1): 167–79.

Velez Arcelay, Yolanda. 1984. "Amenaza ambiental en el norte PR." In *El Reportero de Puerto Rico* vol. IV, 4 de junio, pp. 1–2. San Juan, PR.

Vogel, David. 2005. *The Market for Virtue: The Potential and Limits of Corporate Social Responsibility.* Washington, DC: Brookings Institution Press.

Wade, Mark. 2006. "A Commitment to Sustainable Development—the Long Journey Begins." In *The Accountable Corporation, Vol. 3: Corporate Social Responsibility*, M. J. Epstein and K. O. Hanson, eds. Santa Barbara, CA: Praeger Publishers.

Wailoo, Keith, Julie Livingston, and Steven Epstein. 2010. *Three Shots at Prevention: The HPV Vaccine and the Politics of Medicine's Simple Solutions*. Baltimore, MD: JHU Press.

Wallerstein, Immanuel. 1991. "World System versus World-Systems: A Critique." *Critique of Anthropology* 11(2): 189–94.

Ware, Norma. 1992. "Suffering and the Social Construction of Illness: The Delegitimation of Illness Experience in Chronic Fatigue Syndrome." *Medical Anthropology Quarterly* 6(4): 347–61.

Watts, Michael J. and Hans G. Bohle. 1993. "The Space of Vulnerability: The Causal Structure of Hunger and Famine." *Progress in Human Geography* 17(1) (March 1): 43–67. doi:10.1177/030913259301700103.

Welker, Marina A. 2009. " 'Corporate Security Begins in the Community': Mining, the Corporate Social Responsibility Industry, and Environmental Advocacy in Indonesia." *Cultural Anthropology* 24(1): 142–79.

Welker, Marina, Damani J. Partridge, and Rebecca Hardin. 2011. "Corporate Lives: New Perspectives on the Social Life of the Corporate Form: An Introduction to Supplement 3." *Current Anthropology* 52 (Supplement 3): S3–S16.

Welker, Marina and David Wood. 2011. "Shareholder Activism and Alienation." *Current Anthropology* 52 (Supplement 3): S57–S70.

Whyte, Susan Reynolds, Sjaak van der Geest, and Anita Hardon, eds. 2002. *The Social Lives of Medicines*. Cambridge, UK: Cambridge University Press.

Wilcox, Joyce. 2001. "Vieques, Puerto Rico: An Island Under Siege." *American Journal of Public Health* 91(5): 695–98.

Wilk, Richard. 1996. *Economies and Cultures: Foundations of Economic Anthropology*. Boulder, CO: Westview Press.

———. 1999. "Quality of Life and the Anthropological Perspective." *Feminist Economics* 5(2): 91–93.

Wilson, Duff. 2010. "Risks Seen in Cholesterol Drug Use in Healthy People." *New York Times*, March 30, Business section. http://www.nytimes.com/2010/03/31/business/31statins.html.

Windsor, Duane. 2006. "Corporate Social Responsibility: Cases For and Against." In *The Accountable Corporation, Vol. 3: Corporate Social Responsibility*, M. J. Epstein and K. O. Hanson, eds. Santa Barbara, CA: Praeger Publishers.

Witherspoon, J. E. Allen and C. Quigley. 2004. "Modelling to Assist in Wastewater Collection System Odour and Corrosion Potential Evaluations." *Water Science and Technology* 50(4): 177–83.

Wuthnow, Robert. 1996. *Poor Richard's Principle: Recovering the American Dream through the Moral Dimension of Work, Business, and Money*. Princeton, NJ: Princeton University Press.

Yalamanchili, Chaethana and Michael D. Smith. 2008. "Acute Hydrogen Sulfide Toxicity Due to Sewer Gas Exposure." *American Journal of Emergency Medicine* 26 (4) (May): 518. e5–7. doi:10.1016/j.ajem.2007.08.025.

Zonabend, Francoise. 1993. *The Nuclear Peninsula*. Cambridge: Cambridge University Press.

Alexa Dietrich is Assistant Professor of Anthropology at Wagner College. Trained as both an anthropologist and epidemiologist, her interests are inherently liminal, and lie at the intersections of many fields: culture and health, technology and the natural environment, and qualitative and quantitative methods. She continues to work with communities in Puerto Rico on issues related to environmental health. In the aftermath of Hurricane Sandy she is also working with a number of colleagues to better understand environmental health vulnerabilities and decision-making where she lives and works, in Staten Island, New York.